FROM PEAKS TO PRAIRIE

FROM PEAKS TO PRAIRIE

THE GIFTS OF WALKING IN AN ANXIOUS LIFE

CARA CHAMBERLAIN

Oregon State University Press Corvallis

Oregon State University Press in Corvallis, Oregon, is located within the traditional homelands of the Marys River or Ampinefu Band of Kalapuya. Following the Willamette Valley Treaty of 1855, Kalapuya people were forcibly removed to reservations in Western Oregon. Today, living descendants of these people are a part of the Confederated Tribes of Grand Ronde Community of Oregon (grandronde.org) and the Confederated Tribes of the Siletz Indians (ctsi.nsn.us).

Cataloging-in-publication data available at the Library of Congress.
LCCN 2026024373.

ISBN 978-1-962645-66-9 (paper); ISBN 978-1-962645-67-6 (ebook)

∞ This paper meets the requirements of ANSI/NISO Z39.48-1992 (Permanence of Paper).

First published in 2026 by Oregon State University Press
Printed in the United States of America

Oregon State University
OSU Press

Oregon State University Press
121 The Valley Library
Corvallis OR 97331-4501
541-737-3166 • fax 541-737-3170
www.osupress.oregonstate.edu

In honor of all the dogs I've walked with

Contents

Introduction

The journeys in this book along trails, roads, and rivers are not just adventures into wilderness, riverfront parks, or prairie remnants. They are shimmering rituals, my extra-temporal encounters with truth. But openness to inspiration has a painful side, which, I learned when I was in my thirties and forties, could be clinically defined.

Until then, I thought I'd simply been born nervous. My mother told me I had bouts of colic that kept her up all night. I slept balanced on my shoulders and knees, painful stomach tucked. I grew up nervous, too. In first grade, my school had a Halloween carnival that made me so sick with excitement I could hardly eat a pre-festivities hot dog. Later, my mother bought me a worry stone. She told me to carry it when I was at loose ends. She didn't understand that I was always at loose ends.

As a teen, I was an outcast, a gentile, in a holy place. Salt Lake City was the American version of Mecca, and being non-LDS there meant that some people wouldn't enter our house. Often, my friends' parents barely tolerated me. Dating was pretty much out of the question. My mother's directive was to be impeccable and beyond reproach. In high school, I was sometimes too frightened to eat. Frightened of being seen, being found inadequate.

The earth was charged with a strange luminescence it seemed only an outsider like me could sense. I say this luminescence was "strange," but it wasn't to me. Granite-faced Mount Olympus bent the air above my childhood house with the threat of collapse. The basement "train room" where my dad built his model railroad engines and trolleys on evenings and weekends was a mysterious world of soldering and electrical wiring, charged with masculine creativity and cleverness and made menacing by an Alpine cigarette exhaling from an ashtray. Faithful LDS people seemed as uncanny as Puritans, as if they'd been summoned out of a cloudy past to walk down our street to their church or ward—a place I entered only during summer afternoons to watch matinees like *The Blob* and *King Kong vs. Godzilla* and to buy Jolly Ranchers and Pixy Stix (we called it "going to the ward show"). My present crackled with energy, with a vibrating black-and-white power brought from the past and churning out a hidden future. Eternity and mortality coalesced and broke up again—a spiritual inexorability I couldn't understand or control but that enriched and charged the images I saw.

These days, here in Billings, Montana—a city lodged between prairie and mountains—my ordinary 1950s-era house is sometimes filled with that same dark haze of mortality. Dangerous evanescence glows at nightfall in the sandstone rims that overlook town; pain threatens in the green beauty of June haze over the South Hills; and my spine aches with the appearance of the first bitterroots and the starburst blossoms of Missouri foxtail cactus on the surrounding prairie. The Beartooth Mountains—seventy miles away just this side of Yellowstone National Park—bite at the western horizon as if some cataclysm from the past has never ended. Men in particular are prone to act as if they're in the midst of a cataclysm. Maybe they are. Guys with long beards and giant trucks inhabit town and backroads and seem to keep an eye out if you stop too long on the road. A very few carry pistols into the IGA and on hiking trails. Most prove kind and friendly, but you never know. Being a woman does nothing to assuage the anxiety flowing through me.

Feeling these things so deeply means I live intensely, which has advantages. In the mountains, a malachite tarn and a pearly clump of arctic gentians tingle. A pika, yanking at a tuft of sedge for her winter dining, pulls me into her high-altitude life, bouncing through scree and under drifts all winter, munching on cured stalks. Three hundred sixty degrees of shining surface—tundra, jumbled boulders, granite pinnacles, and bluebell sky—scorch me with cold beauty. I've always been enraptured by the moiré distortions of surface that admit microsecond eruptions of enlightenment into what is supposed to be a material solidity, a calm other. My arms have often felt thin and hurt by that other, that churning invisibility of air.

In its wide and golden loneliness, the Montana prairie is a trauma drifting from the destruction of the seemingly endless grasslands that once stretched east to Ohio and west to the mountains where I often hike. This rarely visited remnant is rich in birdlife and ancient rock art. Its inhabitants are short-eared owls, burying beetles, and bullsnakes. Ranchers, driving the graded county roads, will lift two or three fingers from their one-handed steering-wheel grip to greet you as you pass. I never miss the modest chivalry of their gestures, and the wind's longing and joy as it whispers through wild grasses, the way a lover strokes the hair of the beloved.

A narrative arc is supposed to have a clear beginning, a proximate cause, but I can't find one in my story. "Born nervous" isn't much of an explanation. I do know that after a week when I managed three hours of sleep total—Indiana, 1988—my intensity earned a diagnosis: generalized anxiety disorder (GAD). And I can similarly trace to the year and month (July 2001) when GAD became obsessive-compulsive disorder (OCD) as it blossomed in images of me knifing myself or my dog. But I can't really grasp why these conditions developed, except to fall back on the idea that I was predisposed to experience them.

I have found no cure for either. Medications generally don't work. Fortunately, my version of OCD comes in waves, then recedes and is silent for months, weeks, or years. While there's always a certain level of anxiety percolating under my skin, it can shade into the manageable disquiet many people feel in challenging times. Still—as prevention—I do regularly medicate myself. That is, I walk. It's the way I've found not to eliminate GAD and OCD, as I used to long to do, but to live with them. The single left-right, left-right rhythm of two unwavering and opposing directions operating in unison crashes through such binaries as healthy-and-diseased, good-and-evil. I've dazed along half-asleep due to a bout of insomnia. On other walks, I've silently cursed Oscar Charles Dawson, the disorder that constantly tells me how horrible I am and what awful things I'll do. Walking gets me by. Usually. If it doesn't work—or if it's three in the morning—I might take a Xanax. But I don't take much because medicines make me very nervous—and have twice landed me in the ER with a racing heart. Prescriptions tango inside me in ways I can trace, although I'm pretty sure I shouldn't be able to. In general, traveling the Greater Yellowstone Ecosystem offers a better treatment for my OCD. If for some reason I can't get away from Billings, at least I have the Beartooths on the southwestern horizon, a blue rickrack heightened by mysterious lenticular clouds. Or rain from the prairie might sweep the news of sagebrush and wild rye through an open window.

I offer these trail accounts as that rain offers the perfume of sage, to carry you out to the landscape of eternity and knowledge, to the borderlands of Montana and Wyoming. To the continent's beautiful, if corrupted, heart. This book is a layperson's psychological trail guide, providing impressionistic definitions and descriptions of the mental disorders many of us experience and offering insights for those who inherited a tortured family and societal history. Individual minds can be lonely—and sometimes way too crowded—even in the absence of medical diagnoses. Life, as I've discovered, isn't easy. We all have to walk that lonesome road in our own real or metaphorical ways, through mountains and prairies, and out of ourselves.

ONE

The Analogue Hiker

TRAIL 1

Yellowtail Wildlife Management Area, Wyoming

General location: Lovell and Kane, Wyoming; 98 miles from Yellowstone National Park
Hiking distance: variable over 19,214 acres
Elevation: 3,832 feet
Terrain: River bottomland with cottonwoods, mudflats, and high desert

It starts not with fear but with a mental image that causes fear. Something simple, perhaps, like the head-on view of my car. But the ordinary-enough picture refuses to go away. The image expands and becomes disturbing, and battling it consumes hours. It will not be subdued and soon conjures the thought that I'll be in or, worse yet, cause an accident. That perhaps I'll drive my RAV4 into oncoming traffic. To relieve the anxiety, I will stop driving on freeways. This is what can happen to people like me. The world gets smaller and smaller. I have to fight to keep it wide and open. It's like arthritis. To keep a joint supple, you have to keep it moving.

Usually I can't tell why a cycle begins or how exactly it will end. Events beyond my control might stimulate it. But I don't *always* respond to stress in a clinical way. Episodes can arrive for no obvious reason. Take the first one I had.

It began at a concert by the Israel Camerata Orchestra in 2001. The performance was excellent, perhaps Beethoven or Mozart. As I listened, I focused on different musicians, following their technique and trying to hear their parts above the harmony. One cellist had beautiful red hair.

Red hair and . . . Jewish stereotypes. Fagan and Judas. Magically conjured images, ugly caricatures. "You can see why such people were killed in the 1940s," came a voice from inside me. I quashed the whisper and went back to the music, but the sudden thought haunted me for months, tearing at my core beliefs of myself as a good person. I fought. I felt possessed. The visuals and words were within, and I couldn't get away. If I could generate such violent hatred from whatever interior depths it was coming from, then how could I maintain the illusion that I was a human, let alone a good one? Perhaps I was demonic.

Something was unleashed in me, and after that I saw myself stabbing my dog Rita (the last thing I wanted to do). The unbidden scenarios were so vivid, I wondered about calling the police to report a crime before the fact. How would that work? Should I contact a priest? I'm not religious. Eventually I made an appointment with a psychiatrist. After listening to my story, she said, very calmly, as if such things happened all the time, "You have an obsession."

Scientists describe images as retinal stimulation by photons and neural wiring. But obsessions aren't recreations of an outside world. They seem generated by the brain itself, not by light waves. I can't explain why they are so vivid. One could argue, of course, that the brain generates all images—reasonable blueprints rather than exact replicas of "reality."

As directly received by my retina, for instance, Yellowtail Wildlife Management Area's cottonwood-thick trail, where I walked years ago, would have been upside down. My brain righted it then and rights it now as I remember, differentiating colors and outlines. It gives me names and logical ordering. This much can be studied, but science cannot, I suspect, define or predict why the place my synaptic network makes in response even to properties of matter will sometimes suffuse me with a ghostly ache—an internal, electrochemical conversion of ordinary to mystical or frightening.

Why do crumbling geological layers of the Bighorn Mountains' eastern face still crackle with glare above me and shoot straight down to a desert river whose bottomlands hiss and sparkle with leaves, a boisterous spring flood, and the chords of infinity? And why a few years ago did I repeatedly see myself robbing our local bank?

The memory, though, is textured; the obsession, not so much. "This place is all that exists right now," I might have said about the Bighorn River's meandering, its beaver-cruised shores, its intrusive blue sky. I tallied the birds: cormorants, barn swallows, pelicans. I enjoyed the spectacle, its multifaceted surface. The bank in my obsession lay deep inside me, a movie set caricature, but the one in my reminiscence of Yellowtail was exterior, lapped by clear water. Nothing could be truer than birds and shoreline. To remember past enjoyment is not necessarily to see accurately but to luxuriate in sensory detail. To obsess is to see only one thing—and that darkly.

I've never been above experimenting with vision. I used to let my eyes relax as I lay in bed, their natural strabismus doubling the world. I didn't ask whether it was normal to see two lamps, two dressers. If Shiva wriggled in front of my loosened vision—my hand with its fingers waving times two, some transparent, some solid—I tried to stop the cosmic dance by giving both versions equal substance, by seeing broadly. Sometimes it almost worked. You can try it yourself, if you're slightly walleyed.

Another optical game suited my long-ago walk: parallax. It was fun to play with while following the railroad track along the river. Over the arid and sandy terrain, rails shot ahead. I closed one eye for a certain angle and closed the other for a different one. I usually focus on the middle—the convergence point. Truth, I call it. Stereoscopy: the mark of supposedly advanced vision. But it seemed that with my parallax trick, each angle proved more detailed than the two combined. If it was not more accurate, such vision was at least wider.

My husband Bernie has made do all his life without *optical* convergence. His eyes don't work in tandem and never have. I ask him how he manages depth or drives a car, but he can't explain. The question makes no sense to him. The world he sees is *perceptually* converged, I suppose. His mind takes a mosaic and turns it into a single portrait. It focuses and narrows.

And how, I wonder, might a pelican on the Bighorn River all those years ago have seen things? Better than Bernie or I could, I hope. Her eyes were much farther apart proportionally than ours, ensuring good peripheral vision. But she could also see stereoscopically. If she couldn't have, she'd never have been able to fly. But because her focus converged at about the distance of her beak, she probably didn't see anything smack-dab in front of her forehead. Was she happy with the larger view she monitored for her safety and amusement? I suspect my hypothetical pelican didn't suffer from obsessions. She must have seemed suitably small in a gigantic world.

Internal stereoscopy does not enlarge my view. It puts me front and center, making my obsessions worse. I focus on what is near, not what is true. I am large in a small world. I encompass evil. I might even be the source of evil. The head-on view of my car, hateful antisemitic slurs, or my brandishing a gun at a bank teller are without context and measurable dimension. Plotless but rich everyday reality, with its myriad characters and dimensions, seems far away when I'm in the grip of OCD and closely focused on keeping myself (and everything else) under control. I believe what I've been told by therapists, that 99 percent of OCD sufferers never do the things they fear they might. But what about the rest? Lacking certainty, if I were in the grasp of OCD, I wouldn't be remembering river, sky, cottonwoods. I'd be trapped, dissociated, terrified of finding myself in that one percent.

Might I become more like a pelican? Imperturbable? In the absence of obsessions, my memory uncovers the dancing atmosphere as it roiled Yellowtail's sky, creating spiraling silver herrings. A cubist painting, it was a crumpled, illogical surface I avoided resolving or judging. The memory crowds out obsessions, filling me with the scent of cottonwood, the bright reflections of water, heat waves off bentonite hillsides.

Along these lines, another good visual trick is to try to see all sides of an object at once. Dating from two millennia ago, petroglyphs in the Bighorn Basin near Yellowtail depict powerful two-dimensional beings. Bison horns and the human body come head-on in the same plane. The interior—enfolding, according to Christian tradition, hidden spirit—is irrelevant. As if, with perfect understanding, all things become concurrent and adjacent, nothing hidden in time or space. Interior flattens against exterior. There is no mystery. Or there is nothing but mystery. For artists willing to accept it—and maybe for pelicans as well—surface *is* spirit. On the Bighorn River at Yellowtail, luxuriant surface overwhelmed and crushed my inward images, and I was gloriously free. As I am now, when I reminisce.

From "peaks to prairie," according to the common saying around here, a river like the Bighorn is mountain snowmelt coiling to desert oxbow, an eternal present of enlightenment dispelling internal darkness. I looked into the distance, and yet everything was close. Yellowtail was a whirlwind screen of sparkles and shine, the desert alive with sand and creosote, the river a thread of reality that defied neurosis. My obsessions gasp like stunned fish on this remembered shore of the Bighorn River. That is to say, they're exposed as ridiculous directives of misguided prefrontal angels. Another characteristic of obsessions: incongruity. While a particularly disturbing one might attack my moral core, the signal that an obsession has reached what I call its decadent phase is that my defenses strengthen against it. Logic takes root. Can I really be antisemitic if the very thought of it terrifies me?

Storing up textured experience helps combat obsessions. The desert glare I headed into at Yellowtail is both ever present and continuously receding—and all palpable surface. I can still rise and soar, float and preen, ready to lift far from the trap of obsession, personal or cultural, to achieve true vision—wide-angled, something like a pelican's. The memory of a walk opens four dimensions at once, a single luminous plane of height, depth, and width together with the rushing of an eternally present NOW. I imagine it's the way a dog goes through life.

As I took that desert path years ago along the Bighorn River, Rita, my black Lab/heeler, dashed ahead, turned to gauge how far behind I was, dug a bed in the cool dirt, and waited for me. She sniffed out rabbits, mice, droppings of all sorts, and was smart enough, unlike me, to rest in the shade. She was perhaps a creature not of the catastrophic past, the infinite future, or the self-generated imagery of anxiety, but of rushing-forward-in-stasis consciousness, the phantasmagoria of sensation. She had no obsessions. I envied her.

On that day in 1998, the river's flotilla of white pelicans stirred almost imperceptibly as I watched. Soon a few birds stretched. A few shook their heads and ruffled their wings, and then, with no preparation, no knowing looks at each other, no whispered confidences, the entire flock lifted. They twirled for position and circled and rose with air currents, dipped and swung together, and levitated up and up. They drifted so high in a loose and ever-changing pattern that they became white wimples on the cloudless backdrop and disappeared altogether against the sun until they wheeled around again, showing off the black of their wings. Individuals spiraled, triple-axeled, then formed a rippling union. Eventually, they vanished to the southwest, toward their Yellowstone breeding areas, the whole of their migration palpable.

TRAIL 2

Face-of-the-Mountain

General location: Red Lodge, Montana; about 70 miles from Yellowstone
Hiking distance: 3.5+ miles, one way
Elevation Gain: 1,700 feet
Terrain: Sagebrush flat to lodgepole pine and alpine meadow

The way it works for me is this. Anxiety is the rhythm, and OCD the melody. No matter what, if any, tune is playing, the rhythm continues. I don't know when it started, and I imagine it will go on as long as I live.

The hiker who suffers in this way benefits from having imperturbable companions to help her navigate trails. Not that my dog Luke is imperturbable. But, for more than forty years, my regular human hiking partner has been my husband Bernie—about as unruffled a soul as one could ever find. We met in southwestern Louisiana at an MFA program at McNeese State University—a program we perceived as politically difficult in its infancy at a school whose claim to fame, we found out later, was its mortuary science degree. We'd both been suckered in by a flyer featuring "Leda and the Swan" and the school's promise of French cuisine, "exotic water birds," and jazz music.

Soon the goal became clear: Bring kids from far away, use them to advertise the MFA as "national" and even "international" in scope, and pit them against each other in a kind of versifying gladiatorial contest that would go on throughout the term. There were alternate praise and ridicule and overt student-versus-student comparisons, and heavy-handed lessons in meter and form that relied on performing poems in a way no sane person ever would.

To add to our disorientation, we lived among hostile suburban neighbors who didn't appreciate a bunch of Yankees descending on their quiet subdivision. No doubt the "MFA lads," as the male recruits called themselves, and those few of us who were MFA lasses, were obnoxious and kept late hours. I'm sure we deserved the locals' distain as we tramped over St. Augustine grass, laughing about the Mr. Fish stand down the street and playing "Psycho Killer" into the night.

I lasted one semester; Bernie lasted two.

And now here we are, together, at the Face-of-the-Mountain trailhead in the foothills of Montana's Beartooth Mountains. There's the usual "Hiking in Bear Country" sign and map featuring a reassuring "You are Here" arrow. Instructions tell how to store food if you camp and what to do to avoid bears—grizzlies, to be specific. A friend once did, in fact, see a grizzly on this path. Nevertheless, we sling on our daypacks, suit Luke up, and set out. If, because of anxiety, I avoided trails where there was any possibility of bears, we would never hike in the Beartooth Mountains.

I literally watch my companions' backs: Luke's semi-erect ears, pennant tail, and prance of an undefined, full-body-waved "collie-looking thing" (as one of his sitters referred to him) and, leading the way, Bernie's five-foot five-inch frame burdened by a large blue daypack. For a minute I do what the Forest Service sign warns against. I forget about the here-and-now, the grizzly snuffle, the possible footprint in the dirt. I think about how Bernie and I are a team. And how we have been one for decades, with Luke our vibrant new rookie.

When I first met Bernie, he was somewhat the worse for wear: A three-day Greyhound ride from Rochester, New York, to Lake Charles, Louisiana, had left him short on sleep, long-bearded, and disoriented. The way he parted his hair in the middle bothered me. As did his pipe smoking. Anyway, I didn't pay him that much attention; I was busy trying to acclimate to French cuisine in the form of boudin or spicy blood sausage, to Southern Bell Telephone Company, and to Krogers ("Let's go Krogering!"). Every piece of business I had to attend to involved a long walk down Ryan Street. I'd guess any sizable town in America has one of these thoroughfares where the businesses, fast-food restaurants, and strip malls convene. In Salt Lake, it's State Street. In Billings, where I live now, it's Grand Avenue. In Lake Charles, it was Ryan Street. Unfortunately for me, every walk down Ryan Street involved the sandals I'd thought would be perfect for the subtropics. And thus every walk down Ryan Street incised new blisters on my sunburned toes. Finally I bought a bicycle and new shoes on Ryan Street, and my life improved. On the bicycle, I explored the "rurburbs"—parklike expanses of slapdash houses (in the West, we might call them ranchettes)—and the various lakes around town, all of which, in my memory, lapped at the base of an I-10 or I-210 bridge.

Bernie was far from my mind throughout these early Louisiana weeks. But one night we wandered out independently of each other from an MFA lads party. Not that we didn't appreciate The Clash and Talking Heads and the Ramones (alas, no jazz), and lounging in the "iron lung"—a barrel-like, black vinyl chair the lads had picked up at Goodwill—and tequila-laced punch, and plenty of New Orleans's own K&B beer (another staple of French cuisine). Something about the misty warm evening with palm fronds and blurry streetlights was more compelling, I guess. Together we admired the golden eyes and human-like digits of a green tree frog clinging to a mailbox.

The Face-of-the-Mountain trail starts on private land below Mount Maurice. Here nothing obstructs our view. The flowers distract me, though. Most noticeable at first are the daisies-with-a-vengeance—bright yellow with a poofy rust center. I don't see them high in the mountains; around here they're creatures of the prairie margins. *Gaillardia aristate*, or blanket flowers, like arid spaces where they cheer up the stalwart grasses. Bitterroots, though as tough as blanket flowers, are perhaps not so much cheerful as mystical. I have to kneel for them since they grow close to the earth, pink with twelve or more slim petals. The stems with their bullet buds shoot straight out of the ground.

Although many native peoples understood bitterroot, prepared it as a bear repellent, and liked to eat it, Meriwether Lewis—an early white and anxious wanderer—is credited with the "first" description. He found it "naucious to my palate," which implies that he didn't know how to cook it and failed to ask the locals for help. A specimen sent to Washington, DC, seemed to revive after a year's dormancy. The scientific name honors Lewis and the little plant's intrepidity: *Lewisia rediviva.*

I haven't tried to eat bitterroot. But I don't have to. Just looking at one—let alone a whole patch of them—nourishes. And it does so in a frighteningly ecstatic way. As Rilke says, all angels are terrifying, especially the angel of beauty.

I, of course, kept my weird sensitivities to myself in Bernie's and my early days. Perhaps I couldn't even have defined them or thought them different from what other people experience. Maybe I always assume that I'm the norm. Unfortunately, and not necessarily because of my various anxieties, our first major outdoor adventure was not entirely successful.

The obvious problem was my lack of skill. Bernie had to give me impromptu lessons in canoe handling, as I steered us repeatedly into cypress knees and logs hidden beneath a leek soup of duckweed and algae. He has a certain facility with freshwater. Where he's from, lakes that are large to my arid-trained eye are often called "ponds," but, growing up in sight of the Salt Flats, I'm not and never will be comfortable on water, unless it's naturally buoying like the Great Salt Lake. How we managed a bumpy circumnavigation of Sam Houston Jones State Park's cypress swamp, passing great egrets and nutrias, is a mystery. Bernie remained tolerant of my humiliating ineptitude at the tiller (just now he informs me that canoes don't have tillers—that's how much I know) because he's that way. I would come to rely on his ability to put small difficulties in perspective. "These things happen," he'd say—and still says.

I'm sure he secretly questioned the time we spent on the whole canoe rigmarole. And the thing to do at Sam Houston Jones State Park (where a truck-owning friend had dropped us off) was not to hike but to canoe. Getting our vessel was something of an ordeal in itself. In those days, you had to have a life jacket to rent a boat. The state park, however, didn't have life jackets to offer. It was the sort of pointless bureaucratic hurdle I got used to working my way through in the South. Anything to make life difficult for the hoi polloi. We walked a mile or so from the park office to a gas station life-vest outlet and back, showed off our gear, signed the requisite waiver of liability, and were assigned our sturdy craft. Only then could we set out on our clumsy exploration of the four-foot-deep swamp.

Later that first fall of our infatuation with the land and each other, I rented a car and we drove, more successfully than we had canoed, to Grand Isle, where we walked the sandy beach past houses on stilts that, to my inland eye, seemed clever and are now inadequate. The sea is rising, the land is sinking, and I realize that, like people, places can senesce. The present is destroying my past. But when I think of Grand Isle, that stretch of beach still glows.

I suppose you could say that my various mood disorders were presaged more than two hundred years ago, when my maternal ancestor Patience Throckmorton and her ilk arrived in what she thought of as a frightening kind of wilderness, one full of shadows, devils, and torment. *New* England, they called it. The following generations would eventually swagger across the continent, pushing and driving like Tennessee Williams's Big Daddy, a "fist pounding." Some would marry first cousins, some would throw knives at each other, one would end up in the notorious Topeka State Hospital, many would become Latter-Day Saints, and many would violently oppose Latter-Day Saints. Few would have ridden happily, like Bernie, through a cypress swamp, or strolled over a grizzly-haunted meadow, unarmed and worry-free.

After a meander through sage and flowers, and past a mule deer's silent judgment, we descend to a wooded creek crossing and come out in a wild currant-filled fold between ridges. From here we'll go to the first Face-of-the-Mountain vista point, a mile or so away—as the raven flies. Fortunately, switchbacks keep the grade to a minimum. Unfortunately, they keep us from getting to the top quickly. But Bernie reminds me we're not in a hurry.

The lush, well-watered gully (where a griz might lurk) is one of those things I wonder about. Its virgin timber was decimated to make the old "Black and White Road," the first motor route to the Beartooth Plateau. Minus timber, currants took over, and now, in early June, they're thick, chest-high, covered in fluffy white blossoms. Were the trees used to build what was then the coal-mining town of Red Lodge or the Smith Mine at Bearcreek? Or were they discarded? Blessing or curse, the currants grow so abundantly here because of that decades-past disturbance.

As we follow the old roadbed, I imagine wagons and Model Ts grinding out each switchback turn. We are noisy, too, while climbing, just in case bears are within earshot. In addition to the possibility of lurking griz, giant imprints of moose hooves indent older horse tracks. We don't see the moose. But he or she may see us. An interesting thought.

In one way, Louisiana was like this section of Face-of-the Mountain trail. Neither is a place for long vistas. If here it's geomorphology that limits our vision, along the Gulf Coast it was weather and industry as oil platforms and haze curtailed distance. About the farthest I remember being able to see in those parts was straight up at white pelicans, vanishing and reappearing against the sun. The local marshes and the long bridge over the Atchafalaya River opened things up for a few minutes, but, if you were a Northern, you were more likely to look at the odd sensitive plants and ferns and snakes at your feet. Herons and egrets loomed large on piers and along bayous.

In those days, Bernie wore round John Lennon glasses and a full dark beard—and that central part in his hair. He wore, and still usually wears, blue jeans and plaid shirts, cotton in summer and the South, flannel in winter and the mountains. Unlike me, he was a published poet with a chapbook under his belt. Everything he wrote slid the human into the nonhuman and back, curtailing obsessive thinking. One of his Louisiana poems, "Moving to Marshland," goes in part like this:

> . . . Here, there's no horizon.
> Islands without backbones slump
> In still rivers. A man is a hill by the sea
> Where herons stand like lamps.

Typically, Bernie illuminates surface and does not admit a seething interior.

At Rutherford Beach (the "marshland" of Bernie's poem) and on the Creole Nature Trail, where we spotted our first alligators, we encountered hundreds of waterbirds—at least that part of the McNeese MFA flyer proved accurate—and we realized that our wanderings were taking the form of a shared consciousness that had started with a little green tree frog on a mailbox.

Despite his indispensability to me, Bernie cannot fully understand how my brain twists into knots and my heart swells with torment when anxiety ramps up or obsessions strike. He seems to see the world in much the same way Luke does: It's filled with interesting stuff. Today's failure to relate is minor. When I climb, my right knee hurts. When I descend, my left knee twinges. Says cheerful Bernie, "You have one good leg for each direction!"

Despite my quirky knees, we do reach the end of the switchbacks and a world of delight. We're here at last—the convoluted eastern foothills of the Beartooths push high to our west, with the Pryor Mountains to the east and Red Lodge behind us. Limestone pinnacles flank the trail. And, ah, hell, as perfect as the place is, I can't stay. Is it my family's native compulsion to "get on" or just that old hiker's malady: Let's see what's over this rise, beyond the next bend, down that draw . . . ? "Let's keep going," I tell Bernie, and he's amenable, of course.

We contour around the hillside—the path freshly cleared, the old road above us blocked. We pass two or three abandoned mine adits that have been filled in and walk over a shiny sprinkling of mica, the wonder of which is its friability, making it look as if someone shattered a mirror.

Bernie was, in the ancient past of his SUNY-Brockport days, a geology major. He still takes an interest in rocks. But usually, when I ask, he tells me a particular one looks like gneiss or some sort of shale or something. Granite? But he can't remember. He says that pitch and slope baffled him, and he soon turned to the study of English. He doesn't say what he lost from the switch and what he gained. He does say that he was better with morphemes and phonemes than he was with porphyry, though, poet that he is, the rocks' names, if not their characteristics, stick in his imagination.

Soon we leave the old mines and the mica and head through typical Beartooth Mountain lodgepole pine forest. Wind or fire came through a few years ago and downed small trees, but, oddly enough, the forest remains healthy. Another stream crossing and another climb—and then we're at our second vista point. Here we can see even more as we look at the past, our own and the earth's, with its layers of Mesozoic rock. There are Badger Basin, near where we lived twenty years ago; the Bighorn and Pryor Ranges; and the singular weirdness of Heart Mountain, a massive chunk of two-hundred-fifty-million-year-old limestone that scrambled off the side of the Beartooths while Eocene monkeys darted around raspberry bushes and ferns.

The landslide came to rest. Eons passed. And then, from August 1942 to just before Christmas 1945, almost eleven thousand people lived at the Heart Mountain Internment Camp as prisoners of the United States. Their crime was sharing a Japanese heritage and the desire to immigrate, just as my family had done. But, where my family found a continent to take by force, those first generations from Asia encountered diminished possibilities and unjust incarceration.

What remains of the camp, hidden now by the intervening hills, are a few scattered foundations, some asbestos-riddled ruins, and an interpretive center.

After our MFA fiasco and my return to Utah, Bernie left Louisiana a wanted man. He and the other lads had "abandoned" a rental agreement. Despite the landlord's verbal okay that they could do so, the law was summoned, papers filed. Bernie was never found, though for a while he lived across the street from the lawyer's office. I write this to add the only frisson of scandal that pertains to our story—and because the statute of limitations has probably expired. At any rate, before those marshy lamps of Bernie's poem were extinguished, we faithfully exchanged letters (no email in those days), met in Salt Lake to go hiking in Arches National Park and at Fisher Towers, married in a snowstorm in the Wasatch Mountains, and lived in Denver for a year.

We loved the prairie and the Colorado Rockies, and once saw our orange plastic tube tent, which was all the shelter we could afford and which we'd left at a campsite we'd paid and registered for, converted into a tablecloth by a family that for some reason usurped our spot. That night we slept, uncomfortably, in the 1966 Dodge Dart my dad had given us. I remember angling around the gear shift. But we spent the next day hiking to a head-clearing, cloud-clearing view of the Never Summer Mountains.

One of the only times I've seen Bernie unreasonably angry was when he hurled a snowshoe into February powder. We were on the Ben Tyler Gulch trail west of Denver, and the bindings were, as with many a rental snowshoe, badly designed. He couldn't keep the things on, even though, as he shouted, "Everybody else can use these." I think "everybody else" was me.

Subsequent career choices sent us careening around the country with our son—our only child—forced to go along. We moved from Colorado to California (where Tom was born), back to Utah, to Indiana, Wyoming, Maine, Florida, and Montana. Though Tom has grown, we now have Luke to watch over and (attempt to) train. Rita, the dog of Tom's childhood, never needed a leash, but Luke (a suite of herding dog breeds with a stubborn and lovable disposition—the "collie-looking thing" vibe going for him) is untrustworthy with marmots, deer, and—God forbid—bears. He'll stay leashed until he matures (at six, he's still a pup, right?).

It's usually the three of us, then: Bernie looking for odd cloud effects and rocky outcrops (or maybe not—he tells me he's "just walking" when he's walking); me trying to balance exterior surface with interior depths; and Luke sampling grass, dung, and dirt. Sometimes you enjoy the loneliness of your own perspective. Then again, you can feel alone even in company—what *is* Bernie thinking? Maybe he isn't, just as he claims. In another early poem, "A Walk," he wrote:

> A dog barks somewhere far off.
> A heron takes a long time to cross the sky.
> You turn to face the woman who has appeared beside you,
> whom you have been walking with. A clean night
> drifts down around you. . . .

I admire the clarity of those lines. My poetry inevitably ends up burdened with emotion, fear, convoluted images that twist and turn and open onto a stabbing galaxy of attempted resolution.

Enough, I tell myself. Stop the twisting and turning. Stop the images. Or rather, make them images without meaning or augury. Sacred surfaces. As is.

So, when a white butterfly balances on a balsamroot, demanding more attention than the thirty-mile-wide view, I give her what she wants. A Rocky Mountain Parnassian, she's big by butterfly standards, with a nearly three-inch wingspan; tiny round red spots on each fore- and hindwing, the spots outlined in black; and all the other required dabs and dots of her phenotype. Year after year, century after century for up to two hundred million years (about the time that Heart Mountain's limestone was formed), such angels of beauty have emerged from chrysalises, wearing their genetic codes on their veined sleeves—each species interdependent with a host plant. In the Parnassian's case, that plant is stonecrop—a yellow sedum that, as its name suggests, grows out of rock crevices or thin soil.

What I love about this neck of land between Mount Maurice, with its dense pine forest (destined to burn in the Robertson Draw Fire of 2022), and the prairie-oriented hills is the contrast between a panorama that stretches for miles—and millions of years—and the delicate creatures and plants sipping the present around me. It's an unfathomable mélange of geologic force, human moral and intellectual frailty, and biological persistence.

Bernie early on documented how the wild gets inside us and at the same time resists humanization. As he wrote in "Indian Lake":

> She has driven all afternoon through the heavy skull.
> Trees lean in the blade spaces of her windshield.

With the wild beating inside me and with me seeping into the wild, I settle beside Luke, eat lunch, and pretend to nap while clouds pout, spread, blow away, and reform. It's hard to slow down, relax, stop being nervous, feeling like I should be more, much more—a great hiker, a great writer, a rebellious descendant of Patience Throckmorton, who really shouldn't have come to this continent in the first place, let alone declare it hers.

The clouds darken and mass but soon blue sky, sunshine, and stiffening wind nudge them into better humor. Painful rhythms of inadequacy and the inhumanity of history settle like friable mica. A few feet away, Bernie watches shadows chase themselves over the prairie. Or something.

I stop my self-flagellation. I remember the yellow asbestos-warning tape at the Heart Mountain Camp from our Powell days before the interpretive center was built and the site given a kind of logic. But I'm looking at the mountain, and I feel empowered. Take care of what is good and free, it says.

This is also the advice of the indispensable partner whom I have been walking with. For him, cultivating a sensitivity to the external is one's duty in a place that is neither empty nor howling wilderness. Danger is all around, I think, but there was a time when no grizzlies remained in this area. I'm glad that time is over. Though there might be one on the trail now, there *usually*, as Bernie would remind me, isn't.

TRAILS 3 TO 9

One Summer, Eight Bear Therapists

Late afternoon. DeLacy Creek in Yellowstone. Shadows were long and so was the bear when she stood on two legs to look at us. I didn't specifically think "grizzly," although I knew she was one. When you see your first trail-met *Ursus arctos horribilis* scanning you from about thirty yards away, all the shapes of all your ideas, all you breathe and feel, is Power. In the sun-glinting, ticked fur. In the broad chest. In those knife-tipped paws. In the silent way she rises from the grass, the way she towers, the way she judges.

But Bernie and I and the bear had all been taken by surprise that day, and at first no one could decide what to do. Did that indecision last ten seconds or two minutes, Bernie and I paralyzed, the bear judging us from her bipedal height, perhaps calculating the possibility that we carried bear spray or posed some other threat? Her curiosity satisfied, she lowered into the grass and sprinted across the meadow away from us. She was beautiful, and her power left a twang after she'd gone. We didn't stay to ponder it but glided back to the trailhead, enjoying the efficacy of adrenaline. We were high on bear.

Fight or flight. A grizzly arrives out of a forest into a green meadow just as humans are on a perpendicular course, skirting the grasses. The obvious best response for the bear is flight. It will save her life in the long run. For the humans, doing nothing, at least for a while, is the answer. Doing nothing, that is, with bear spray in hand. And then, when it's safe, the flight to the car and a cathartic release of tension. What amazes me about our griz encounter is how human control was subsumed by the bear's intentions, the bear's will. And we let it be. And it all turned out okay.

Allowing someone else—especially a bear—to take the lead doesn't come easy for me. When I was a kid I was troubled by compulsions more than obsessions—the other side of the OCD coin. Very early in my anxious life, I embarked on the difficult task of controlling all outcomes of all events, and compulsive behavior was the way I managed to do this. Once started, my compulsions were a powerful fight response against dangers real and imagined. I might have looked perfectly calm or simply prone to weird habits, but my mind was a raging battlefield. I had to count the schoolroom tiles I walked on to make the world run correctly. I had to play a new piece on my guitar perfectly to keep my family from harm. I had to count to a certain number before I walked into a room. I had to sleep facing a certain direction to ward off evil. These rituals stopped the unspooling of events, bending the very direction of fate. Because of me, an aunt and uncle would not be in a car wreck as they drove from Reno, Nevada, to visit us. My dachshund would not eat toxic foot powder again as she had when she was a puppy. Satan would not sneak up on anyone I knew. I believed I could fight disaster by keeping my behavior and words in order. My cosmic battles weighed me down, generating even more anxiety. It was like meeting a grizzly in every meadow, in all the random thoughts my mind launched. Against them I used a psychological equivalent of bear spray: repetitive behaviors meant to calm the mind and save the world.

Not all compulsions are obvious, and mine became less so as I grew older. I hated Wasatch Junior High School and fervently agreed with the poem etched on a bathroom stall door:

> Spring has sprung
> The grass is risen
> Here we are
> In Wasatch prison

School's confinement and social stuff bedeviled me. I might as well have been an ethnographer in another culture. As a gentile, or perpetual outsider, I didn't want to call attention to myself by angling across a room to step only on white tiles or to avoid cracks. Reading and writing became my compulsions. I read books and wrote stories to order my disordered loneliness and to stop bad things from happening, but no one would have counted those behaviors as compulsive. I didn't. Until now, when I revisit that era.

I loved new texts, the way they felt in my hands, the way they smelled, and how they could take me far from the indiscernible cause-and-effect of real life to the controlled causality of plot. But one particularly glorious book in our eighth-grade curriculum wasn't a novel. When you're fourteen years old, you're probably not supposed to get all shivery about *Thirty Days to a More Powerful Vocabulary*. How could I, though, resist the paperback's examples and exercises studded with words like "brio," "sub rosa," "tyro," "bête noire," and "bagatelle"? Hardly good additions to casual conversation, I admit, even if they come in handy for crossword puzzles. But they helped me see different hues of awareness, helped me gain control of my adolescent feeling of being "de trop." If I could put a word to something, then that thing was mine to order.

Consider a German term writers Wilfred Funk and Norman Lewis sneaked in as if for me. It defined an emotional nuance I had long felt: "weltzschmerz," or "world-pain." The word's phonemes alone fascinated me. That knot of consonants mirrored my idiosyncratic psychological realities, my oddness and sense of impending doom. And my need to struggle.

Naming this emotional state, like naming a bear, diminished its power, made it comprehensible. Oh, it's just my weltzschmerz, I could say. As now I recognize, "Oh, not that obsession again!" And, really, how frightening can even great beasts be if they have names like Smoky, Ben, Old Ephraim, or the famous Grand Teton Bear 399, if they're brought into human consciousness and shrunk to size? Just use one of those *Thirty Days* words like "bête noir." Or, like a psychiatrist, contain a patient's misery in the diagnostic term "obsession."

Back at DeLacy Creek we didn't have the luxury of naming. We let the bear make the first move, taking the middle path between fight or flight, which is maybe the only thing to do in the face of overwhelming power, because on that day, in front of us—head raised, body a mass of fur and flesh—was simply Bear, a force, not the word. Over the retellings of her story, she remains nameless, becoming, at most, "the" bear. An adversary who isn't. A ground-zero griz, who defies numbering, naming, and climax. A few years later, over one amazing summer, her avatars continued the lesson: Fear and paralysis, let alone compulsion, needn't be my only reactions to things I can't control.

Bear #1
Hayden Valley, 2017

General location: Yellowstone
Driving distance from Gardiner (north entrance): 29.5 miles
Elevation: ~7,707 feet
Terrain: Subalpine meadow

Our first bear of 2017 lives in Yellowstone's Hayden Valley—one of only about a thousand grizzlies in the greater ecosystem. Westerners often call for the animals' elimination, or at least for a smaller population of them. This one, ensconced in the middle of the park, is lucky. She won't be hunted, but if she becomes a danger or a nuisance, she could be managed, which is a nice word for "killed." Essentially a ward of the state, she's not endangered anymore, just threatened, because the federal government judges the numbers of her kind sufficient. That is to say, she exists at the whim of the politicians. Like the rest of us.

Identified as a sow by a park ranger whose job is to manage the humans lining the roadside to gawk, this grizzly suffers hominin attentions with noblesse oblige. Early-season tourists train an arsenal of optical equipment at her, but she's unfazed. When I give a stranger a look through my scope, the woman, tearing up, turns to me afterward. "This is what I've always dreamed of," she says.

As we watch, the bear takes brunch—a meadow's worth of tastes and smells, succulent tubers, savory broadleaves, sweet bulbs, sprigs of fresh spring grass, and the occasional unfortunate ground squirrel whose winter diggings have loosened the soil and made berms through the pasture. Sometimes the bear leaps on a little rodent. Sometimes she scoops one up with her three-inch claws. Sometimes she swallows one whole from a mound of dirt she excavated. I imagine she has nothing against gulping any delicacy she can find—larvae, boreal frogs, mice, voles, worms. Her forepaws work methodically. She's in no hurry, surrounded by the largesse of May, the good dark smells of sodden grasslands and sage, the warmth of early summer. She can exert hundreds of pounds of pressure with one swipe of her giant forepaw. But she can probably also extract a caterpillar from his home twig with a tender tug of her flexible lips.

Her quick mind undoubtedly assesses the humans, analyzes the prospects for bitterroot bulbs, takes in the coalescing but still innocent clouds, knows where the local boar grizzlies make their daybeds—places she will want to avoid. She may even be using the proximity of the road as a shield against presumably wilder and more aggressive bears. She may or may not be burdened by knowledge of her rarity, the possibility that her power—like that of a great democracy—could be overthrown. A dark form against the radiant pasture, she looks up occasionally to take in any threats. She seems far from fighting or fleeing right now. On the edge of the abyss—like the rest of us—she runs out the clock in style as she savors the valley's delicacies. I want to be like her.

I grew up in a sacred place, too. But mine was the LDS Jerusalem, Salt Lake City. A gathering point for the end times. The Zion my ancestors worked so hard to reach and defend, and change. Unlike the bear, they did not belong but warped the place around them. As with any American holy site—even Yellowstone—the arrival of white settlers meant the oppression of the Indigenous population and reengineering of the affected biome.

In Salt Lake, righteousness diminished the awareness of oppression—if you were LDS. But how could I, whose family had fallen out of the Church aristocracy and who didn't believe in Zion anymore, be at rest in this stolen place? Unable to accept the ideal of conquest, I felt (and still feel) that my childhood home—built over the site of a pioneer orchard in Shoshone land—was haunted. It wasn't until I was older that I understood the source of this feeling.

One white neighbor family (the whole subdivision was predominantly white) took in a succession of Navajo kids, presumably wrenched from their families, to prepare them for their roles as Lamanites in the Church. While these little boys and girls were often out playing basketball or bicycling, they never stayed long enough for the rest of us to get to know them. They were much younger than we were anyway, or so we rationalized our indifference. They were "those poor Indian children," in my mother's view.

I focused on my own trivial problems: acne (I hated my mother's comment about the "underlying redness" of my complexion) and social pressure. I didn't belong to any group, not to the anti-Mormon-devout-anyway Protestant clique, the tough-girl-smoker clique, the wealthy-gentile clique. I had no boyfriends. I wasn't pretty or cool enough to be in the desirable-though-heathen clique. I was neither Lamanite nor Saint nor categorizable gentile. Mostly, I wanted to be away from my peers and out hiking, which *was* where I belonged—with mule's ear daisies and scrub jays, hard pressed though they were as more people (including me) visited the mountains.

And that's where the beauty of "weltzschmerz" came in.

Experience settles far below the ideal, and the emotional pain of living in such a disillusioned state creates sadness not just for oneself but for the world. Finally, I could name how I felt. With the coming of the LDS, many beautiful things vanished or were hidden. Not just open spaces but Indigenous lifeways and languages. In Utah, these processes were called "making the desert bloom" and turning the fallen Lamanites "whiter and more delightsome." If the resulting flowers were less numerous for gentiles like me, they weren't even budding for the appropriated children. At least I would have the luxury of choosing between fighting for what I loved or flying from post-pioneer Zion. Not yet counseled by the Hayden Valley griz, I would choose flight.

Bear #2
Bear Canyon, 2017

General location: Pryor Mountains south slope, Montana; 105 miles from Yellowstone
Distance: 4.1+ miles one way
Elevation gain: ~400 to 1,400 feet or more
Terrain: Juniper desert to alpine "prairie"

The old road follows sparkling orange rocks and dull white ones, and it feels good to swing along with my two usual companions—dog and husband—in the sun while morning shadows stick to the hollows. To Luke's canine consternation, Bernie and I sometimes make him stop as we flick over a dried cowpie—about every third one yields a small northern scorpion, a handsome creature with black stripes and a central spot on a tan exoskeleton. The little manure denizens seem more perturbed than aggressive—they scootch under loose soil when their shelters are violated. We carefully replace their roofs.

This first real hike of the summer is up Bear Canyon in the Pryor Mountains, giant hills to the west of the lofty Bighorns. Despite their lack of altitude, the Pryors are in no way lesser. Their base rock is venerable, about 2.5 billion years old. On top of that, the limestone-sandstone geology is so complex I can't ever get a handle on its folds and warps. This newer rock shows that cataclysms come and cataclysms go—inland seas, floods, dry periods, extinctions. In the future, Yellowtail Dam will certainly break; the water in nearby Bighorn Canyon will flow unobstructed again. At some point, the local towns will vanish. Deaver, Frannie, Lovell, Powell—with their approximately eight thousand human inhabitants, all told—teeter in the desert even now. Will it be drought or political upheaval or earthquake that will whisk away their stories, like sagebrush pollen in an October wind?

I suppose my own story will last a fraction of that time. Parts of it are long gone already. How salient is it anymore that in junior high school my weltzschmerz involved Wasatch prison—halls filled with people who might insult my looks; gym classes filled with girls who'd been playing on their LDS ward softball teams for years and taunted me for my poor fielding; classrooms in which I might have such a horrible gushing of menstrual blood as I sat through a lecture that I'd be afraid to stand up when the bell rang? And what was under my control? Reams of writing paper, the beautifully empty notebooks I'd soon fill to save the world—compulsive writing never stopped by any blockage. I envy people who have that trouble.

I'm far from my adolescence. I left Utah, if not its anxieties, years ago, and I find satisfaction in an adulthood untroubled by whether my friends are popular. In some ways, I'm walking in the best of all possible worlds—a Utah vibe without Utah's fraught religious history. These are the semi-arid southern reaches of the Pryor Mountains in a late spring when the high country is too snowy for easy walking. The car waits behind in a flat dominated by sage, yucca, and prickly pear cactus that, by June, large yellow rose-like blossoms will dress. We're too early for them, though, and the cactus is easy to step on by mistake.

Entering the sharp rock gates of the lowest reaches of the canyon, I feel all but beamed up to my home state: Horned toads, not to mention those little scorpions, live in these parts, and there are red sandstone and a stubborn seasonal wash mostly dry already. Lark sparrows join gray flycatchers and blue-gray gnatcatchers, birds I associate with the Colorado plateau country. We round a bend, and the world expands to a view of Red Pryor Mountain, still snow covered. Cottonwoods crop up, and lazuli buntings' sonatas overlap in a contrapuntal chorus. The suave males pose on bare limbs. Turquoise with white wing bars and a splash of orange on the pale breast, they seem to have arrived before the women, maybe to prepare and mark off homesites. I remember lazuli buntings from the outdoor lunch area under scrub oak of the Wasatch Range at one of the many temporary jobs I held as an undergrad at the University of Utah. I don't remember what the job was, though.

In Bear Canyon proper, the view contracts again. Rock walls close in, dented by caves and alcoves of all sizes. Cockleburs that in fall lodged in Luke's curly brindled fur and drove him to hysteria and an impromptu haircut with the tiny scissors on a Swiss army knife are still soft. Cottonwoods hoard the tender yellow-green of early summer, delicate against the rock as if they could be bruised. White-throated swifts, lemony chats, and more lazuli buntings dazzle the cliffs.

We eat lunch at the table someone built beneath cottonwoods, its top made of two-by-fours laid on end and about rib high. The Pryors are famous for their "Little People"—uncanny beings about whom Apsáalooke culture has many stories. But this is a table for giants. As we spread out sandwiches, apples, and dog treats, Luke barks in anticipation. And then keeps barking as we eat. It's one of his more annoying traits.

After our repast, we skirt the canyon's western margin. The steep dirt road takes us through junipers, past lichen-covered rock, and to expansive views of the highest Pryors ridge, a few thousand feet, it looks like, above us. From here, we can tell that Bear Canyon isn't a single defile; it's hardly a canyon at all but a network of sunken arteries hidden below forested cliffs.

When we get to the firs, there's still too much daylight to stop. We eventually climb beyond them into an arrowleaf balsamroot meadow glowing yellow with accents of lupine blue and larkspur purple. To the northwest and across the desert, treeless plateaus and rocky spires of the Beartooth Mountains shimmer—Whitetail Peak's pyramidal summit a whirlwind of blown snow visible these tens of miles east. To the south, ditch burning smudges the dry expanse of the Bighorn Basin, and I imagine farmers with acetylene torches incinerating weeds, similar pyrotechnics undoubtedly a beloved hominin activity since *Homo erectus* mastered ignition.

The mystical eternal perfection of petals and stamens, of desire and space and freedom and desert, lights my soul. We're far from human suffering, from geopolitics. Anxiety recedes. And my episodic OCD is currently in remission. The Xanax bottle sits untouched at home, and mostly full. Still, compulsions stir. I tick off bird, plant, and insect names. To me "bear," "wood nymph," and "short-horned lizard" are hedges against my anxiety and their extinction, as if by learning the names I can keep myself and the animals alive.

As a child I probably didn't know many names. But I remember being crazy about the swallows that dove and wheeled around a cave opening in the Wasatch, and someone was able to tell me what to call them. Later, in the 1970s, I wrote letters to protest the trans-Alaska oil pipeline and steel-jaw leghold traps. As if my words—and mine alone ("hubris," according to *Thirty Days to a More Powerful Vocabulary*)—could save the world.

I felt the gap between actual and ideal on many levels. Time was, for instance, when my dad could take us to Yellowstone and we'd see bears all along the road. By the era of Wasatch Junior High, the bears were gone; garbage pits had been closed throughout the park, and many biologists were afraid the cold-turkeyed animals would die en masse. Their numbers dropped to around one hundred fifty grizzlies. Yellowstone wasn't the same, my parents said. My dad didn't want to drive there anymore. Utah's own great bears had been extirpated for at least fifty years, but we never thought about them, as if they'd been erased from the land. In the 1970s I'd have argued that Utah was never home to grizzlies.

I can't shake the familiarity of this place in the Pryors. So much like Utah. Even to its lack of griz and its limestone cliffs. Our turnaround point is where a single last deep chasm of Bear Canyon separates us from the highest ridge and the snow. We settle by a wind-sculpted juniper. I dig a treat out of my pack for Luke and a bag of trail mix for me. Mid-chew, I notice some kind of shrub—a skunkbush sumac, maybe—moving along the other side of the canyon. It has quite a stride. I raise my binoculars. No—the sumac isn't a sumac. Monstrous, oblivious, it strolls along a line of firs, stops, continues. My heart speeds. My arms and cervical spine tingle in a healthy way. I'm looking at a five-hundred-pounds-at-least black bear. Naming him makes everything click, but then he goes beyond the naming. He vibrates, radiates. His nobility polishes this ridge and this juniper, shrinks my ego and quiets my fears. I point him out to Bernie, and then the bear is gone.

Bear #3
Roberts Bench, 2017

General location: Pryor Mountains off Sage Creek Road, Montana; 105 miles from Yellowstone
Distance: 3–6 miles round trip
Elevation gain: 200–500 feet
Terrain: Lodgepole pine and fir forest to grassland

If a raven had bothered to look down right then, she would have seen an improvised choreography, symmetrical, somewhat silly, and, by mere chance, well executed. Here's how the dance happened.

We've not gotten the Pryors out of our systems this year. So we go back—still early enough that the "good" road to Big Ice Cave (aside from a population of wild horses, the Pryors' only tourist attraction) is closed halfway up. We park at a wide spot by the barricade and go on foot along the more-than-a-two-track until a jeep "route" breaks off uphill. That's the direction we want.

Red cliffs and a tangle of wildflowers. And a harrier drifting down the gully. In most of my time outside, I see animals lazing, playing, talking, bathing—rarely fighting or fleeing. Maybe Robinson Jeffers had it wrong about the "equally earnest elements of nature." This hawk, anyway, seems light-hearted, taking a chance on the morning breeze.

There will be a plausible sighting of a grizzly in the Pryors in 2023, a lone adult moving through the area, perhaps looking for prairie on the other side since, until they were driven into the mountains, that's what the West's grizzlies were: a prairie species. But on this hike, we're innocent of the future. My alertness is low. We watch for rattlers and black bears but not that overwhelming, snuffling presentiment of power.

I grew up hiking with similar unconcern, though I didn't realize why. Utah in the 1960s and 1970s was a place trying, as I was, to come to terms with its limitations. According to legend, Frank Clark, a sheepherder and trapper, shot and killed the state's alleged last grizzly, Old Ephraim, in 1922 or 1923, after years of trying. But even some fifty years later, recreationists and hunters, not to mention eager kids, could still find seemingly wild land and abundant wildlife. Floating in the Great Salt Lake as a child, I was surveilled by flocks of gulls, buzzed by brine flies, and surrounded by the miniature red commas of brine shrimp. *How can such amazing creatures exist?* I wondered, as the serum of brine bit my lips. But the smelter stack at Magna and the world's largest open-pit copper mine at Bingham Canyon were gazing over my shoulder. That should have been a clue that weltzschmerz was creeping in.

The copper mine held a bizarre fascination for me. You could see it from all over the valley, an amphitheater dug from the side of the denuded Oquirrhs (ironically, "Oquirrh" means "Shining Mountains" in Ute). This structure, though vaguely Delphic, did not honor Aphrodite, Zeus, or any other god—except for the almighty dollar. At the turn of the nineteenth century, as tribute to capitalism, Japanese laborers were dangled from baskets to chisel out new levels. It was the most dangerous work around. In that way, the mine was a multiethnic, gentile endeavor, an abomination—and a beautiful, multi-toned pastel marvel driven by a societal compulsion: greed dressed up as inevitability. Fighting the terrors of darkness required electrification, and electrification needed minerals. A true wonder of the world, Bingham in my day had a visitor center that I remember from a school fieldtrip. An interpretive movie told us that the pit provided a good portion of the world's industrial copper. The men who worked there (they were all men, of course) were as godlike as Vulcan with their khaki pants, hardhats, and biceps.

The transformation of Utah began decades earlier, with my ancestors' arrival in the valley. Pre-industrial Salt Lake wasn't built by prayer alone. The LDS downtown department store—Zion's Cooperative Mercantile Institution, or ZCMI—used to be decorated by giant wooden columns taken from the now-denuded Oquirrhs. Construction of the Tabernacle and the Temple ate lumber as well. And Mormon farming projects depended on irrigation.

Far below the copper mine is that saucer of water I floated in so many years ago—the Great Salt Lake, now dying of drought and overuse. Nonetheless, the state is planning to dam one of its major inflows, the Bear River. With the lake's passing would go the remnant of a great Pleistocene freshwater lake. Migratory shorebirds and ducks. Pelican rookeries. And yes, brine shrimp. And up would come winds of arsenic-laden sand to whip across the Wasatch Front and into the lungs of its million people. The sardonic joke is that the metropolitan area may have to change its name to Dust Lake City.

The Pryors, too, were and are the site of mine workings: scattered, abandoned uranium diggings, and a large quarry pit that keeps growing just like any open-pit mine. Blooms and rusts. The well-known cycle. Ironically, the company looking for a foothold in the Pryors—its name splashed on announcements of pending permits tacked to posts along the lower Crooked Creek drainage—now owns the Bingham mine. Based in Australia and the United Kingdom, Rio Tinto is a major multinational corporation. State Farm Insurance, Goldman Sachs, and Morgan Stanley are significant investors. Rio Tinto's worst act of destruction isn't the Utah operation, though, or its desired incursion into the Pryors, but the demolition in 2020 of an Australian cave that contained artifacts from forty-six thousand years of human residency. The company expresses regret for "the distress we caused," but not, as the *Guardian* points out, for "the destruction."

Rio Tinto is everywhere, apparently. Humans are good at searching for minerals, and corporations specialize in processing landscapes into money. All this digging and draining can be seen as a way to control earth's processes, to fight entropy and catastrophe—and even stasis. What Rio Tinto and other corporations are doing is no more effective than my teenage compulsions were. Earth simply uses our own excesses against us in the form of climate change and water degradation.

On our hike today, I honor what is near and still free. Sugar bowls, otherwise known as "vase flowers," "lion's beard," or the wonderful "leather flowers," are dark purple with deep cups folded over at their white brims. I easily find them pictured in my field guide.

Our destination is off-trail to Roberts Bench—which off-trailness lends a roguish quality to our hike and tells of the world's nonlinearity.

We soon reach the broad plateau overlooking a piece of terrain called the Punch Bowl. Above us, a high ridge deflects bubbles of thunderclouds that, in the end, don't amount to much, and aspens daub a green valley below. A road in the hollow winds and lazes, minus cars or trucks. We squeeze under the barbed wire of a grazing allotment fence, and inevitably I tear a small hole in my pantleg.

We follow where the grassy, flat hilltop meets the trees that skirt it—a tangle of firs and pines—until we circumnavigate all of Roberts Bench. Bernie wanders down the hill. Luke is peaceable and willing to sit with me. All is green, buzzing, happy. Distracted by the sun's warmth and the acrobatic chipping sparrow who grabs a large insect mid-flight, I forget to make noise, forget to be alert. When Bernie rejoins us to continue our walk, I see her: a little glistening black bear, as sharp, tidy, and clean as a person can be. How I stand up, put on my pack, juggle Luke's leash and my hiking poles, and admire her appearance, I've no idea. Because this is where the dance occurs.

Bernie, Luke, and I, on the one hand, describe a perfect 180-degree arc as we turn gracefully away. The bear, on the other hand, describes a similar delicate arc in the opposite direction. A paw de deux. Cream-colored snout leading, her face declares a certain embarrassed admission that she let down her guard too and almost ran into us.

What I like to think about now is that bear and non-bears were imperfectly in perfect sync. On a nice day, it's easy to loll—and then something happens to snap you back. In the Roman myth of Actaeon, Diana—the goddess of the moon and archery—transforms a hunter into a stag when he happens upon her bathing. As goddesses are wont to do, she gets her panties (the ones she'd flung into the olive trees) in a twist about such a mortal access of hubris. She makes sure that Actaeon is subsequently torn apart by his own hounds.

You might blame the goddess for being too persnickety. But Actaeon violates one of the cardinal principles of the woods: Pay attention! His punishment, though severe, is not undeserved. I suppose the myth could serve as a warning to any individual or corporation so self-absorbed that it forgets to watch where it's going. A cautionary tale about mental landscapes. Thinking you're in control, which is not a cure for anxiety but its stimulus. Because control is a mirage.

This is all to say that I felt somewhat like Actaeon. The bear was a small, fierce creature confused by our appearance but clearly the star of the drama, ready to set us straight. If not the bear herself then perhaps her mother in the trees nearby.

Bears #4, 5, and 6
Yellowstone River Bridge, south of the confluence with the Lamar River, 2017

General location: Yellowstone, northern route between Gardiner and Cooke City
Driving distance (Gardiner to Lamar River): 28 miles one way
Elevation gain: ~1,141 feet
Terrain: Sagebrush and shortgrass prairie through lodgepole pine and spruce forest to mountain meadow

When I was a teenager, there were two close destinations for family outings: the mountains and the lake. The Wasatch were green and cool and relaxing. Sometimes we even went to the High Uintas, which I thought of as the Wasatch's bigger sisters. These were the ideal—Bald Mountain and Mount Agassiz, with their pikas and talus and lichens and fierce winds and glaciated views of twelve-thousand- and thirteen-thousand-foot peaks and tarns and swirling clouds and turquoise sky.

The Great Salt Lake was the actual, a trenchant source of weltzschmerz. I-80 zoomed alongside; Antelope Island State Park's causeway shot across the brine to a forlorn group of metal picnic tables; Morton Salt carved disease-tinted industrial evaporation ponds along the shallows; the city with its Temple and corporate skyscrapers hung on the horizon; and the ruins of shoreline resorts that had come and gone for a hundred years were drowned or exposed, depending on the whims of snowmelt.

But the odd thing is, even dearer to me than the wide freedom of the mountains was anything left of the ideal wild lake: avocets, gulls, the winter bald eagle roost at Willard Bay—and the unearthly tourmaline waters themselves, loitering around barren islands. Here, where people had been driven to fight nature by the magical thinking of Manifest Destiny and the LDS concept of latter days, these isolated facets reflected more brightly by contrast.

Yellowstone, too, is an indefinable mixture of the real magic created by water, rhyolite, lodgepole pines, and ospreys, and the superstitious stuff created by laws, prejudices, and the human mind. Specifically, much of what the boundaries of the national park contain is just the world going about its business. But that business is imprisoned, defined, political.

Not that any of that seems to matter to the mother black bear and her two cubs. We see them twice, a stalwart figure and the two scrambling toddlers—the first time, they're crossing the Yellowstone River the civilized way, on a bridge. They cause a minor traffic jam, their power animating gray-green firs and grasses.

On our return trip, the mother and cubs are still bewitching drivers. They've gone up a gully by the side of the road not far from the river. Mother bear searches the bottom of the gully, cubs jumping and tumbling behind. Horsetails are her vegetable du jour. She deliberately seeks them out and plucks the stalks. I've never imagined that horsetails could be tasty. They sure go down easy for her.

Humans pour from their cars to stand within ten feet of the tolerant mother. Languages burst out—Japanese and Chinese, Spanish and French, German and Swedish. I'll bet the bears have curtailed some family squabbles: children warring after a long drive, spouses getting on each other's nerves. I won't say the bears are a tonic for our troubles. Still, there must be something in humans that craves transformation beyond struggle, ennui, or compulsion, and something in our world's remaining bears that offers it. The ideal, maybe, or Hemingway's grace under pressure. You can't kill the anxiety, but you can live with it. Especially in the presence of black bears.

Bear #7
Lost Lake Trail, 2017

General location: Roosevelt Lodge, Yellowstone
Distance: 3–4 miles round trip
Elevation gain: 300 feet
Terrain: Lodgepole pine and fir forest with mountain lake meadow

I listen to my instincts enough to let them make me nervous, but I don't do what they tell me. So here I am—the Lost Lake trail, an easy, crowded path, at 4:30 in the afternoon. Bears get active around this time—our DeLacy Creek grizzly came out of the trees in early evening. But we aren't going far, just two miles or so to the lake and then back. We'll be okay, Bernie says.

From Roosevelt Lodge in the heart of Yellowstone, the steep trail ascends via switchbacks through lodgepole pines. After an earlier nine-mile jaunt through bear country around Garnet Hill, whose most dangerous sights were a mass of bitterroot blossoms and a solitary bull bison across the river, we're feeling both lucky and talked out. We have a touch of Actaeon's hubris. We walk quietly, emerge from the woods, and then, of course, it happens.

Weltzschmerz's opposite: Eden and shimmering surface and eternity appear. Through no effort on my part. My thoughts, images, behavior, attempts to single-handedly save the planet shrink to nothing. My own personal magical thinking—jacked up by mental compulsions—is exposed in its usual absurdity. Keeping the world together is a pretty big responsibility. But I do it diligently. And to no effect. And now here I am again, not in control at all. Not even subject to the illusion of control.

In my family, it was "Cara's thing" to love animals, champion the underdog, crave the outdoors. My earnestness and ambition to save the world must have been hard to live with. Once, I hosted a vegan party, and I tried to found an international organization called SOW (Save Our World—I wasn't great with acronyms). My junior high school friends soon dropped away. So I trained my sights on family members. I lectured my mother about detergent phosphates and sent my uncle, who worked for the BLM, petitions about saving prairie falcons. I even scolded the neighbors for using lawn chemicals and wrote bundles of letters to presidents, governors, senators. In high school I volunteered for the Youth Conservation Corps, a Jimmy Carter initiative to teach young people to care about and be cared for by the outdoors.

We YCC kids helped the US Forest Service build trails and bridges in the Wasatch and Stansbury Mountains west of the Oquirrhs and the Bingham copper pit. We also walked around Salt Lake and Bountiful foothill neighborhoods in hardhats and hiking boots, handing out flyers about wildfire in the transition zone between mountain mahogany and McMansions (what we would now call the wildland–urban interface, or WUI). Our pay was room and board at Brighton ski resort, a $400 monthly stipend, and the rudiments of a natural history education. Though our grunt work saved the taxpayers money as we ticked off the jobs for which highly skilled, salaried employees would have been paid regular wages, Ronald Reagan later eliminated the program.

We learned about forest succession and watersheds, but why the YCC director chose two University of Utah scientists to discuss an esoteric subject that summer is a mystery. Few of us high school freshmen gathered one night in the resort's dining room had any notion at the time of what carbon dioxide even was. The audience picked at sunburns and thought about budding romances, while the professors disagreed about whether the disaster should be called *climate change*, *global warming*, or *the greenhouse effect*. But both said we had to do something within ten years if we wanted to survive the next hundred. This was, I recall, 1976.

For whatever reason, their conclusion washed over most of us. Somehow it was just as important in those days to wonder selfishly if I, for example, would be lumped as an outcast with the ostracized "stinky girl" I took dance class with, if those rich cheerleaders driving the family Mercedes to school were laughing about me, if the boy who smashed his fist into the wall in history class and complimented my hair was trying to impress or insult. My activism ran up against selfishness and vanity. And, of course, to combat the vanity, I needed to get out of bed or go through doorways just as I said the correct word: *light* or *life,* rather than *death* or *devil.*

This remnant-of-Eden bear on the Lost Lake trail requires no words—until now as I try to write about her. She's tall and young. Blonde. Happy. She dances across the yellow-green meadow marking the boundary between forest and lake. Her face is open, pleased. She's out for an impossible solo prance on flat feet—darting in and out of shadows, about to pirouette. But she sees us. Those pesky bipeds. She heads toward the lake, so we head toward the trees. She changes her mind and makes an escape to the trees, so we go for the lake. She disappears. I mean, she dissolves. She's that fast. The entire encounter lasts about two minutes, the place reverberating longer with the echo of her jolly presence than with the time it took her to exit. I think she was a griz—I swear I saw the scooped face, the shoulder hump. Bernie says she was a blond black bear. I say she was thirty feet away. Bernie says a hundred, no less. I saw her eyes. He didn't.

Either way, I'm not going into the woods again. Despite a feeling that I ought to be brave, to be a man like Bernie, I rush us along the calm lake. Another solitary bull bison, much more dangerous than the dancing bear, grazes in a meadow. We skirt him respectfully, since he could charge us at thirty miles an hour if he wanted to. Apparently he doesn't. He keeps munching, muzzle-deep in grasses.

At the end of the trail, near the Petrified Tree parking lot, we decide to complete the four-mile loop over sagebrush hills and away from the bear. Two female tourists from Hamburg seem uncertain about how to get back to Roosevelt Lodge. We offer to guide them. Suddenly, we're talking about German newspapers and the German healthcare system. I feel safe in a company of four humans, surrounded by an aura of words. And now I miss our *bär,* the happy blond dancer's challenge: Relax, why don't you?

Bear #8
Emerald Lake Campground, 2017

General location: West Rosebud Creek, Beartooth Mountains; 170 miles from Yellowstone
Driving distance from Fishtail, Montana: ~20 miles
Elevation: 6,400 feet
Terrain: Lodgepole pine forest

Hubris gets you killed, according to the ancient Greeks. Pride goeth before a fall, say the Christian sages. In many Eastern religions, god-envy and -emulation kick the ass of anyone trying to ascend to the realm of the immortals. Even excessive self-abnegation is egotistical—or at least attachment to illusion is. And OCD? Yes, it's a kind of self-involvement bordering on pride, its compulsions giving the illusion of power.

My hubris today is a belief that I understand bears after this haunted summer, that somehow we have a rapport, a relationship I understand. The creatures have been wandering out of the bushes for months, after all. I admire the pluck of the black bears, the presence of the grizzlies. Of course, I'm still afraid of them. But they strike me as generous free-thinkers, jolly gleaners, good mothers, pleased and happy with the riches of summer. Plus, they'll never know the hardships of winter. They'll be dreaming deep under the snow in comfortable earthen dens. Pretty damn unweltzschmerzy of them.

It seems that something always quashes my self-confidence. What I think I'm good at turns out to be my greatest weakness. Thus, my last bruin of the year abolishes all such self-congratulatory confidence—and not in the standard *Field and Stream* outdoor adventure sort of way. No, this bear gifts me with understanding and humility, neither of which I've ever had much of. Negative ego is still ego.

When my sister and I were little girls, my mother decided to counteract Mormonism by taking us to the Presbyterian church. It suited her interest in her Scots ancestry. My dad sometimes went along—he'd just as soon have dispensed with all religion, though he loved conspiracy theories about LDS politics.

Far from giving me something to belong to, it was the Presbyterian church that finally put me sideways to spirituality. I must have been ready to dangle over the abyss. I can blame hormones, the bursting of childhood rationality, social isolation. But the proximate cause of my dislocation was the pastor of my mother's congregation, who sounded like a Baptist preacher. When I was a teenager, one of his sermons featured Satan as a spider in a web. This was somehow enough to set powerful religious impulses in motion, impulses that threatened to overburden my life. In addition to silent counting and Bible reading, I used to do penance on my knees for hours at night. I still had to play songs perfectly on my guitar or repeat them endlessly until they *were* perfect. I feared my dad's book of Doré engravings of Satan from Dante's *Inferno* and made sure to avoid facing it, not just when I was going to sleep but during the day as well. I thought I ought to sacrifice myself, that I was evil—but I didn't want to and felt that perhaps the impulse itself constituted hubris. I couldn't get right with the world or my own mind and all its swirling, anxious dust.

I kept much of this struggle to myself, including most of a two-year-long dark night of the soul. I felt in direct contact with what I defined as "God," but I was also, like a medieval saint, beset by demonic incarnations and fear of suicidal thoughts. I had to count or recite magic words to keep them at bay. One winter afternoon, I remember going for a walk—my usual respite—and finding no border between my anguish and the way the icy world seemed unkind and terrifying. I'd been cast out. I walked in a dead land.

If Old Ephraim, that legendary Utah bear, had had descendants who were still around with their surrounding forests and meadows, I might have been able to shrink into the far-from-grandiose being I am. But the world I grew up in magnified me and my spiritual responsibilities. My fears multiplied and grew, spawned new ones, and never ceased. I scratched burns in my thighs with my fingernails to relieve the tension and to make me seem heroic, but it didn't work for long, despite the temporary and perverse pleasure I took in surveying the brown tracks I'd made in my pale skin. Surrounded by ordinary houses and roads and cement, I was shut out from that normality by vivid images of grace *and* damnation. The cross. The cloven hoof. The streets of gold. The leathery-winged Satanic temptation of Christ. Clichés, maybe, but nonetheless overpowering. These were not simply *visual* images. I *felt* eternity twisting inside my gut, tingling along my arms and legs. Not even the Wasatch peaks could pare me down to safety. This bombardment by religious icons, I decided, was the nadir of my existence. (I liked the word "nadir," which, of course, I plucked from *Thirty Days to a More Powerful Vocabulary.*)

Lacking a twenty-first-century lexicon of mental illness, my parents—given what little I told them—were resigned to a "teenage girls are moody" approach. Besides, I'd always been "flighty," according to my mother. My sister lectured that I had a "negative self-image" and needed counseling. Where or how I would get this counseling, I didn't know. Nor, I suppose, did she. I talked to the youth minister at Wasatch Presbyterian Church. He was much less intimidating than Reverend Dowdy, but he suggested physical and social activity rather than a profound exploration of spirituality. No matter how logical, his reasoning disappointed me.

To their credit, the LDS seem more concerned with Christ's resurrection than with his death. Though kitschy and exceedingly Anglo-Saxon, their Jesus is alive and loving, outwardly focused. He often sits in a flowery meadow, arms open. No dreadful wounds suppurate on his palms and feet. Neither crucifixes nor crosses mark LDS wards. Once, the LDS were my people. Their cheerfulness may have rubbed off on me or my alleles, at least a little. I owe them one. My dark night ended eventually.

As I grew into my late teens, I stopped going to church. I went hiking. I read *The Tibetan Book of the Dead*, which, by showing me a non-Judeo-Christian, nonbinary way of thinking, bucked me up. Perhaps I owe the Buddha one, too. I managed through months of mental struggle and attention to life's exuberance to ditch organized religion and its attendant magical thinking.

This isn't a happy ending. I'm still prone to hidden, mental compulsions and to the anxiety they cause and that they are caused by in an eternal feedback loop. I stopped worshipping death, scarifying myself, worrying about torture on the cross, and dodging infernal enemies. But climate change and the Sixth Extinction now bare apocalyptic wings I feel obliged to defeat. Single-handedly. It's a struggle in an uncertain sea of tempests and near-wreckage, but, when I worship bears and meadows, the violent rant of spiritual and ecological doom recedes. As does my ego. I am, essentially, competent, in a small way.

We drive from the Mystic Lake trailhead this August evening after a bearless hike, and I *know* I'm going to see one. It's a fact. I scan the bushes across West Rosebud Creek for signs of movement. I'm more expectant than hopeful, even as the creek widens into a shadowy lake, green and soft. Fly fishermen wade what might as well be a reflecting pool. Families wander the shore. Campers tend their evening cooking fires, welcoming that primordial hominin world. And against this domestic activity is, in all his reality, what I knew I'd see because, yes, I am that gifted. My ego is exceptionally large tonight. The bear of my premonition focuses himself against the trees on the opposite side of the lake.

Equal in size to our Pryors behemoth of May, a large onyx boar heads toward the campground on a trajectory that will run parallel to tents and RVs. Should I stop and warn people? I ask Bernie to pull over, and we admire him—a shadow among shadows, a survivor. Magnificent, black-robed, one of the immortals, he telegraphed his presence fifteen minutes before I saw him. But the message wasn't intended for me. It was a quasar's energy, blasting into the cosmos.

The omen flashes like a synaptic connection: The bears will come back and stop being tragic. Non-Indigenous Americans will learn the right names for the world and its beings. We'll stop being exclusive, frightened, and compulsive. There's even a recent and credible sighting of a grizzly in Utah. Something weltzschmerz doesn't account for is the irrepressibility of living things.

The Emerald Lake bear, it turns out, doesn't care about humans at all. He ignores the campers, who will have no knowledge of him as he heads now to the forest edge.

TRAIL 10

Analogue Hiking on Basin Creek Lakes Trail

—In memory of Burt Bradley

General location: Beartooth Mountains near Red Lodge, Montana; about 70 miles from Yellowstone
Hiking distance: 7–8 miles round trip (field guides and Forest Service signage disagree)
Elevation gain: 2,000 feet
Terrain: Lodgepole pine and fir forest to krummholz

1994

The moose leads two calves through timber on the Basin Creek Lakes trail, contouring around a steep hillside, coming our way. My friend and I and our dogs, Gila and Rita, stop to let them pass. I can't speak for the dogs, but the humans are tense. It's late, shadows are deep, the sky golden, and the moose trio very, very large and now very, very close. The twins are leggy, the mother massive. Her stride is powerful and deliberate, her back legs folding and unfolding with the angles of a Swiss army knife. Somehow humans and dogs manage to remain absolutely still as the family crosses our trail about twenty feet away and vanishes, in the inimitable style of moose, into the lodgepole pines.

Like the bears I've seen, these moose remain vibrant and active in my memory, not at all like the granular manifestations of OCD flare-ups.

When I try to explain how it *feels* to have an obsession blasting away at the cohesiveness of my personality, most people say they worry about things too. Certainly, I worry about moose encounters when they happen. Moose can kill, though most of the time they don't. But obsessions are something else entirely, a shrinkage of vision, an inwardness, even as they produce greater and greater fear and disgust. They involve an extreme digitization of experience, a playlist of the same tones used over and over in the same way, a focused convergence of loathsome scenes. Uncanny in their targeting of the sufferer's vulnerabilities, they trigger the fight response that creates ineffectual compulsions rather than positive (or negative) action. Eventually, most become ridiculous. I interrogate them: Now, just how are you going to have me rob a bank? Am I going to wear a red bandanna? Will I ask for all C-notes? Have a Model T getaway car waiting on Broadwater Avenue with the rest of my gang? And just how far will I get before the G-men catch on?

I'm not the only one who suffers from OCD. Millions do. The suffering is embarrassing and lonely. Flare-ups alienate us from the sensory world that can be corroborated by others and that offers artifacts for us to see, taste, smell, hear, and touch. No one is ever going to grasp an obsession's physical reality, though, because it has none.

As you scramble out of an episode, you find that there *is* somewhere else to be. You name your illness, recognize it for what it is, and let nature convince you that its conjured images are specious. The knowledge doesn't cure, but it gives you back the ability to be here, open-eyed, in the world, and ready for moose.

I've hiked Basin Creek, about five or six miles out of the eastern Beartooth Mountains' ever-handy gateway town of Red Lodge, too many times to count. I mentally follow the trail when I can't sleep. I know the place in all seasons and moods. I know it when the forest is intact. I know it after a storm sculpts a slope of blown-down pines. I know that a wooden water trough marking the halfway point will gradually disintegrate. I've missed the path and found the path. I know the trail with its first half mile burned and denuded after a late-summer fire. All its conditions are normalized and characteristic of its "true" nature, enriched by that moose-calves-humans-dogs encounter.

Even on trails they know, seasoned nervous hikers carry good maps, ones with contour lines and land features, ones that represent the latest route changes and illustrate through color and icons trail hazards and highlights. Topographical maps are as close as you can come on paper to a 3-D view, and I highly recommend them. But I'm interested here in a greater-than-three-dimensional guide—an interactive map of Basin Creek, say, that relies on analogy and metaphor, time and memory and experience, not the metrics of mileage and isoline. Nor is this at all similar to the map of an obsession, which is abstract and stark, with the lines of a graticule and a directive, or with the bossy voice of a car's navigation system.

For a map you can play with, start with a moose or a stand of whitebark pines. Whatever you want. But let's not call it a *start*, a *point A*. For ease of thinking, we could call it *swirl A*, or just a never-ending rhythm of swirls within swirls that starts any old place to make up the blended topography, ecology, and companionship of a trail. Rare moments of transcendence (or abject incompetence) form the key, but these "plots"—both linear and lumpy with "events"—only momentarily obscure the swirling.

A moose story is an alarm. An eidetic image. The X on a hillside. An eddy in alternately shadowed and sunny coursing mountain streams of memory. Other experiences rush by, charted by color, temperature, odor, but mostly as a mass of sensation that washes through, around, and over us, shaping and polishing and displacing—although, I suspect, the nugget of individuality remains digital and elemental. As do moose. Centers of multiple swirls.

Everywhere-rushing sensation hardly notices the pebble of anecdote at whose heart lie genetic predeterminations known as "human" and "moose." Our features, mine and the moose's, are no different from those of a wildflower's replicable design, a Parnassian's species-specific daubs and dashes of black and red—patterns that look inevitable and immutable but that arose through millennia of accidents and chance occurrences. It may be that obsession is a dark metal pocking the stream, but perhaps in the rounding flow it shows up for what it is: obstruction. The task is to make the obstruction fail. It shouldn't be impossible. Mountain streams flow many ways. Evaporation and condensation are multidirectional. Erosion happens.

Separating consciousnesses—mine, moose's—seems like plot, seems digitized and parsed like obsession. But what if discrete sensations are factitious? Analogue offers a much better rendition of things, according to my son Tom, an electrical engineer. If recording technology were up to it, analogue could *almost* capture the way the world sounds. Analogue could *almost* graph the way we work when we're healthy, with forward momentum and distinct eddies, overlapping stillwaters, backwashes, countertides, and cycles. This isn't a new way of mapping. Not by any means. It's probably quite common in non-Western societies. Maybe it was de rigueur in the Pleistocene. But it's not the norm in America now, especially not in Montana, where sporting goods stores offer steel cabinets full of USGS quadrangle maps and there is a shortage of mental health professionals.

Analogue charts vary from region to region, person to person, hike to hike. Occurrences are superimposed on previous ones. Walking a short trail again and again defies the natural linearity of hiking. We're no longer talking about stimulus (the trail) and response (your enjoyment, or fatigue, or awe), about trailhead and destination. We're talking multi-way communication. Swirls. You get personal with one place and it gets personal with you. Such a map does not represent the quick-and-easy epiphany that mountain lakes used to bring me to when I was younger, when the narrative of rocks, clouds, whitebark pines, and Clark's nutcrackers led me—and me alone—to discern discrete forms until story and characters followed the inexorable arc to ecstasy, the flip side of obsession. These days I'm as likely to see ecstasy flowing back and forth from me to the trail.

An obsessive map will not document change, because obsessions are stuck in place. An obsessive map is not intended to be used by anyone but the sufferer. It is, more or less, a dark spot on a blank page. Or, if it is more complex, it is static. Blue lines indicating anxiety will not tell *how* the nerves swell, tumble, widen, and interact with seasons, humidity, other hikers, or the fern frond bobbing in the current.

So why not, as the remembered topography of the Basin Creek trail erodes and reforms, let the creek and my sensations draw an analogue map, an authentic Basin Creek cartography suggesting something of all of us who've gone there, if only as an unconnected dot-to-dot of footprints, hoofprints, pawprints, and floods? My map will not define something completely contained, like an unbreakable capsule, inside the human psyche. My map will depict emotions, though, and show the trail holding all of us, the wild raspberry bushes knowing that some have picked their tart-sweet fruit and that others have passed it up. This would be neither epiphany nor the digital precision of a mental image, but liveliness and love.

Love at first sight, I'd say, in my case. Years ago, I came to Basin Creek from our home in Powell, Wyoming, over desert and badlands and into cottonwoods and canyon. I was thirty years old. Bernie and I led our first-grader son to the lower, lily-pad lake, urging him along with games and imagination. We were space explorers on an alien world. We were mountain men (and woman). We were young, and the trail wasn't steep. I was between bouts of GAD. The place was beautiful, and it made me beautiful too, albeit sweaty and footsore.

Later, at some point, the three of us backpacked to the lower lake to camp in an orange two-person tent I'd inherited from my dad. After canned ravioli (which never quite got hot, despite the industriousness of our Coleman mini-stove), we lay under a night of clarity and stars, and above the leaf-studded water (over twenty years, I've noted the gradual invasion of more lily pads). Next morning, the air remained clear, the earth silent and benign, sunlight knocking on the tent flap, turning the cheap cloth roof into a rind of energy. Bernie and Tom remember this too, but in their own ways. They also remember exploring unknown regions as far as the larger Upper Basin Creek Lake, a mountain laurel- and boulder-bound route that was new to us then and is familiar now, and was once—and only once—graced by a dusky grouse. One or two years later, on that very stretch between the lakes, Rita found the trail when we lost it beneath two feet of sloppy, late-spring snow, and I could understand why humans domesticated dogs (or was it the other way around?) and why Aztec mythology gives every dead human a canine guide to the underworld.

I can't picture the wide view at the upper lake without remembering how a friend and I, near the end of my time in Wyoming, brought our dogs and lounged for hours on a sun-drenched boulder in the kind of mountain heat that softens skin and muscles, inoffensive gnats and unhungry mosquitoes dancing in sunbeams over the water like small quasars. The moose were waiting below.

I've seen that lake roiled by storms. I've stood in the rain while the surface went the color of lead solder. I've seen snow chutes lingering into July, and I've seen the canyon crowded with ambitious snowflakes. I've seen the cirque bare and harsh in late summer. I can't say that I know Upper Basin Creek Lake or that it knows me, but its remembered mossy shore still yields under my feet, water clapping and sloshing with spring when it's shelved in ice, the lake burning in aluminum-foil-shining summer, lolling in fall's recession and solemnity.

Obsessions might have the precision and unidirectional quality of anecdote or parable, but on a true map of Basin Creek Lakes trail, few images fit a reliable sequence—here, mountain avens lingers in sharp relief against cold water, and here, I step over exposed roots of twisted krummholz. At some point (when?) Bernie and I explore dark forest on the far edge of the upper lake—a sorcerer's grove of twisted trunks and mucky shore yielding one fresh moose track. Memory slips, with some vignettes subsumed into others—as if a fault bisects them. Sometimes Tom is small, skinny as a pixie. Sometimes he's an adult with a long ponytail tied at his nape. Sometimes I'm with Rita. Sometimes her successor, Luke, bounds ahead. Sometimes blue butterflies dance. Sometimes an olive-sided flycatcher flies in the burn. Sometimes the burn hasn't happened. Sometimes, I'm with our friend Burt Bradley, a poet and college professor we met thirty years ago. And sometimes I stand by the waterfall and reflect that Burt has been dead for a year.

2013

A second moose story? For that, the Beartooths send me one drainage over, enlarging my map to include another trail. Swirls cycle and gyre outward.

Deep into January, Lake Fork south of Red Lodge is snow-packed to the point where Bernie and I don't need snowshoes. In fact, I wish I didn't have mine. It's hard to keep one-year-old Luke from tangling in the trekking poles. I've fallen a few times because of his odd habit of stopping, staring, crying when he sees that Bernie is ahead and then bounding like a simple-minded jackrabbit along the trail to reach him.

When I can, I admire how beautiful, if stark, the woods are, the pines and firs blue-black against snow kept white by a constant refreshment of new storms. The stream below to our right is open though lined with lacy hoarfrost, ice bridges, and valences. We tromp along in the shadows—shadows that never go away this time of year, an observation my map notes.

The trail is quiet, lacking even chickadees, and that's fitting because a yearling moose lies dead in an opening we enter. *Enter* implies a seriousness, though, that my progress lacks. Luke augments his usual lunging to reach the corpse—the calf's body, extended, flattened, and unmarked in death, blocks the trail. The fur is dark, clear of snow. I don't know how or how long ago this young one died. I wonder if the mother is mourning close by.

Like most dogs, Luke is ecstatic about dead things. He'd like to sniff the carcass, roll on it, eat parts of it, carry off bones. It's the greatest thing he's ever seen or smelled. When I hold him back, he pulls me onto my stomach—a soft landing in the snow. He keeps pulling, my shoulder and arm straining to stop him from desecrating the corpse as he plunges toward it. Bernie says, "Do you want me to take him?"

After we gather ourselves together, silence crashes in on the calf. Cold nudges him as his mother's muzzle must have. All the work of life undone by winter, and quickly. We leave him and walk on through the multifarious map of memory that now incorporates a dead moose calf.

Real narratives, unlike those of OCD, are studded with intersecting surfaces and significance that defies summary. It's always one season in an obsession, but Lake Fork has aspens that bend away from the wind and burst into gold in fall. It has scree fields farther up where we spoke with Forest Service summer interns doing trail work one July. It has an enormous blowdown. It has a great widening of the fork, commonly known as the Broadwater. It can host the cool-hot summer sun of a typical Beartooth place. Yet, unlike the wearying retelling of an obsessive story, nothing about it is typical. Nothing stays the same. The moose carcass was gone by spring.

Lake Fork enters the heart of the Absaroka-Beartooth Wilderness area, but Basin Creek trail, no less "wild," actually, lies outside the boundary line because it's not a footpath at all—at least not for most of its first three miles. Instead, the route follows an old dirt road, and its ascents are designed for driving. I know when I'm about to reach the lower lake because the old road tears right across the side of a steep slope, my hip joints mapping that stretch or vice versa.

In this spot, surely, a 1940 International Harvester once complained and stalled, the miner—fedora-wearing, hand-rolled-cigarette-smoking—cursing the final uphill before his claim. His angry "damn truck" echoes and fades and echoes. He was after silver, or maybe chromite. The European war demanded minerals. He could almost make a living, his ore shipped long distances to be smelted. He stopped under this double-stemmed pine to let his truck engine cool and study a map he'd drawn. Lines and endpoints. He pulled another folded piece of paper—a dearer one—and a dull pencil from his pocket and added, in a letter to his girl, a few more hard-earned elliptical lines about cold nights and unfailing stars.

The old mines along the Basin Creek trail are filled in now for public safety, and cabins have over the years shifted, listed, and finally collapsed. Miners' shadows inhabit these hills. Here, you can imagine, was where a tire went flat. Here someone wondered if a mountain lion was close. A few may have wanted to save democracy from Hitler; the ore they mined would make anti-fascist cannons, guns, and other equipment. I hear them sometimes standing outside their unchinked cabins, singing "Mexicali Rose" or "Beautiful Dreamer" or "The Prison Song." Perhaps they were in thrall to a certain cultural notion that twinned war and romantic love. Still, I bet they were clear-eyed about the clouds beaten high like egg whites, just as they are today. But then, not like these at all.

A lot of hikers don't get much higher than the waterfall, about a half mile up from the parking area and almost hidden in the hillside. I've found the cornhusks of packaged tamales scattered below. I've found fishing line. I've found snow caves and arches in winter. I've waded back as far into the alcove as I could go, back to the rocks where water ouzels nap in snow or summer heat until their white eyelids blink them awake.

How to map the waterfall? As far as I know, no plots impede the rush. No one's been killed here. No one's been married. Still, it's possible to imagine a scene: two lovers rising into each other behind the sheet of spray, below the ferns and touch-me-knots, cradled on moss, or, more likely, sorry they started the whole thing because the rock is so jagged.

The water is analogue action, suffering, let's say, a cataclysm in three movements: the first, a dramatic tumble over a cliff; the second, a gentle unveiling down fallen boulders; the third, a series of acrobatic stunts punctuated by meditative poolings. In summer it's shady and refreshing, and the water lingers between cascading stairways. In winter the current is encased in a clear tunnel of ice. For some reason, cold creates wildness and distance, and the world seems far away. It's easy to imagine that the water has no inkling of its future.

But on a hot day in summer, hydrogen and oxygen atoms may sense their destination in the Gulf of Mexico's toxic dead zone. They'll travel across eastern Montana, turn sharply north toward the little prairie town of Sydney, join the Missouri in the heart of the "maturing" (rather than booming) Bakken oil play of North Dakota, split Nebraska from Iowa, bisect Missouri, mix with heartland chemicals down past St. Louis and a union with the Mississippi, and roll on to the Delta where their predecessors once told Mississippi Fred McDowell the story of the blues so that he could slide it "pure and natural" off his guitar and onto high-fidelity thirty-three RPM records that would spin and crackle on turntables around the world.

Think digitally and obsessively, and you'd have to use smaller grammatical units. Basin Creek Falls enlarges a weak spot in the rock. Gravity and physics determine its path. It could be mapped centimeter by centimeter. It could be mapped angstrom by angstrom. That sounds tedious. It might be impossible to understand a Borgesian map like that. Could one be made? Minor errors might compound into nonsense. Just like the errors of an obsession. Errors that trap you in a tighter and tighter box.

Despite all their seeming reality, obsessions are not complex, and they are exquisitely detailed only in their most disturbing particulars. If, for example, I obsess about stabbing someone with a knife, I will fight against that image of blood spurting from a wound, but if I stop to examine the scene, I will find it myopic, clichéd, lacking in practical specifics: What is the knife like and where would I get it? How would I have the strength to stab someone (anyone?) and where? What would be my motivation? Why wouldn't they fight back? The story is simplistic, composed of unrealistic bits.

At waterfalls, on the other hand, I've seen cascades pulled and bent, twisted and shocked and crashed in, and turned to mist. They are more fractal than digital, which is nice because fractals offer some fun things that I don't understand. Infinite replication. Self-similarity. Randomness. Irregularities.

Obsessions are ugly, with impoverished storylines that nevertheless mechanically pop up with each attack, like one of those inflatable clowns you can punch and punch, to no effect. But complex math and physics swirl beautifully at a waterfall.

1993

This moose story is my best. Set in yet another part of the Beartooths, its analogue vibrations shake any trail I walk. Surely the seismic echoes lift and fold the ground, even as far south as Basin Creek.

We're coming back from Elk Lake, in the East Rosebud drainage, in late afternoon. Already, shadows are long, luxuriating in the shorter days of October. Rita leads the way with Bernie. The two have vanished from sight around a curve. Unlike Luke, Rita is a dog we trust. She's never leashed, so it's unusual to see Bernie and an attached Rita coming back to join seven-year-old Tom and me. "There's a moose near the trail ahead," Bernie confides, with typical understatement, "and he doesn't look very happy."

After the manner of adults who pretend to know what to do while their child looks on, Bernie and I confer. The path cleaves a narrow way through a rocky cliff on the right and a muskeggy stream on the left. It's getting dark. We'll hew to the path. Rita and Bernie first, me next, and Tom last. If the moose is going to charge, we agree, Tom will be spared.

We do not understand moose psychology.

It goes almost according to plan, though. Rita and Bernie lead us—our trusty dog skirting the bull, whose antlers, though impressive, show that he's young. I go next, observing him with a strange, detached scientific interest. He, too, seems studious, musing over the evening shrubbery.

But in the cervine world, studiousness turns to annoyance with the scuffling of one leaf or the fluffing up of one fair-weather cloud. Without signaling his intention, the moose lowers his head and lunges at the space where Tom should be. But our boy somehow anticipates the charge and hangs back. Now we have a moose between us. Though I'd like to relate that my maternal adrenaline rushes to Tom's defense, it's the moose and the boy who figure things out. Satisfied with his display, the young bull goes back to browsing and studiousness, almost literally shrugging with a trembling of his withers, and Tom calmly joins us.

The ways of moose are inscrutable. Nor are the ways of children any more transparent. My son is alive not because his parents were wise or acted heroically but because he and the moose made intertwined decisions not to engage. The bright center of an enlarging swirl, their miracle lights every Beartooth trail.

At the end of another trip to Basin Creek, new self-similar details blur and collide with memories. My analogue map, thick with experience, is more than moose calves and an intractable cow, climax and resolution.

It's bricolage, a mashup of Burt's baseball stories; discussions of Milton, Keats, and Frost; and young people's complaints about sore knees and boredom. Here a little boy named Tom stalls beside me, curious and frustrated by turns: "I'm tired and my shoe is rubbing." Here the lily pads of the lower lake bloom and drift on their tethers. Here Bernie takes a photograph that can be superimposed on a *nearly* identical one he took five years before. Here an adult Tom walks with his partner.

My memory maps chipmunks and yellow-rumped warblers, fiery sunsets and clearing rainstorms, varied hiking companions, and many versions of my "self," each following a hypothetical vein of riches, each with an eager thesis to prove, each looking for an angle, a glint of alchemy that will turn life into plot and danger into cathartic humor and the rush of sensuousness into digitized bits of meaning. Of course, that's the last thing I want to do. And I can't anyway. If I have any mining acuity it's the ability to dig out images from experience's flowing veins. But despite my best efforts to hold them, they swirl, coalesce, dissolve, reform. Obsessions don't. Ever. Even when they cease to bother me, I can call them up again in their entirety, if only to mock their absurdity. Oh sure, I'm going to start screaming on a plane and end up duct-taped to my seat. The plane will have to be turned around, and everyone's life will be ruined.

Each analogue hike offers a healthy rushing, cool-water gigue, a wild raspberry tang, chromite-bearing outcrops, moose consciousness, conversations whose content vanishes though their flavors remain. These are the scenes that filter out obsessions, if only for a while. Exposed to the richness of analogue recordings, digitized bits of mental overwork stand like a trapped beam that resolves into invisible dust particles when the sun of anxiety leaves the window. My analogue map contains sacred swirls and transforming surface, light and shadow, snow and rain. And it never resolves. It demonstrates more than what I know. It locates and loses and relocates. It's not self-aggrandizing. It shows the tracks of moose who have their own destinies.

TWO

Roots and Stems

TRAIL 11

Off-Trail in Search of Mainsprings on the Line Creek Plateau

General location: Beartooth Mountains High Plateau off the Beartooth Highway, 26 miles from Yellowstone
Hiking distance: 4+ miles round trip
Elevation gain: 300 feet
Terrain: Krummholz and tundra

His head fills a varnished wooden box. Women I don't know croon over their "sweet little grandpa." His white hair sparkles—has someone tossed a handful of glitter over him? His eyes are brown, though they were once blue, and he blinks slowly, awakening. He's been dead for twenty-three years, and I've never dreamed about him before.

I could dismiss the whole thing as macabre. But the vision won't fade. It's so incongruous. Although religious enthusiasms permeated his family history, my grandfather was a practical man, not an Orpheus to star in a dream. I'm not sure what his prophetic appearance could possibly signify. Perhaps I'm to take it at face value: The great beyond is just odd. He had a dry sense of humor. Maybe the dream is his idea of a joke.

In life, my grandfather escaped the spiritual inclination and could, like Bernie himself, sleep well despite ongoing disasters. He told my exasperated and anxious grandmother during World War II, when their oldest son was a Marine in the Pacific, that staying awake all night wasn't going to help anything. So, genetics alone may not explain the origins of my psychological disease, which has no obvious precipitating event, though individual bouts of it might. Inheritance may refer to something larger and more convoluted, an aura that surrounds the unique history of a family and occasionally rests in the nervous system of a member here and there. An inheritance too subtle to trace via DNA or a particular grandparent.

It is possible for me to find analogues of that family history and the origins of my OCD up here near the top of the Beartooth Plateau where goat kids scamper along the ten-thousand-foot heights, leaving tufts of their soft wool on ancient, dwarfed willows that grow for two snowless months every year. There are older relics, too: rocks dating to almost four billion years. When I hop over these remnants, risking a sprained ankle, I wonder why their Precambrian granite sits twelve thousand feet in the air. Like my own family's odd propensities, why is this stratum still palpable?

The answer, for the granite, at least, isn't hard to understand. Though the Beartooths were once at the bottom of an ocean, they were uplifted in the Paleocene, a time when tapir-like pantodonts may have grazed among gingko trees several thousand feet above the wobbling boulder I now balance on. After the peaks rose, their delicate sandstone coverlet eroded, exposing this much older rock. Glaciers worked, then, to pound, gouge, and decorate.

It's not just the rocks up here that are primal. Life is, too. Oh, in summer you'll see plenty of recently evolved angiosperms in the form of tiny forget-me-nots, fluted arctic gentians, white marsh marigolds, and puffy bistorts as new-fangled dinosaurs—white-crowned sparrows and pipits—blip from meltwater to snowfield to tarn. But in autumn you'd be forgiven for thinking that the most colorful and dominant life forms are the lichens radiating in orange and red and emerald and lime on almost every sizeable stone surface. They're hard or brittle to the touch, flaking off if you're not careful.

Lichens are duos of algae and fungi. They colonize seemingly unlivable surfaces, industriously manufacture sugars, and even absorb pollutants. Both algae and fungi have been around a long time. Their partnership is younger but still venerable at four hundred million years, more or less. Theirs is a successful marriage, a plural one at times. Lichens are sometimes a threesome (add bacteria) or a foursome (add other types of fungi, such as yeast). Thus, you might think of them as polygamous enterprises pioneering ever-new frontiers, as my grandfather's people thought they were doing.

When we drive over the dips and ridges of the Beartooths, we can see that the range, much like a family's story, is subdivided into plateaus. I'm thinking not just about the switchbacks, the possibility of brake failures, and the beauty of mountaintops that resemble the backs of floating manatees, but about original causes, mainsprings, my uplifted layers exposed in a dream, in my memories, online, or in LDS archives. Often in the mountains I think about my grandfather—a logical portal into the deep time of my living geology, and one of the people who taught me to love high places.

Born in 1898 to a polygamous Mormon family, Alma Allen Tripp was a rancher, miner, and seed packer. In his semi-wild backyard in the heart of Salt Lake, he planted tomatoes, pruned apricot trees, squeezed yet another highbush cranberry into an already overcrowded garden. He sowed wild columbine seed, and the delicate yellow and red blooms punctuated what he referred to as "orchard grass." He once gave me a two-gallon pot of columbine, one of my favorite gifts ever.

My first hikes happened in his backyard. Followed around by a gentle German shepherd, I threaded raspberry canes and hip-high matrimony vine to find archeological objects: a rusty lard pail, an old wooden duck house, the wire remains of a previous fence, some iron piece of equipment whose purpose I could never figure out. On a disastrous afternoon I stepped in one of the dog's messes, and there was a frenzy about how my shoe would be cleaned. The frenzy, of course, involved my mother and grandmother—not my imperturbable grandfather.

For her part, my grandmother raised a screen of irises and peonies to hide the jungle effect farther back, watered the grassy civilized foreyard, hung clean laundry to dry, read me terrifying non-Disney folk stories while we drank root beer floats at a massive picnic table on "sultry" (her word) summer afternoons, and once a year attacked her most-hated job—preserving pie cherries the robins hadn't eaten. My grandfather abhorred waste, but canning was women's work. And my grandmother couldn't entirely screen out that wild urban orchard he'd grown.

Alma Tripp never adapted to city life. It wasn't his idea to end up in Salt Lake. He'd have owned a horse ranch near the Deep Creek Mountains along the Nevada border, if he'd been able to argue successfully against the need for his children to go to good schools. His heart was with the desert and its island ranges. When I was a kid, he owned a yellow Chevrolet Impala, the kind with fins, a black faux-leather interior, and built-in silver cigarette trays whose spring-controlled lids were fun to flip. He drove through town as if he were on a dirt two-track, turning left from any lane he chose and reaching speeds of sixty in residential neighborhoods.

Right after my seventh birthday, my grandmother and I went with him and my uncle Jeff to the Stansbury Mountain foothills. After parking, my grandfather immediately took off over rocks and through sage, with my uncle following, while Grandmother and I stayed in the car. Out of sight, the men shot targets so far away that the pop of their guns didn't reach us. Why couldn't I have gone with them? Were they afraid I'd cause trouble? And my grandmother? Maybe she didn't want to go out in the harsh air. She'd broken her hip the year before and would have had a hard time walking the pathless benchlands.

For a while, I amused myself by watching her, so studious in her black-rimmed reading glasses, perusing what must have been every line of text in the *Salt Lake Tribune*—she'd wanted to be a journalist like her father. Later, I went outside a few times, staying, as she asked, within ten or fifteen steps of the Chev and shining a toy flashlight on glittering rocks, as if I might look inside them. Every time I opened or shut the car door, the heavy thud signaled my grandmother's wordless irritation. Nowadays, a child and her grandmother might wear ear buds and listen to the music of their respective generations, separate and interested rather than together, gloriously bored, mildly annoyed.

On that long-ago fall day after my seventh birthday, my uncle brought me a jar containing a sci-fi creature from the target practice site: a two-inch-long Jerusalem cricket with a giant orange head and striped abdomen. Jeff's gifts were usually perfectly geared for kids. But a Jerusalem cricket pet was too much, even from him. My grandmother remarked that she'd been bitten by one once, and the welt had lasted six weeks. To my shame, I later abandoned the jar and the cricket in the farthest back corner of our yard. Over weeks, the poor innocent creature became an empty exoskeleton. My grandfather wasn't the bearer of the gift, but he did, sometime later, show me another jar with a dog tick inside. "The most dangerous animal on earth," he called it.

I came to remorseful adulthood just as he began to recede from view, to be buried under layers of silence. He seemed a hard outcropping, losing touch with human interaction, colonized by the barebones work of biology, by colorful lichen he could no longer tell us about. He was a monument, and it took my mother to interpret his meaning, to recover his significance as a post-polygamy, second-generation bridge from Utah territory to the contemporary world.

Alma Tripp grew up one of six children (a seventh died in toddlerhood) on a ranch where things were never flush. His father, Christopher John, outdid him with dashing good looks and flamboyant habits—and general toughness—but not, perhaps, industriousness. Depending on who's telling the story, Chris was a kindly lover of children or a dictatorial womanizer chasing nurses around his hospital room in his last illness. He wore his teeth to nubs by gnawing on raw root vegetables from the kitchen garden. He laughed when my mother—his favorite, I suspect—put a horned toad on a visitor's mashed potatoes. She even braided his beard while he napped; waking up, he was amused by his small stylist's work. Her older brother, though, lived in fear of swift and corporal punishments. I don't believe Chris Tripp was any harsher than my grandfather. Both men worked too hard to expect less of my uncle than they demanded of themselves. But both could afford to be indulgent with my mother, who labored only under the administration of female justice. Discipline did not mean lack of concern. After all, my grandfather once carried his teenage son on his back up out of the Hell Hole mine after he fell twenty feet (so the story goes), badly spraining both ankles. Whether Grandpa later punished him for carelessness, I don't know.

Indulgent or violent or both, Chris was, above all, a survivor. No doubt about it. The ranch folks my grandfather came from needed to be tough if they were going to thrive on an alkaline plot of land a few tens of miles from the Utah/Nevada border. It took a ruptured appendix two weeks or so to do Chris in—when he was 92. This happened the year I was born, 1959.

Chris's wife and Alma's mother, Artamissa Reynolds, was a hard-working, irony-spouting farm woman who cooked all day every day and wore her life out too soon. Reflecting the family's focus on the male line, not many stories of her survive. She was called "Artie" or "Aunt Artie." My mother inherited her beautiful deep-set eyes and high forehead and cheekbones, and her acerbic turn of phrase. Once when she'd cooked up a big batch of canned oyster stew for seasonal haying crews, someone didn't appreciate the oysters and spat one out. "Might as well eat the devil as drink his broth," Artie noted. She died at a mere sixty-two, younger than I am.

Work dominated Alma's upbringing. He never shied away from tough jobs. His life started with cattle dips and the planting of orchards and later morphed into mining with dynamite, stone boats, and donkeys. After he moved to Salt Lake, he worked until he was seventy-five for Porter-Walton Company, a nursery operation with the motto "Every Seed a Sturdy Plant." He barely had time to worry.

He would have taken even today's route to the mountains as just another chore. But because you can drive to ten thousand feet in the Beartooths, it deserves a catch in my breath at least to come up over the pass, where tundra falls steeply below, and the Bear's Tooth itself chomps at the horizon. Often the hairpin turns will make a passenger dog (our Luke included) puke. It's reassuring to park at an overlook, change into hiking boots, and as you do assess the route you're going to take from your car to the Line Creek Plateau. I fancy I adopt Alma's discerning miner's judgment.

For starters, there's no trail. It looks like you'll bob down on your own to a silvery, willowy, unnamed lake. Good enough. If you're caught in a thunderstorm there, God help you, though. Without cover, you'll crouch in the runoff, as Bernie and I did once, pre-Luke, while lightning boomerangs and the temperature drops twenty degrees in twenty minutes.

Today's weather is fine. It's a warm autumn morning, with grasses orange and yellow to match the lichen. Hiking the trailless terrain that straddles the Montana-Wyoming state line is straightforward—a lot of people have gone down to the first lake, and we easily—or as easily as we can at this altitude—reach the willows. The unofficial path falls apart after that, but it's obvious how to climb through a narrow defile, pass a sentinel whitebark pine, and turn around the bend at the top. There we confront a series of gorgeous lakes, the first of which is home to a delicate western grebe bobbing solo on wind-scalloped blue. Bernie and Luke and I will follow these tarns and see what happens. No other humans or dogs are in sight. It's us and the water and the rocks and the willows and the black-and-white grebe and the incessant musical contributions of white-crowned sparrows. Sans trail, we're down to elemental interactions with air, soil, rock, and water. Following a gentle rill from lake to lake involves little more than reading the land. We can hardly get lost.

Wyoming Creek's dale protects us. The jumbled rocks of the Beartooths are replaced here by actual soil and sedge. Relaxed and lazy, we explore each small body of water the creek flares just for us: this one with a dwarf willow fringe, this one all rumpled, this one a slate mirror. I pretend I'm the first woman to balance over this crossing, the first to see a spotted sandpiper on this shore, the first to use this pointed rock and these lichens as a sundial. Why it's important to be first may have to do with freedom. If you're first, no one is ahead of you to mess you up. But, in fact, there's something to be said for *not* being first. I imagine a woman, twenty thousand years ago, pausing in this spot. Her dreams and breaths quiver. I walk through her comforting aura. And then I imagine not being a human at all. Why has biochemistry resolved into this particular body of mine? Why was I not born a grebe? Or a fungus? For that matter, why was a heartbeat contrived for me, who could otherwise have been a fine granite boulder staring for eons at the sky, tickled below by melting snow and pika claws? Unlike my grandfather, I'm essentially lazy.

As I go farther back in the Tripp branches of my family tree, I find veins of possible spiritual obsession and rebellion. Consider that when my grandfather's parents named him after a figure in the *Book of Mormon* (his brothers diminished that heroic moniker to "Almy"), the LDS Church was not the well-established, prosperous mainstream institution it is now. It had been less than a decade since it renounced polygamy. In Alma's own father's lifetime, the US Army had invaded and tried to overrun Deseret, as the LDS called their Great Basin kingdom. As late as 1887, the Edmunds-Tucker Act sought to seize the Church's assets. Fresh on the heels of the Civil War and the massacres of Plains Indians, the Union was wary of religious separatists. The goal became policing morality and marriage and the human body, imposing uniformity on renegade, plural-marriage-practicing, sacred-underwear-clad Saints. This is a history that many current LDS people would probably rather forget, just as the lichens up here on the Line Creek Plateau are slowly erasing their rocky berths, eroding the past.

Alma's parents, Chris Tripp and Artie Reynolds, were both products of spiritual wifery. They wed in 1889 on the cusp of historic change—the moment when the Church capitulated to federal demands and outlawed polygamy. Had President Wilford Woodruff not issued his 1890 Manifesto banning plural marriage, would Chris Tripp have taken other wives? I would guess so, which makes Church history personal, the basis from which individual psyches and the course of individual lives and loves spread, just like lichen.

Not only were Chris Tripp's patriarchal powers limited, but his father and father-in-law both had more than one wife simultaneously, intimate relationships that in an instant became suspect. In fact, Chris's father, Enoch Bartlett Tripp, wed five spouses. In the LDS Church of that time (Enoch's matrimonial proclivities spanned pretty much its entire nineteenth-century history and geography prior to Utah statehood, from 1840s Nauvoo, Illinois, to 1890s Salt Lake), men acquired wives based on their status. So, having five of them was a pretty big deal, though not as impressive as Brigham Young's fifty-five. Nonetheless, when he had to renounce polygamy, Enoch must have feared for the legal status of his children and felt his own social standing plummet. That descent seems to have echoed through succeeding generations, which became increasingly alienated from the Church.

Much of his story is documented in Church archives. Of his early years, Enoch noted that his father was a circuit-riding Methodist preacher in southern Maine and that people referred to his young self as "the deacon ... on the account of my Still, Stedy & trusty habits, while the rest of my Brothers wer vary wild & rude." He learned the shoemaking trade from his father and got caught up in the religious fervor gripping the Northeast during the Second Great Awakening, but "after the excitement was over I cannot Say that I felt eny change." What troubled adolescent Enoch was that his new Protestant "church Could not do mericles, like Christs Church of old, according to the record in the New Testement, & that seemed a great mistery." Like so many of his time, Enoch craved inspiration. Contrary to my own teenage experience, though, it sounds as if my great-great-grandfather felt too little religious fervor.

Standing in front of the beautiful white temple in Nauvoo, Illinois, still and steady young Enoch's skin crawled as he studied its imposing spire—something like a pagan ziggurat. From its perch on a hilltop above town, the temple seemed to track his every move. Visiting his aunt Patty Sessions in Nauvoo after the death of Joseph Smith, as threats and counterthreats shot back and forth between Mormons and anti-Mormons, Enoch watched his step and his back. The Mormons, after all, might have wanted to kill him, a nonbeliever. He trod carefully.

But Enoch stayed on. He heard about the Haun Massacre of LDS fathers and sons in Missouri, about the mobs that had chased the Mormons from Kirtland, Ohio, whose temple—white and plain as any New England church—still stood. After several weeks, he concluded that the Saints weren't blind followers of a martyred fanatic, they weren't a danger to him, and they needed strong young men to help them build a sacred empire in the West. He may even have found the refreshing power of speaking in tongues, something practiced by the early Saints. But perhaps that was not a ritual he would personally have been able to attempt, "still" as he was. At any rate, when God spoke to him, Enoch found his life's calling if not his soul's expansion—and he married his first wife, an "orphing" named Roxanna Sophia Billings. I sometimes wonder if it was the God of love that called Enoch into the fold rather than the God of Nephi and Lehi, Moroni and Mormon. Or did he simply realize he could make a good income selling shoes to emigrants on the Mormon Trail, which he soon took to as part of the LDS exodus from the Midwest? Enoch did not leave any clues about that in his diary.

Unlike my hypothetical, eons-past, mountain-explorer, first-discoverer woman, Mormon polygamy, though it seems unique, did not blaze a new path. In fact, polygyny—marriage between one husband and multiple wives—was and still often is a common practice throughout the world, from China to the Middle East, from Africa to the Great Plains of North America. For my great-great-grandfather Enoch Tripp, the possibility of engaging in plural marriage must have seemed like a return to that "Church of old," that time of "mericles," he'd craved as a teenager coming to manhood in the "burned-over district" of the early nineteenth-century Northeast. That he had found a church to bestow on him the blessings of the patriarchy enjoyed by Solomon and Judah must have cemented his personal revelation, whatever form that took.

If his first marriage fulfilled the romantic promise of traditional European unions, the second surely amazed him with its evidence of God's (and the LDS authorities') favor. The third established his standing in the community. And the fourth?

I wonder if by the time of his fourth sealing, Enoch Bartlett had moved beyond romance, amazement, or pride. Concerning wife number four—my great-great-grandmother—his diary sandwiches a brief account of their marriage between Civil War news and the announcement that "I have made a trade for 20 cords of Bark." He describes Catherine Jane Allen as "formley of Jersey Island neer France. . . . She is Scotch desent."

According to popular gentile literature and political rhetoric, Mormon plural marriage was little better than child abuse, its victims living like sex slaves in sultanic harems. But when Susan B. Anthony and Elizabeth Cady Stanton visited Salt Lake in 1871 to drum up support for universal suffrage, they did not find a cowering sisterhood. They found instead a Tabernacle full of cheering, ardent female supporters and a lifelong friend in Utah suffragist Emmaline B. Wells.

I don't know if Enoch's wives attended the spectacle. But I can bet that Alma's grandmother, Catherine Jane, was not the sort of child-bride caricature decried in anti-LDS literature of the time. No, she was hard-as-nails Scots-Irish from Temple Michael, Longford, who would bear six children and would, like her son Christopher, live to be ninety-two or more (her date of birth is given variously as 1837, 1839, and 1840). She and her family sailed to North America on a ship called, icily, the *Antarctic*. Judging by her subsequent life, she wouldn't have been one to succumb to seasickness. In 1863, she and a whole passel of Allens walked or rode or somehow or other reached Salt Lake. How she caught Enoch's attention one year later, I don't know. Perhaps a bishop here or there suggested the union.

What might be a wedding photo depicts a formidable, if dapper, couple. Enoch has the close-set, piercing eyes of all the Tripps I've known, and their luxuriant wavy hair. The bit of stubble on his face is fashionable even by today's standards. His waistcoat looks to be silk, a black tie is snugged under his chin, his right thumb hooks his jacket lapel, and he's staring ahead. With her hand planted on his left shoulder (he's almost a foot taller than she is), Catherine announces her authority with perfectly parted hair, a crisp plaid dress, and hollow cheeks. These features tell of a stern young woman, someone the old narratives might have called a "personage." She's up to the second-generation pioneer life, aptly equated with the beehive adopted by the LDS as their motto for converting the West into a self-sufficient, agro-industrial paradise.

As far as I know, the Enoch Bartlett Tripp family with its eventual five wives flourished. And then, in middle age, their settled domesticity was ripped apart. Enoch may have clandestinely married a young woman (his sixth wife) in the 1890s—*after* the anti-polygamy Manifesto. For this, I believe he was excommunicated.

What it all meant for Catherine Allen is unclear. Perhaps the sundering of her marriage or being predeceased by six of her seven children (including one in infancy) chilled her. At any rate, all she could say when she saw her grandson Alma after a hiatus of several years was, acidly, "You're not as handsome as your father."

Overall, it seems that these Tripps were hard-nosed people, pushed and pulled by an interest in getting ahead. They counted spirituality by productivity and the stoic handling of personal loss. Among them I don't see a kindred OCD sufferer. Mostly, I read into these ancestors' actions a need to prosper on both religious and economic fronts.

Warren Ford Reynolds, Alma's other grandfather, isn't as celebrated in Church history as Enoch Tripp, though he was a polygamist also, being the husband of two women. He was perhaps less prosperous, if no less devout. He'd grown up on an Avon, New York, farm near Palmyra, the site of Joseph Smith's visions of the angel Moroni. Baptized in the Mississippi River near Nauvoo along with his first wife, Edna Merrell, Warren was part of the first pioneer migration to Deseret.

In her single extant photograph, Edna looks plain and grim—perhaps toothless. Her sister-wife, Christina McNeil, on the other hand, seems kindly and downright beautiful. The marriages lasted fifty and forty-seven years, respectively. Those images—one showing an unattractive woman, the other a natural beauty—were included in the annual McNeil-Reynolds Family Reunion invitations sent to my grandfather by Christina's descendants. I used to laugh at them, but now I wonder. What led these three people to marry, produce seventeen children total, and believe they were fulfilling prophecy? Surely something more was involved than a metaphorical "Algae met fungi and they took a lichen to each other." And something even more than the prodding of LDS General Authorities. On these points, Edna and Christina left no written record.

But I have clues about Warren. In 1854, having been in Utah eight years, he tells his brother in a letter, "Asa, I am proud of my religion—it embrases every good thing under the hull heavon." Though he has "had sum harde times … I hav no reson to com plane for the God that I serve & worship the God of Abriham Isiek & Jacob has precieeved and led me carefully to these peacefule valleys of the mountains whare thare is rest at least for a season." Passion, gratitude, and love spin from his poor spelling and burn

Warren's eyes in an old photograph (his chest-length beard is impressive, too). A fanatic? Maybe. A formidable soul? Certainly. Someone who didn't mind being led only by what he called spirit? Absolutely. Someone whose propensity for magical thinking burned a channel through time to lodge inside me? I think: Here's my man, a fellow lover of "valleys of the mountains."

My own struggle has taught me to reject directions, scriptures, churches. I don't want to understand what God shouts down at me or shoots into my brain. I want to ache as power rises through my feet to my tailbone and sacrum and neck and skull from mosses, liverworts, and lichens—the rich symbiosis of ancient survival. I *have* inherited Enoch Bartlett Tripp's desire for the "mericles" of old and Warren Ford Reynolds's embrace of "every good thing under the hull heavon" but not their need for a patriarchal deity. I crave revelations but not those of a God busy with politics, gender identity, marriage customs, and wealth.

When I'm away from roads, trails, state-line signposts, and other markers (go here, turn here, backtrack there), spiritual luxuriance takes over, especially in expansive weather with a lazy breeze and a clear sky. Here there is "rest at least for a season." I stretch into a bountiful world, temporarily safe from anxiety, following humans who've been here before, ancestors of today's Indigenous people crafting a route over living boulders and through mysterious valleys.

I appreciate the seasonality of Warren Ford Reynolds's "rest." When you go hiking above timberline in early autumn, you find few blossoms. Most of the birds are quiet, except for the cheerful, white-crowned sparrows. Everything draws down into the drying soil it's come from—what soil manages to accumulate, that is, between boulders. The grasses are yellow, the dwarf shrubs wise in their clinging just a little longer to still-photosynthesizing leaves. Yet they will soon give up even these and sink into their roots to sleep.

The sky is vivid today, brighter than it ever is in the summer and unburdened by moisture-laden clouds. Those fishtail-looking cirrus formations? They billow and shrink, leaving a sky of pure "heavon." But the brightness and the rest from obsessions may dim in a week or two and grow over with winter storm clouds closing up the business of life—at least for a while. Dormant under the snow, lichens create shields of ice and wake up to the elixir of June meltwater, creatures of the past but fully open to the new. Industrious, elemental beings.

My grandfather had a lot in common with them. He was bound to the earth, more interested in hunting trips, mining, and gardening than in religion. When he talked, it wasn't about Joseph Smith, the Saints, or the past. In his later years, he was mostly quiet and still, emitting only an occasional wry observation about my grandmother.

It wasn't always that way. Throwing off his pioneer heritage, Alma left the Church as a young man, whether for love of the woman he would marry and cleave to for more than fifty years or as his own form of rebellion, I don't know. But, in keeping with his Book of Mormon name, he was as restless as any Saint. He drove to Idaho in the 1920s for the potato harvest in an open-air, homemade car he called "the Bug," which in the photos I have looks like a soup can on wheels. He made his way farther north to Burke and the Hecla Mines. Even after he came home to Utah, he worked hard. He reclaimed alkaline soil on the family ranch, extending its orchards, and prospected in the mountains above. He didn't believe in much except the enjoyment of squeezing utility out of a place. The only religious ritual I ever saw him engage in was taking communion at the Presbyterian church my parents attended. He wasn't a member, and so it seemed as if his lifting a glass of grape juice from the salver as it passed down the pews was more of a "when in Rome" sort of deal. Or maybe he was thirsty.

With an eighth-grade education, Alma learned how to prospect and do it well. He loved any place dry and far from a road, and lonesome. In his day, Utah's Deep Creek Range fit the bill. He'd turn a wild place like that to use. The last time he went out to his mining claims for assessment work, he was, he said with disgust, too old even to fish. I remember him standing beside Tom's Creek, at the mouth of Goshute Canyon, having a devil of a time putting a grasshopper on his hook. How worthless he seemed to feel he'd become.

I thought of him as a grand old man (he achieved his father's longevity), someone fittingly born in the previous century, now the century before last. Alma Allen Tripp, yes, with his donkeys and ore carts and cabin and mountains and his thick hair raised straight up when lightning played around the guy-wires of his tramways. No one was ever struck by lightning at his highest mine, the Eagle's Nest, but it was often a very real possibility, and he made his entire crew find shelter whenever a storm beat down from the peaks.

Alma loved the hawks and the bobcats and the coyotes and the Bonneville cutthroat trout. He loved supervising five families who worked his mines and lived in boxcar houses or cabins like his own. He loved sitting above a hole sawed in the ice of Bear Lake, hoping he'd tap the storied cisco run with his rod and reel. He loved hunting, or even just tracking, pronghorn and deer. He also loved blasting adits and cutting switchbacks from wild hillsides. He loved planting tomatoes and cherry trees in his city garden.

That ambitious strain brought Catherine Allen to America on a ship called *Antarctic*, led Enoch Tripp to seek God in the desert, filled Warren Reynolds's life with blessed work and visions, made Chris Tripp build a ranch on alkaline soil at the base of the Deep Creek Mountains. Maybe they were all compulsively working to build some structure their thoughts created. "Deseret" they called it, land of the honeybee.

By the time Utah was on the verge of statehood and the LDS church was threatened with federally orchestrated financial ruin, the world had gotten too small for polygamy, for people like young Enoch and Catherine Allen Tripp. Maybe by the end of the nineteenth century, the world was too small for their grandchild Alma. When rock-and-ice wilderness areas are all we have left, it's easy to say it's even too small for ne'er-do-well descendants like me. I'm not charging westward toward glory. I'm trying to let things roll along waterways, past western grebes, through wind-rumpled sedges. I'm poking around in the ruins of yet another boom-bust delusion. I'm counting on the resilience of lichen. Because, when I go home again, I'll be on the downward slope of Manifest Destiny's crumbling freeway overpasses, train-mad freight yards, mercury-tainted working-class neighborhoods, oil refineries, and upscale subdivisions that squeeze out the last remaining prairie dogs, deer, and sparrows.

I'll never shake Alma Tripp's legacy—wildness intertwined with (even dependent on) human ambition: the mines, switchbacks, cabins, and miscellaneous junk (including old shoes and even a vintage typewriter) that, according to recent bloggers, still scar his Goshute Canyon haunts in the Deep Creeks. When I hike to an old homesite, ghost town, or abandoned ranch in Montana, I feel at home. Those rough wood floors and walls, those tailings piles and those rusty, unidentifiable bits of equipment remind me of my grandfather's claim, his ore bins and compressor shed, and even his backyard. I recognize the tar paper, planed wood slats, and cheap, warped-glass windows—just like those of his cabin—and the hopeful poverty and driving hardship.

After two centuries, my family's westward push—once a pioneering march to the prophesied future—has become a backward-looking path of confusing polygamous genetics, patriarchal spiritual and physical passions, symbioses and antagonisms, industrial litter and religious enthusiasms strewn from the British Isles to Bethel, Maine, from Nauvoo, Illinois, to the arid American West.

Unlike those pioneers, Bernie, Luke, and I wander for no practical reason. Why *Line* Creek Plateau is freshened by *Wyoming* Creek—and, indeed, whether we're in Wyoming or Montana as we wind along the border—is a cartographical puzzle I don't want to solve right now. We relax to the freedom of going wherever we want, without routes to follow or "recommended" contours or switchbacks. Set loose, we climb a massive but gentle rise. At the top, we eat the snacks we've brought and overlook the scene.

Bernie takes photographs and studies all kinds of things he doesn't mention or point out to me. Luke rolls in a promising pile of marmot scat. He turns his face to the wind, nostrils quivering. Bernie and Luke seem to accept *Everything as It Happens* (the title of one of Bernie's poetry collections). Me, I wonder how to interpret dwarf willow and orange lichens, and I look for revelation sparkling on every surface.

At the end of the hike as Luke and I head to the car, which we can see for the final mile or two, that odd LDS past churns inside me, and it inflects my relationship to the land. Do I belong here? Can I accept it without wanting to do *something* to it?

Since Bernie has had to go back a ways to retrieve his forgotten hiking poles, I take time to scope out blue-winged teal deep in the canyons of the first lake, whose water is now whipped by a late afternoon breeze. Luke is worried enough about Bernie's absence to sit calmly while I wonder what it's like to be a teal, to bob and rise and spin as the wind-driven waves allow. Would all the history of development and its attendant guilt drop off my feathered shoulders? But there it is, our car, waiting for us ("There we are," I think, as if the car *is* us)—waiting to take us back to where we make our living. Down the switch-backing highway, down from the mountains, and out into the expanding wasteland.

I hope Alma Allen Tripp shows up in my dreams again, to the soundtrack of one of his favorite songs: "Oh, if I had the wings of an angel / from these prison bars I would fly." He'll explain lichens' lithic connection. He'll scatter wild columbine ("Every Seed a Sturdy Plant") and get a chance to tell me he's discovered where veins run deepest and riches are inaccessible and how to climb a scree slope without setting off a rockslide.

Soon Bernie joins us, and we struggle on the last little rutted bit of tundra. Everything is hard after a day at high altitude. Especially leaving.

TRAIL 12

Thinking of the Trees on Nichols Creek

General location: Red Lodge, Montana, Beartooth Mountains; about 70 miles from Yellowstone
Hiking distance: 6+ miles round trip
Elevation gain: 1,100+ feet
Terrain: Sage, aspen meadow, and cottonwood to lodgepole pine forest

Nichols Creek is the first trail on the north as you go along the National Forest Service access road from Red Lodge, Montana. The route's not spectacular, but I like going uphill and transitional from sage and junipers to willows and aspens, and farther to pines and firs. It's October, my birth month, and Bernie, Luke, and I have the place to ourselves, if you don't think of the trees.

At the trailhead, junipers grow no bigger than shrubs, gray and loden. Willows come in as wraiths edging the creek. Taller and thicker are the aspens, which I pause to admire. Yet numbering the latter among the "trees" would be a mistake. What looks like a hillside of modest individuals is a single being, clones branching from the mother root. There's less dependence that way on sexual reproduction, seeds, and iffy germination. It's an Edenic arrangement minimizing the painful cycle of birth, reproduction, and death. But Eden, I think, isn't all harmony and forest bathing. Eden is a place to fall from.

One of the enduring beliefs permeating most origin myths is the idea that female egos are not just inferior but dangerous architects of those falls. In Christianity, Eve is the stand-in for all females, and motherhood is her punishment. Over the centuries, she has been judged an evil succubus or a gutsy heroine, and everything in between. In getting us kicked out of Eden, she introduced change, progress, and evolution—all aspects of human, and aspen, identity. Still, the heart of the Genesis story is always that sharp division between primary man and secondary woman—a seemingly inescapable truth for the agrarian people who composed the book. The Old Testament talks a lot about seeds.

I can only now hold Christianity's fundamental sexual dichotomy at arm's length. I grew up in the 1960s and 1970s, and fully absorbed the "girls were girls, and men were men" lessons from the Bible. It's hard to climb out of that sort of indoctrination. Societal obsessions of woman-as-other formed my maturing ego, taking the shape of a deep-seated, almost unconscious loathing of my physical appearance (unlikely to attract men) and a desire to emulate male success. Anxiety and OCD may have roots in an inherited fear that I won't live up to expectations. I don't know what male ego is, but my female one was formed by the patriarchal structures I grew up inside. It's taken me a long time to realize that plants, animals, and places can pull me out of unhealthy dependency and into communion. This tree-dominated path on the edge of the Beartooth Mountains makes me think about ego as a social thing, not a singular "me" deal.

Imagine Eden as a lodgepole pine community hemmed with aspens and junipers. Pygmy owls here and there. A hum of blue horseflies that won't bite (it's paradise, after all). Vultures circling and bored. The ground littered with needles. The soil springy, infused with algae, mosses, fungi. And the snake? A cool-eyed, arrow-headed, cynical rattler or maybe a kindly bull snake. Even better, a diminutive garter, which is more likely here, anyway.

Pick juniper berries, the snake would tell Eve. *Smash them. Mix them with grains or potatoes. Steep them for a month. Strain the mixture. Drink it, girl, and you'll be a god. You'll have visions.* A child, really, Eve is already running to find a basket for harvesting and misses the snake's appended warning: *Don't share with Adam.*

Of course, being an ego made of someone else's rib, she won't drink alone. When her concoction is ready, Eve gives Adam a sample and another, the two of them on this rocky outcrop overlooking West Eden, tipping back amateurish clay goblets fired in his kiln. They giggle at each other's bodies, the two so different. But they're discovered soon enough. The boy blames the girl, and the girl blames the snake. Miffed, God sends them both off to live in a delusional, pain-beset world.

No oracle, no hermit, just a kid in need of a friend—that's Eve, the snake decides, shaking her head, stretching her tongue once or twice, then settling under the tree of the fruit of the critique of binary but unequal genders. She's fine with God's "punishment"—a long, lean body and exquisite heat-sensing organs, beautiful soft scales and the possibility of renewal as she shimmies herself out of one dulled old skin after another. She thinks of the trees, the fallen ones like these on Nichols Creek that change from month to month.

Though they are generally uncommon in the Beartooth Mountains, there are several aspen stands along the trail's first half mile, and they call attention to themselves. At least, I notice them. Growing up in Utah, I learned aspens. They flourished throughout the Wasatch Range, creating October style. Their half-dollar leaves turned yellow, orange, dark gold. Some were speckled with black. And they danced, spinning in all directions with a slight buckling of air. A delicate petiole attached each to its twig. The leaves' particular talent in the summer was to photosynthesize on either surface. Together, they sounded like someone shuffling a gigantic deck of cards made of dragonfly wings. In autumn, their rifflings were nostalgic reminders of summer industriousness.

I used to think of aspens as female. I don't know why. Maybe it was their flashing leaves on fairy-white trunks, so delicate they scarred, a phenomenon that induced people to carve initials in their flesh. Or the sociable groves of them. Maybe it was that my dad didn't like them much and my mother did. Maybe it was that, in my mother's family, men worked in mines with rocks and metal and failed at pruning, and women admired trees. I think now that aspens paralleled something quintessential in my mother's mother's lineage and in me.

I go back, for example, to watch a particular sixteen-year-old with a middle-class life and a seventy-two-year-old scarred by early loss and poverty tackle kitchen cleanup on a hot July evening in the mid-1970s. Some family gathering or other continues in the living room, but the girl loves being with her grandmother and has volunteered to help. If she's lucky, the grandmother will talk about the past, about philosophy and the occult. Tonic for a teenage ego.

In front of the two—my grandmother and me—are gritty reminders of material existence: pots and pans to scrub, eight place settings, the good silver, my great-grandmother's gravy boat, colorful iced-tea tumblers with matching spoons, bits of food drifting in the plastic dishpan. Without air conditioning, the kitchen swelters. Perspiration gathers on my grandmother's upper lip and forehead, and her hair, bluish with a rinse she uses to temper the white, is damp. Few wrinkles cross her face. In window light speckling through the gingko tree, she looks vigorous even though she broke her hip ten years ago and has limped ever since.

When at last we hang up our aprons (I have to wear an apron in my grandmother's kitchen), we go out on the side steps to cool off. The rest of the family chats inside. We don't tell them where we're going, a perch on the cement, city noises fading with the evening. Occasionally, a motorcycle percusses or a mufflerless car roars. But, even at dusk, the major constellations are visible in town in those days, and the evening freshens yards and parks. The quotidian slides away. I think about nearby Sugar House Park, site of the former Utah State Prison, where Wobbly songwriter Joe Hill was executed.

My grandmother continues our never-ending conversation about the supernatural. Self-taught after having to drop out of school at sixteen, she's become an amateur Egyptologist who collects ankhs and reveres the sun-god-worshipping pharaoh Akhenaten—one of her historical heroes. She rather likes Napoleon, too. She reads Romantic poetry, particularly Percy Shelley, and her books cover Gnosticism and 1920s theosophy. She loves arguing with Jehovah's Witnesses and LDS missionaries who come to her door. But now her talk is personal: "I saw a ghost once."

Her words jolt me, and I no longer sag after our marathon dish-doing. She explains how my aunt as an infant was often sick. And how one night, my grandmother, near despair because of the Depression and the child's ailments, lay awake in bed and saw, standing behind the crib, her own mother—almost two decades dead and the baby's namesake—smiling at her and very clearly corporeal, reassuring her that the Depression would end and the baby survive.

Time slips. The past isn't over. The present peels back, exposing layers that reassemble on one eternal plane. My throat clogs. Tears start. My grandmother's eyes redden. We float into a world of never-ending relational presence. My grandmother isn't one to make up a ghost story, so the veracity of it hits like a branch from the tree of knowledge. Her confession is something rare, a watershed vision joining four generations: my ghostly great-grandmother, my grandmother, my aunt and mother, and me. An aspen stand of roots and stems. The aspen mother and her fatherless offspring. Not exactly fatherless, maybe, but female nurtured. Survivors—somehow.

Nichols Creek aspens are on the sparse side compared to the giant groves of my Wasatch Mountain childhood. In fact, one of the earth's largest, oldest, and most successful life forms is the Utah aspen "grove" known as "Pando" (Latin for "I spread"). Growing near the center of the state, it is more than twenty-six times as big as the United States Capitol grounds and heavier than six thousand bull bison. Its miraculous tens of thousands of interacting stems came from a seed so small you couldn't find it again if you dropped it on a polished floor. Unfortunately, this Edenic plant is in trouble now. Drought and high numbers of sucker-eating deer and elk threaten its vigor—as much as sixteen thousand years of growth, knowledge, and openness to rain, sun, moonlight, and wild mint.

In the great world religions and myths, Pando would be the faith that grew from a mustard seed, the multi-pronged arms of Shiva, the multifarious ranks of Arhats. But Pando might, after all, shrug off metaphors. Its arms and legs and heart are entwined in the earth, not in the abstractions of humans. Though people have tapped into and recorded Pando's low-pitched-humming circulatory system, the being itself defies definition. A nonbinary maternal lineage.

Cradled at first by two ridges, the quivering October aspens here on Nichols Creek are much more obscure than Pando, but golden leaved and sociable nevertheless. As the trail crosses the stream, juncos dart and fireweed is royal purple with autumn, blown seedheads dispersing under the auspices of the aspens. Coming out of the healthy groves and creekside willows, we pass a few isolated, dying, and twisted trunks—remnants of other once-thriving root systems now overshadowed by the betraying pines they'd sheltered. They exude age and time, worthy little sisters of Pando. Even the human inscriptions in their scarred bark are old and blurry. How did they begin their lives? Were they among the first pioneers after a fire? Did their origins set them up for a lifetime of struggle?

Like these remnants, my grandmother Helen Irene McLaughlin knew loss and trauma. She was born in 1903, when there were virgin forests, horses and carriages, passenger pigeons and small family farms, linotype presses and steam-powered trains. Geronimo and Chief Joseph were alive. Theodore Roosevelt was president. Performing circus elephants pounded along the main streets of small towns. Like Mark Twain, my grandmother saw Halley's Comet.

For a while, her father ran a newspaper in Randolph, Utah, but due to its anti-LDS columns, local Saints threatened to burn it. After that, he worked as a schoolteacher and an office manager in Salt Lake. Coming from a Kansas Jayhawker family (he was born in the middle of the Civil War) with a brother named Darwin, William James McLaughlin didn't fit in well—Utah was much more conservative and devout than it is now. He seems to have been a sensitive and passionate man. I have no idea how, as a boy, he or his siblings (there were nine of them) reacted to their mother's death in the Topeka State Hospital, then known simply as the Insane Asylum—a cruel place whose former grounds are said to be haunted. Martha Dooley McLaughlin lived there a scant three months, dying on October 7—the date of her discharge. She was fifty-three years old. Was mental illness the reason for her confinement? Early dementia? I know nothing else about it and only found the information online. I do know that my grandfather William James was shipped off to relatives for a year or two. Was Martha Dooley lost to shadows, strapped to a chair, never to be mentioned again by her many children? Was she, lacking modern psychological care, my precursor in anxiety?

As it has come down to me, the personal disaster that first opened Helen's heart to her own tragic sensibility was being told that she was the "replacement" for a brother who'd died at two and whom she'd never known. The replacement was incomplete: She was not a boy. And her family subscribed to the rule that stipulated the superiority and greater value of the male. Then, as if this simultaneous sense of mortality and inadequacy were insufficient, she lost her mother to the H1N1 flu pandemic. A touching letter from William James to his relatives relates how he held his wife's hand as, both of them very ill, she died. Mamie McLaughlin was forty-five; her daughter Helen sixteen. The family fell to pieces. Helen's older sister ran off to California to become a professional pianist (they didn't speak to each other for decades), and her father died in 1926. Helen was left with an orphaned little brother and sister. Somehow, like a stalwart aspen root, she held things together. She refused victimization. By the time she was twenty-four, she'd married a handsome young miner and had him and four youngsters to look after, her own and her siblings. My mother said Helen was cross. I can see why. She raised them all successfully, as well as two later arrivals. It's not that she didn't fight anxiety, but her strong will wouldn't bow to the judgments of others. "Consider the source," she'd say about criticism.

As if the Nichols Creek trail were a metaphor for Helen's young adulthood, it soon turns steep, dry, and coniferous. Out of the aspens and the meadowy stuff and into the lodgepole pines, we can't see much but the trail and the trees—rough-barked trunks and thick-needled crowns. I'm sure young Helen was equally pressed in and probably wondered how she would find her way. I have a small notepad she wrote out in pencil, ticking off every purchase and expense of the week: coal, sugar, coffee. By then, she'd entered the thicket of the Great Depression. One late fall, my mother, a child at the time, found a twenty-dollar bill lying in slush on the side of the road. When she asked whether it was real, Helen broke down in tears.

Every so often along our hike today, there's a limber pine, kinnikinnick, spent fireweed spikes, and old, shrunken, colorless stems of the dead summer's pinedrops, which are easy to miss. The flowers aren't showy. When they stop blossoming, they turn especially cryptic. The plants may not bloom again for a year or more. Phantom-like inflorescences are left scattered under the trees, reminders of beauty thwarted. But dormant pinedrops eke out enough nutrition from their association with fungi and pine roots to get by and reappear again someday as supple, living stalks. My grandmother, like those intrepid plants, became a powerful force in our family—even after she broke her hip, her autodidactic charisma gathered us around her. She was the smartest woman I knew, and I'm grateful I told her so.

My mother's personality, unlike my grandmother's, seemed constrained and narrow. The way she sat—legs crossed, hands clenched—and the way she refused to accept or ask for help armored her against pain, disappointment, revelation, embarrassment. She'd been a child who took to heart adults' offhand comments. Someone once told her she had a "moon face," and for the rest of her life she remembered that injustice. She also held tight a memory of unfairness in a Salt Lake school after she'd moved from her grandfather's Six Mile Ranch. She was in first grade, and the students, most of them LDS, had to say what religion they belonged to. When she offered up what my grandmother had told her—that she was "a Christian"—everyone laughed. "Nobody can be just a Christian. What do you mean by that?" the teacher asked. My mother didn't know. She hoarded that humiliation, as an oyster hoards its particle of sand, but no pearl ever formed. Her shell was real, and the ego inside, though vulnerable, grew tough. Once, when I was in my thirties, I stood by the kitchen table after breakfast and put my hands on her shoulders as she sat reading the paper. She almost jumped out of her seat. "Don't you EVER DO THAT!" she snarled.

A friend of mine said she thought of my mother as "distinguished." With her love of high heels, perfume, ironed A-line dresses and skirts, Mrs. Chamberlain, as my friend called her, was shielded against any public display that would rumple a fine appearance and open her to the kind of criticism that had wilted her in first grade. She didn't play board or card games with my sister and me for fear of doing something wrong. Perhaps she suffered from what one of my counselors called obsessive-compulsive personality disorder (not to be confused with OCD), which speaks to her use of order and composure to ward off unwanted social interactions. More than anything, she was impeccable. When a coworker told her that she had a poker face, my mother took it as a compliment. My dad was shut out of her affections, too—or so it seemed when I was growing up. She resented the fact that *he* had shut *her* out, she told me later. I now imagine the missed communication there, and the anger. But despite all of that, she was fiercely loyal in a superior sort of way. My sister and I called her "the martyr."

Unlike my grandmother, my mother didn't care for philosophy and metaphysics. She sewed our clothes and cooked my dad's favorite roasts, delicious egg-and-cheese dishes, and that most dreaded of all dinners: the Swiss steak that would be so tough I'd have to secretly spit a mouthful or two of it into my napkin at the dinner table. She mowed the lawn; pruned the shrubs; and in all sorts of little ways helped "the folks," as she called her parents, during their later years. When it was time to shovel snow for them, she made us all pitch in with just the correctness of the thing. If they had a doctor's appointment, she gritted her teeth and drove the folks downtown, white-knuckling it because she was terrified of heavy traffic. If she watched *The Mike Douglas Show* or *One Life to Live* or *Wagon Train* reruns in the afternoons, she had a stack of ironing to do or a pile of mending to justify the diversion. Only occasionally, when I stayed home from school (I had to have a fever or be vomiting for this blessed occurrence) would I see her take up a mystery or historical novel, lean back in a chair, and read silently for an hour or two. I remember that her lips moved to form the words, as if she were pressing them into her mind. I liked to follow her progress along the page.

Her hugs were few but significant: before I went to kindergarten after my goldfish died, and years later at my grandmother's funeral. I vowed I'd always love her for it and never forget how she cradled our dying dachshund on her lap and gave her sips of water throughout a very long night when there were no such things as emergency vet clinics. She hugged me after the vet's devastating phone call the next day—and even she and my dad embraced, the only time I remember that happening unless they jokingly put their arms around each other for a photograph.

My mother loved infants—she could be freely affectionate with them. As a youngster, she'd done a lot of babysitting, but after my sister and I went to school, she undoubtedly felt motherhood and housewifery as burdens. Because she could go into a towering rage without much warning, I kept a doll-blanket bindle in a corner of my room filled with toy dishes and a jacket—in case I had to leave in a hurry. It was the worst and best feeling in the world when she once punished only my sister for something we were both doing—I don't remember what. Before I was born, she'd turned the front-yard hose on my sister. The neighbors were shocked at her cruelty, but, as she told me later, what else could she have done when the two-year-old was running toward the street and wouldn't listen to her shouts, and she heavily pregnant? I didn't escape her attention all the time, and more than once felt the wooden-spoon force of her wrath on my derriere, as if she would shape me into perfection.

She criticized my dad. She implied that he was weak because he didn't hunt and fish as her father and older brother did. No one ever reached the high standards of masculinity they set. She didn't like how Dad shirked duties due to back pain, which I don't believe she thought was real—and maybe she was right about that. She was frustrated by his dark moods when he didn't talk much. She wanted to entertain, but he said he saw enough people at work to last him. Above all, she hated his cigarette smoking and once pointed out to me how a nicely dressed woman "ruined the whole thing" by having a cigarette "dangling" from her lips. Of course, she didn't want me or my sister to smoke. But the issue was like a wedge to pry us from our dad's sphere, to assert her correctness and forcefulness against his ineffectuality because he couldn't just quit. She also complained that he'd passed up promotions because he didn't want to hire and fire people—and now his trainees were his bosses. Whether that bothered him, I don't know. But it bothered her. Still, let anyone outside the family criticize one of us, and her anger flared in deep sarcasm or bitter asides.

When she was in her fifties, my mother learned to drive, bought her own boxy Ford Fairlane, and, in addition to taxiing the folks, worked as a church secretary. After my dad died, she revamped the yard and redecorated the house. She was physically fit until her last illness—and even then she didn't complain or show weakness if she could help it. In fact, her brain cancer embarrassed her. She told me that if they knew about her tumor, people would think she wasn't competent anymore and would belittle her. And maybe they did, as she lost physical functions one by one. Confined to a care center, Mother was still talking about "getting back in shape" and walking over to the grocery store again. She was like an aspen who remained visibly unscarred though bowed by storms. She expected love but would never ask for it.

I think she looked down on many women and craved a strong male presence—which my emotional dad did not provide. In effect, she was tougher than the men she idolized. A hard-nosed Eve. Even my dad acknowledged this. She'd conquered female stereotypes and anxiety by outwomaning all the other women I knew. When, on my sixteenth birthday in an October long ago, the neighbors' chihuahua was hit by a car, I stood frozen at the window. Then, as I'm ashamed to recall, I turned away to tell what had happened. My mother didn't wait for the whole story but rushed past me through the front door, picked up the dog, led our wailing neighbor to the trusty Fairlane, and drove to the vet. Of course, it was too late.

When Mother died at eighty-three and my sister at the funeral said she'd lost her "best friend," I wondered. I'm not sure my mother would have wanted to be *my* friend. And, undoubtedly, I never thought of *her* that way. She'd created the substrate on which my life grew—a bit warped, perhaps, but upward nonetheless. I owed her everything, for good or ill. No, I think she was *not* my friend. And, no, she was not, in this regard, like an aspen after all. She was the forest giant, the nurse log, who prepared my possibilities of stunting and growth, anger and acceptance, resentment and anxiety, and love.

Despite my mother's determination to do nothing wrong or be exposed as flawed, which undoubtedly rubbed off on me, I've learned that it can be a good thing to make a mistake, to, in this case, lose our way. Feckless Luke with his high-cocked flag of a tail and eager prance doesn't help, no savvy guide as his predecessor Rita was. We had two choices when the path forked, and, as my son says, given a fifty-fifty chance of being right, you'll always be wrong. But sometimes wrong turns out okay.

Stumbling onto a rocky view overlooking the West Fork drainage, we lounge in the coolish sun and eat lunch. I play with slow-moving grasshoppers, and admire the mica scattered around and the glittering crystals in the foundational granite. A flock of black rosy-finches flies over—a species I've never seen before. I compose an impromptu oral poem I won't remember except that it's very good. Brilliant, even. It drifts down the hill toward the aspens as I say it. I feel like Basho, creating on the spot, unencumbered by a clouded mind or ego-protecting armor. My mother would not approve.

But she never failed me.

Consider Eureka, California. 1985. Just before 11:30 a.m. I sit in a birthing chair and push into pain and fear and the arrival of my son. I don't think about Eve's curse or original sin, or about compulsions to avoid the unpleasant. Or about flight. Whom can I battle? Where am I to go? There is an anxious bit of hyperventilation and a seconds-long dagger-thrust of pain as the baby's head crowns, but the birth happens no matter what. The logic of physiological processes overwhelms anxiety. The baby is, unexpectedly, a boy and human (I dreamed once or twice in the third trimester that I'd give birth to a giraffe). Briefly, I worry about his hesitant breathing and modest Apgar score as he's whisked from me. I see blood and vernix and a weirdly ropy, white-and-purple umbilical cord. And the bluish child. But soon we know that that little bit of new human life is doing well, and the pediatrician takes him off for a thorough exam—with Bernie following and later marveling at how the doctor turned Tom over and over and upside down.

Alone, suspended in the chair, I have no connection to the nurse stitching me up or to her Demerol injection. A long-anticipated event has come and gone. I'm alone. But … not really. As I float beyond time and space, it's easy to see that I'm at the apex of an aspen trunk, part of a complex, part of the mother rhizome so far below, part of an unbroken branch stretching back beyond Eve to mitochondrial Africa. I'm not *a* mother ("Tom's Mom," as I'll be dubbed when he's in high school) but *the* mother. Archetypal. Mythic. Creative. Heroic. A friend of snakes. Awash in emotional wisdom, feminine power, matrilineal joining, true ecstatic revelation, Demerol side-effect, loss-of-blood giddiness, I float ever higher above my emptied body. I'm great.

Until I get shaky.

The nurse puts me in a wheelchair, whisking me to a hospital room in time for lunch. I face my first juggling act of motherhood: how to hold a baby and devour in a few bites a massive piece of chocolate cake because baby and I have arrived in the room at the same time as the cake, whose sugar overcomes my hypoglycemic tremors and egoistic delusions. During that postpartum lunch, Bernie daintily consumes the sandwich and salad I can't eat. He looks like he's had a day of it. He denies this; when I ask what it was like to see our son for the first time, he shrugs: "He just slid out." No problem at all. He holds Tom—wearing a white knit cap and wrapped in a cotton receiving blanket—like a football, baby head under his palm, baby feet at his ribs.

You might think it strange that we have such stamina, but that night after visiting hours and with partners absent, I talk endlessly and elatedly with the new mother in the bed next to mine. I guess we're young and exhilarated. Our babies are healthy, so are we, and on top of that the consciousness returns that I'm one stem in a complex self that includes not only this stranger but my mother, grandmothers, great-grandmothers, and on and on. What a line of witches and crones and sweethearts and femme fatales and nervous wrecks and cooks and seamstresses and laborers and poets and chemists and athletes we are, going all the way back to our sinless Eve, who gathered baobab pods while her baby rode in a fiber nest on her back. Good company. I think about my grandmother and how she'd done this job of labor four times. And about my mother, who'd done it twice. There's one root. Every woman—mother or not, to be sure—is a stem growing to the sun, scarred by the ache of birth. And so is everyone else.

Ah, but anxiety returns when I'm home alone with a neonate suffering from a slight case of jaundice, the first of many common health issues most parents worry about, some more than others. Bernie told me years later that he thought I always had things under control. He perhaps doesn't realize how the arrival of my mother—who'd flown in from Salt Lake—was like a visitation by angels. If Eve made us suffer in childbirth and got us kicked out of Eden, she was also the first mother to help her daughters bathe and comfort and soothe a slippery infant. My mother was a mature, competent version of the silly girl who once talked to snakes and shared their secrets with men. My mother had grown out of her rages and come to rescue me.

On the Nichols Creek hike, thinking about tree destinies, the anguish and fervor of individual pines, is hard at first. When you leave the aspens, you sink deep into a shadowy forest, aware of its overall shape and uniformity—those dense armies of identical trunks, those boring reproductions of each other similar in shape, size, and age because virtually the whole generation burns in this habitat about every hundred years, when the next forest is born. While pines don't send out suckers from a central root like the aspens, it's somehow easy to think of them as uniform ranks, background scenery to animal dramas.

But look again and you are *inside* the whole. Individuals take shape. Near one shagged crown there's a witch's broom—a twiggy mass formed by a fungus, virus, or pest. The top of another was sheared by a long-ago windstorm and makes a nesting platform for falcons or goshawks. This trunk was bent and broken by snow and whips in a knot of branches. Protective sap drips from another to ward off infection or infestation. Shelf fungi attack an ailing pine. Another unfortunate supports a partner who died—when the wind blows, they keen together. Still other trees, well situated or lucky, puff and swell in perfect health. Neither lodgepole nor aspen is long lived on its own. You have to think of "forest" or "grove" as the organism that persists.

But what if it doesn't?

If Eden is about eternal, forbidden trees that survive our mortality, it's a gentle myth compared to Ovid's story of Erysichthon, which tells of arboreal murder and of how to fall beyond redemption. Along Nichols Creek, it's easy to imagine Ceres' sacred tree as neither aspen nor lodgepole but as a massive limber pine, growing like a colony, its many trunks joined. The weight of roosting birds means nothing to it. Of the seeds it makes, some fall and grow, only to die in their mother's shadow. Squirrels carry many others beyond the colony.

Erysichthon's daughter Mestra loves the tree. But her father talks about the board feet of lumber that can be his. A sacred pine, yes, claimed by Ceres. It troubles him in the morning—Mestra sees his hand shake as he drinks his tea. It preoccupies him at noon when he eats raw cheese and flatbread. At evening, when he drinks wine, his lips smack over the thought of that tree's clean heartwood. He'd leveled whole fields, entire forests. Why does this pine matter?

Mestra goes out with him in the moonlight. Her cotton gown flutters and glows, her bare feet stung by rocks and nettles. He's brought his axe. They stand beneath the tree—its whispering boughs, the lullaby it sings. Such waste, Erysichthon says. Where's the goddess, anyway? He's never seen her. Has Mestra? She shakes her head. He raises his axe, hesitates as it flashes under the moon, and then strikes.

Once he starts, Erysichthon can't stop. He slashes at the massive trunks. He calls for his employees in the morning. They top branches, lop twigs, harass the main bole until they find a hidden pocket of heart rot. The tree groans, gives up, implodes. Mestra puts her hands in the cool shavings. It's like putting her hands in the tree's—the goddess's—soul.

Cutting the pine doesn't satisfy Erysichthon. He chops and eats, ploughs and consumes, and imports and eats. He's ego gone wild. He even sells Mestra to buy scallops, eels, prawns. She discovers shapeshifting and returns home, thinking she can stop her father's madness, only to be sold again. And again. Why does she come back? Duty, she says—you don't abandon family.

Erysichthon is insatiable. He eats his fingers, his arms, his toes, his legs. Ceres laughs at the bargain she'd made with the goddess Famine, as Erysichthon gnaws his torso, his intestines, his stomach, his tongue. He's a jaw chewing itself to bits.

The birds and squirrels vanish. And, finally, Mestra won't return either. As she stitches her footprints into Rock Creek's shoreline, seeing her whole life represented by a whorled eddy, trying to arrive at some straight and rational path, she's swept away.

I find it disturbing that when Ovid told the story, he focused on Erysichthon and did not explore Mestra's motivations or even explain what shapes she shifted into. Maybe he felt that a woman naturally bends and transforms to stay just this far ahead of injustice and destruction. As if a woman's malleable ego is uniquely qualified for this skill.

Recently, someone pointed out that beneath all the pleasant 1960s and 1970s holiday get-togethers at my grandmother's house, hatred smoldered. Perhaps "hatred" is a bit strong, but there were jealousies and disillusionments. It seemed that female relations felt this more and worked harder to cover it up. My mother was, for one, acutely aware that she would never top her older brother's talents: his artistic skill, his intelligence, and, above all, his good fortune to have been born male. She knew very early in life that males were privileged. After she was hit by a car at the age of seven, she was never taken to a doctor but had to scoot along the floor on an improvised cardboard sled. Her brother, though, merited such visits. She adored him nonetheless, especially after he became a US Marine who fought on Guadalcanal. Rather than rebel as some in her age group did—Betty Friedan, Bella Abzug, and Shirley Chisolm were all of the 1920s generation—she acquiesced, vaguely resented it, smoldered.

Her sister-in-law's captivity was more extreme. A gifted athlete, she'd come down with polio in her teens. With my uncle's help and the aid of crutches, she taught herself to walk again. She excelled at needlepoint, housewifery, and conversation while, I would guess, burning to be active again, to smash tennis balls at opponents on the court.

You'd think an alliance might have formed between sister and sister-in-law, but the relationship between these women, and between them and the world, was marked by a deep antipathy coated with bantering civility. It was as if they could never allow anyone within their own personal eddies of solitude, jealousy, and despair. As if reconfiguring one's outward life to fit—even surpass—an ideal was part of being female.

At a summer gathering, perhaps another Fourth of July, my dad snapped one of his patented 3-D photographs, this one of my mother, her sister (young enough to have an envied career in nursing), and her sister-in-law. Seen in three-quarter profile, they look into the distance rather than at the camera. The scene is a backyard picnic, greened by unpruned dogwood. How youthful those stoical faces are! The women sit like strangers on a bus, avoiding intrusions into each other's space. Dogwood shadows, 1960s floral-print sleeveless shifts, permanent waves, and dark hair. It's like a scene from a Stanley Kramer movie. None of the women exhibit a shred of humor or friendliness, though I'm sure that before and after the photograph they chatted amicably. Their isolation in interconnectedness is very much like an aspen stand or a pine forest—various branches, one root system, with the axe lifted above them. My mother's and aunt's ability to perform what we might now call code shifting represents an apparently shared desire to appear impeccable and avoid societal judgments reserved for women who "act up," not realizing that in this very endeavor they were becoming superior beings. Multiplicity with a similar goal, burdened perhaps by a hunger to win out, to be loved, and to love more. Or at least to be more perfect, more correct—and less transparent. I'll call it the Mestra imperative. Outmaneuver your society's collective delusions as you change your appearance to meet them. It's a recipe for nurturing GAD or OCD in one's daughter. Or it was in my case. You had to control every situation. Yes, you did.

With my grandmother's death, such family gatherings stopped. My grandfather was sent to live with his sons and then to a nursing home near his youngest daughter. The folks had been the tree nurturing all of us, and when that tree fell, we scattered like so many Mestras.

The day lazes by. Bernie, Luke, and I climb into dense brush, landing ourselves in a tangle. We retrace our steps and eventually discover the flags and freshly turned earth of the new trail segment, forged by volunteers from the Absaroka-Beartooth Wilderness Foundation, that will connect to the ski resort. It's a much easier walk than the bushwhacking we've been doing. But evening comes faster than we expect—this being our first autumn hike—and we stop exploring when the new trail gives out. Going back to the car, we startle two white-tailed does, mother and yearling. We also meet two camouflaged men with heavy-duty bows and arrows. I'm not unnerved. They're just hunting. Of course, I have Bernie and Luke to back me up in case of danger. Well, Bernie. Luke barks a good game, but I don't think he's much protection. I'm glad to have sent the deer bounding off, and we don't let on that we've seen any when the hunters ask.

A fragile moon rises over the aspens. The season seems advanced even from what it was when we started. The stream exhales chilled air. Late sun churns quaking leaves. I think about the trees, the flexibility of the aspens and the shapeshifting transformations of the lodgepole forest. Egos stretching and changing to win.

Nichols Creek Winter Addendum

We haven't snowshoed for a few years. As usual, Bernie struggles with the bindings, and, as usual, I lose my patience as our hours of light shrink. I tell him we could dispense with the shoes since the snow is spotty. I plead, nag, rail, "Let's just go." Luke, meanwhile, pushes his muzzle under a drift, digs his paws into the cold. He's at home in winter. Exhibiting admirable (or annoying) persistence, Bernie finally secures his snowshoes.

Our plan: travel up Nichols Creek again from the West Fork Road. We won't have time to reach the ski area, four and a half miles along. We'll be in it for the existential journey, that's all. As Luke dances, we humans heave ourselves up the first absurd two miles, my thoughts all the while of Suzanne Somers's old gizmo, the Thighmaster, and the virtue of a bourgeois American woman "getting in shape," *viz.* reducing the circumference of her legs. We've rented these snowshoes from our neighborhood outfitter, and they're about what you'd expect of rentals—heavy, ever-loosening, clumsy.

Altogether, Bernie and I fall twice each, shoes entangling or slipping downhill without warning. Luke stepping on the webbing, his leash catching under a frame. Our progress is slow (as might have been foretold by our difficulty putting the darn things on in the first place). Plus, let me say that peeing in the woods is not so liberating as it might be, not when you're on snowshoes, hitching up a coat, unzipping waterproof pants and jeans, pulling down long and short underwear, and hanging onto your dog's leash.

But. The lodgepole pines are beautiful with yet another arboreal transformation. Snow has gathered on their boughs, and looking across a hillside gives an impression of lace on denim. Nutcrackers squawk in their friendly-mean way. The trail eventually gives up switchbacking and opens to a wide and sunny view of Mount Maurice and the faraway Pryor and Bighorn Mountains. Close at hand, poking their delicate heads from the snow, seedling pines struggle. It's good to see them, wistful and delicate but driving toward the light.

TRAIL 13

Shiloh Conservation Area
(Honey, I Shrunk the Prairie)

General Location: Billings, Montana; distance from Yellowstone, 172 miles
Hiking distance: 1 mile round trip, with possible extensions
Elevation gain: Negligible
Terrain: Prairie restoration with grasses, cottonwoods, and urban sprawl

Billings, Montana, is a hardscrabble town, nicknamed "The Magic City" because it grew so fast from a waystation of the Northern Pacific Railroad that its expansion seemed like magic. These days, it claims several oil refineries and a sugar beet processing facility, I-90 with its attendant chain restaurants and motels, and a gritty downtown of casinos and bars. More trimmed is the "medical corridor" with Billings Clinic and St. Vincent's Hospital. There are also a few excellent locally owned eateries, a French bakery, and more than a handful of independent breweries. If human population growth is any measure of magic, then Billings is still sleight-of-hand savvy. New subdivisions tumble westward, flattening prairie and farm fields.

My completely unscientific theory is that such chartering of streets does not undo the riotousness of nature but supercharges it. Compare the phenomenon to dealing with anxiety. The first counselor I went to said that I should act "as if." As if, in other words, I wasn't anxious. Don't fight or deny. Pretend the disturbances weren't there. She said that, even though I might not sleep for days on end, eventually a tired body would give out. Conversely, I suppose, the harder I would shutter the lid, the more pressure would build up in the pot, and the more explosive would be its eruption from subterranean passages of my nervous system.

I wasn't ready for her spiel. Maybe I'm still not ready. Because there are scary things in the pot, you know? I wrestle and half-nelson and fireman's carry those hidden things, and just when I have them whipped and tell a healthcare professional that I'm perfectly calm, anxiety flares as a racing heart, a sleepless night, and, eventually, perhaps an obsession.

Batting down life systems disfigures the land just as containing anxiety warps the psyche. Like my attempts to contain GAD and OCD, the birth and growth of Billings have involved compression, in this case the containment of grasslands. Old photos show a wide expanse below the sandstone rimrocks where Billings will later be. Wagons crisscross the valley, bringing the literal seeds of its destruction: Russian thistle, corn, wheat, and Norway maples. Cement and stone. The rifle and the railroad. And shrinkage.

I've always thought I had to man up, stop being a wimp, contain and control my weaknesses. Like mother, like daughter. But checking energy of any kind results in tension and fear. Because I don't like what seethes under my skin or in the soil, I turn away, pave it over, hide from it—but it will show itself with all its hateful prejudices, random thoughts, and fierce love. We've mangled the earth in and around Billings with the spread of asphalt, monoculture lawns, and roads—and dust still rises in houses and cars. Channeled streams eventually flood or clog with branches, old mattresses, and random school compositions. Suburban pools birth mosquitoes that carry West Nile Virus transmitted from other similarly squashed ecosystems. Oil and tar spill into the Yellowstone River. Someone is murdered in a casino parking lot. Young men and women take meth or fentanyl.

After a hundred years, there aren't many accessible holdout spots in Billings, places where things are encouraged to go along as they always have. Anti-anxiety and OCD-erasing spots. Luckily, I can get to one of the largest of such places from my house by taking a series of bike routes that eventually join the broad trail paralleling Shiloh Road, a newish thoroughfare designed to accommodate growth. After the dental surgery place, the Assembly of God church, and REI, whose massive rectangular architecture and landscaping have ironed out old farms, I pedal beside the outdoor mall with a Kohl's, a fourteen-theater movie complex, and a Scheels—where statues of Washington, Jefferson, Lincoln, and Reagan sit on outdoor benches. My destination is directly opposite the luminaries: Shiloh Conservation Area (or SCA) on Shiloh Avenue near Shiloh Crossing.

Why so much "Shiloh"? The original was where, according to Joshua 18:1–10, the tribes of Israel set up a tent meeting after the conquest of the Canaanites. There they parceled out land among themselves and planted the Ark of the Covenant. By the time of Jeremiah, that Shiloh had been laid waste, as had, by the end of April 7, 1862, the Civil War battlefield of Shiloh, Tennessee. Billings's SCA still fits the biblical meaning: a place of peace, a respite from societal compulsions of containment and organization, some original settler's ideal. It contradicts the drive to render all living things dead or tamed. It resists prophesied destruction, despite the exigencies of real estate development.

Progress takes many forms, including the spiritual, which is not as easy to trace as new interstate routes and subdivisions. But it is every bit as powerful. My LDS ancestors, for instance, believed not only in commercial advancement but in the perfectibility of mortal humans, a doctrine encapsulated in the late-nineteenth century by Church President Lorenzo Snow with the phrase, "As man is now, God once was. As God is now, man may become." Although gentiles like me often make fun of the "law of eternal progression," as it's known—the tenet that a human soul can reach divine understanding and run its own planet as Christ runs this one—it's really not that different from the Buddhist concept of satori. As I've discovered, this spiritual striving for perfection, even if we no longer believe doctrinally, runs in my family—and, according to the law of eternal compression of one's faults, causes a good deal of anxiety. A collateral maternal ancestor, Patty Bartlett Sessions, centered her life around ushering humans into this religious evolution. While I don't know whether she was particularly anxious herself—she might have had too much energy to ever sit still—thinking about her certainly works at my nerves.

Often referred to as "Mother Sessions" in LDS lore, she seems a complex woman. An early Church member who converted her nephew Enoch, my grandfather's grandfather, she kept a diary for most of five decades. It provides invaluable documentation of early Church history. "I have drove my wagon all the way [from Illinois to Great Salt Lake City] but [for] part of the two last mts," she recorded of her 1847 journey along the Mormon Trail, having previously relocated from Maine to Far West, Missouri, and thence to Nauvoo, Illinois. She'd made that last move due to Missouri's anti-Mormon sentiment and its attendant violence. In 1838 at Haun's Mill, seventeen Saints, including three children, were killed by a gentile militia. After various skirmishes in Illinois and the martyrdom of Joseph Smith, the LDS could no longer hope to establish a new Garden of Eden in the American Midwest.

Not to be kept down, Mother Sessions continued working for decades in her Great Basin home as a midwife, delivering babies for two dollars each. In this way, she was key to the spiritual journey of many LDS souls. She was also an important figure in the prosperous enterprise of the Church and its capture of the Intermountain West under Brigham Young's authoritarian direction. In Great Salt Lake City, his planned streets were laid like a grid over the desert and were wide enough to turn a wagon around in. Babies in that wild and rigid town must have leapt like William Blake into the dangerous world, only to be processed by Mother Sessions, Brigham's organizational equal. According to her own estimation, Great-Great-Great Aunt Patty's total birthing count was a little shy of four thousand. Having arrived in vernix and blood, umbilical cord dangling, the neonates fell into her capable hands. She cleaned and packaged them as Latter-Day miracles to be nestled in the arms of adoring biological mothers. Soon they were named and put to the breast to, like all LDS enterprises, "blossom as the rose"—not, that is, as prickly pear blooms, though some were undoubtedly (neu)roses waiting to happen.

The most surprising thing about this can-do sort of woman was that in 1842—before the trip West and while legally married to David Sessions, with whom she had eight children—Aunt Patty was "sealed" to the Mormon prophet and founder Joseph Smith as one of his more than eighty spiritual wives. That would make her a polyandrist. What passions seethed under her very proper bonnet, shirtwaist, and gathered skirt? What wild pulse beat in her capable wrists as she turned a breech birth or gently wiped a laboring mother's forehead? Would Mother Sessions be proud of the growth she helped inaugurate in the West—with Billings's LDS Temple just up the way? Or would she miss the wildness she once literally walked through? Or both? It's impossible to clear away contradictions. I have no answers in regard to Patty Sessions.

I turn off the Shiloh bike trail and onto SCA's paved routes that weave around sedimentation and filtration ponds, cattail and cottonwood restoration, and wild grasses bounded on the south by the Knife River gravel pit, with its mounds of rock and its metal silos, and on the north and east by those big-box stores I've just cruised past. To the west there used to be wet fields of geese and alfalfa, replaced now by a housing development with an artificial and rather sterile lake.

Unique among Billings open spaces, SCA actively nurtures native plants and birds. Avocets, yellow-headed blackbirds, spotted sandpipers, even soras live here in the summer, along with whirligigs of barn swallows. I lost my heart to the place the day I saw a mink *and* a fox loping along Canyon Creek, which joins the Yellowstone River some two or three miles from where I ride. The city even put in bridges with wrought-iron railings designed to look like cattails, a nod to aesthetics usually lacking in local civic projects. But SCA is an island now. Huge power lines run along the north boundary, and apartments and condos burst like acne on the previously unbounded western margin. I doubt there's enough open space for the minks and foxes I used to see.

One cold January day, with the wind blowing straight in my eyes and aching ears, I investigated the new streets named after college basketball teams: Blue Devils Way, Ducks Way, Tar Heels Way. There were barracks rows of featureless $1,200-plus-per-month apartments and brown Kentucky bluegrass. The neighborhood was raw—an ugly, angular reef of developer profits rising with tidal winds. If this was magic, it was the dark kind. Nor was it an answer to the city's need for affordable housing, though I guess these places were more affordable than some.

It's spring now at SCA. I enjoy the mile-long outer loop trail as it circumnavigates ponds and cattails. Ibises flock, brilliant cinnamon teal dabble, a meadowlark flashes white tail edges as he demonstrates his best come-on lines. Muskrats float, leaving wakes that tickle a great blue heron's ankles. These creatures may suffer from compulsions, but I like to think they are clear-eyed and clear-eared and understand their surroundings without the fog of disturbing impulses that must be tamped down or sublimated. Perhaps I'm wrong. But surely they wouldn't pursue anything as intangible as God's favor, which, I like to think, they already enjoy.

Mother Sessions, on the other hand, was indomitable in her service to a deity she couldn't see, touch, or hear, though, to read her diary, she was a practical-minded Saint. Even as she packed for her trip to Deseret and a new spiritual home, she managed, by her own reckoning, to "put" two women "to bed" with their babies. Along the way, she not only drove her wagon but attended to miscarriages and live births, knitted mittens, waded through mud, and sometimes walked just to keep warm. Maybe if I'd had her inspiration, I'd have grown up capable rather than nervous.

Patty Sessions holds an honored place in LDS history not only for her midwifery but also for her relationship to Joseph Smith. Whatever that relationship was. When a woman marries in the Church, she is sealed to her husband for "time and eternity," but it's commonly held that Joseph's plural wives were sealed to him only for eternity. I find it hard to believe that the very handsome, energetic, and charismatic Joseph abstained with any of his eighty-plus wives, including Patty Sessions. His first, Emma, felt strongly enough about the carnal nature of polygamy that she refused to move to Great Salt Lake City after Joseph's martyrdom at the hands of a mob who broke into the Carthage, Illinois, jail where he was being held. She and her son and their followers founded a monogamy-promoting Reorganized Church of Jesus Christ of Latter-Day Saints, now known as the relatively lowkey Community of Christ.

Flamboyant Joseph may have become a liability to a faith looking for bureaucratic stability and independence. Before the LDS exodus to Deseret, Joseph ran for president, set up his own bank, wore a military uniform, and instituted polygamy and polyandry, which became both detrimental and indispensable to the Church's survival. If it hadn't been for plural marriage, I imagine, Joseph wouldn't have been assassinated, and the LDS Church would have become just another midwestern Protestant denomination listed on small-town signs welcoming visitors. Clearly, spiritual fervor is antithetical to the establishment of lasting religious and financial organization, which relies on the fantasy of order and progress rather than inspiration. Thus, Mother Sessions industriously brought more Saints into the world and Brigham Young designed cities after Smith's demise, and the Church prospered without its founder. But, as with any taming, passions would break out, as they have from time to time in LDS Zion—first with polygyny, then with the often violent Reformation of the 1850s, then with the killing of 120 travelers from Arkansas in what has become known as the Mountain Meadows Massacre, and, more recently, with the Cliven Bundy family's lawless anti-government efforts to wrest complete control of public land.

I was taught in my tenth-grade Utah History class that Mormon polygamy began because there were more female converts than male. Very practical. Very logical. Farming with lots of women and children to share the duties and exploit whatever might be their peculiar talents is an efficient plan. Later I learned that the Church encouraged white men to marry Indigenous women in addition to their white wives to speed the conversion of the Lamanites—descendants of blasphemous Laman from the Book of Mormon, namely Native Americans and Pacific Islanders.

So, here was the faith I grew up just outside of, my maternal grandfather Alma Tripp having renounced it a few decades after Mother Sessions's era and my dad having stopped going to the ward in his teens. The faith that eventually realized how bad the urge to make Lamanites "white and delightsome," as specified in the *Book of Mormon*, sounded and made sure, beginning in 1978, that the passage read "pure and delightsome." The faith that dominated my childhood. The faith that might have colonized my psyche. The faith I have forgiven in light of the many kindnesses its adherents have shown me over the years.

I dismount by the SCA fishing shelter at the large front pond. I sit on the riprap and look into and over the water, focusing on small dramas of uncontained liveliness. Wriggling larvae curl in still harbors. Dragonflies dangle over algae. They pulse against the wind. They raft along the cattails. They shoot by like military drones. They alight on floating leaves. They clasp each other and mate. They are red striped, lightning blue, sequined gold, their wings clear or patterned.

I look up after a while, The Magic City still symmetrical and angular all around me, red letters of the Scheels sign burning like revelation shot up from some deep well of greed. How far I have fallen from my family's spiritually ambitious pioneer days. And how small and relaxed my ego is right now as I watch the hydrological cycle—cloud to pond to dragonfly-escorted evaporation.

If Mother Sessions had been a simple partaker of LDS marriage customs, that would be one thing. But what seems explosive to me is that her daughter Sylvia Sessions Lyon Clark also married Joseph Smith—and at about the same time as her mother. On top of that, Sylvia's marriage to Windsor Lyon had been performed by Smith himself four or five years earlier. Was Sylvia's daughter, born posthumously, Smith's biological offspring? Sylvia obviously thought so. She named the baby Josephine—my mother's distant cousin, perhaps?

In photographs of Patty and Sylvia, neither seems alluring, which might speak to the "spiritual" nature of Joseph's many marriages. Of course, Patty was quite elderly and probably almost toothless when her picture was taken—she looks every bit the archetypal mother of her people. But even in the prime of life, Sylvia, though beautiful, is austere. Were the two polyandrous wives driven by coercion, faith, love, ambition, devotion, lust, some hereditary kind of mental illness—or all of the above? In those days of redemption with spirituality hanging in the air they breathed, LDS pioneers were ready to die—and marry—for their industrious and prosperous Zion.

As a student at the University of Utah, I took an anthropology course called "Primitive Religions." On the first day, the professor noted that the course title was misleading. All religions, he said, are primitive. And, I would now add, all depend on some form of obsession, the magical thinking that entwines mental creations and physical laws and tries to bend them both. I'm still prone to that approach, to using my "good words" and routines to keep myself on the right side of universal power.

Their lexicon of glory didn't work for the early Saints. Disaster led on to disaster. After the retreat from Missouri, there was Joseph's murder in Illinois. There was the exodus to the far desert. And, finally, there was the ruin of polygamy, forced upon the Saints by the federal government. How did the post-1890 church accept that retreat? I suppose one consolation was that it could buy into the American ideal of progress and follow that playbook as devoutly as it followed the *Pearl of Great Price* and the *Doctrine and Covenants.* While the Saints became what we might term normal Americans, their early strain of fanaticism, taking one form and then another, swirls through the West, through my heritage—Puritan and LDS—and settles in my brain as a supersensitivity to what seems a simple material reality but actually is not. Sometimes a dragonfly is not just a dragonfly?

On the far western horizon, the Beartooth Mountains tease with draperies of cloud. Their waters are fresh and multi-directional. By the time these flows combine into Rock Creek, Clark's Fork, and the Yellowstone River, they'll be through with their initial clashing. They'll be ready for slower subsidence, local tragedies of pollution and channelization, and union with low-key prairie streams like Canyon Creek. All these waters carry the wild into Billings. Last winter, a moose wandered from the mountains via the Yellowstone River only to starve to death in the labyrinthine residential neighborhood a mile from my house. Given a little luck or more sangfroid, the moose could have made it to the Bighorns.

Just like the moose but for different reasons (or maybe not so different, really), those first devout LDS settlers to Utah could not be contained. The Salt Lake Valley, the kingdom of Deseret, expanded to include Provo in the south and Ogden in the north. Eventually, small mountain valleys and sprawling sagebrush and salt-ridden flats throughout Utah, Idaho, Wyoming, and parts of Montana filled with Latter-Day Saints. The mandibles of faith reached out to snag whatever prey of land and resources the General Authorities directed them to.

My own Tripps and their contemporaries, the Bagleys and the Timms, sprang like a new hatch toward the Nevada border. LDS gunman Orrin Porter Rockwell and LDS President George Albert Smith (a friend of the family, whom my great-grandfather called GAS) came out for visits at Chris Tripp's Six Mile Ranch near the Deep Creeks and the state line. One can read a fair amount about Rockwell's controversial career as an assassin and bully—my great-grandfather made him sleep in the barn—but the studious-looking Smith is more obscure, despite having served as the eighth president of the LDS Church from 1945 through 1951. His major claim to fame was attending the 1901 Pan American exposition and hearing the shot that killed empire-building William McKinley, whom he'd campaigned for.

Truth be told, all that LDS industriousness ran aground right there on the eastern slope of the Deep Creek Mountains. The desert defeated it, refused to be understood according to macroeconomics. Most of the white families—including mine—who'd over the decades made a tenuous living on the border moved back to the city. With a greater depth of practical and spiritual knowledge, the Goshute nation is still there.

Billings has yet to become disillusioned and probably won't anytime soon. What was religious fervor in early Utah is simply commerce in The Magic City. Here progress doesn't rely on faith in supernatural forces. Here we have industrialized expansion. While there's plenty of Christian organizing around Billings—we're sandwiched off Shiloh Road between the Baptists, the Bible School, the Assembly of God, and the Methodists, with the local LDS Temple a few miles to the north—Billingsites are more likely to spout the names of their favorite stores and restaurants than those of their favorite Old Testament characters. The official religion of Montana might be the Western mystique denoted by the state's popular nickname, The Last Best Place. And to service that mystique, we have the previously noted Scheels and REI, but also Cabela's, The Base Camp, and a new Sierra—every bit as imposing as Billings's largest churches. Here we talk about city fathers and name the streets after self-promoting imperialists such as Nelson Miles, Philip St. George Cook, William Clark, and George Armstrong Custer—or favorite NCAA men's basketball teams. The Last Best Place can, of course, erupt in violence or alcoholism more often than anyone would like to admit.

Despite all this industriousness, the wire-mesh sculpture of an angel, erected atop the sandstone cliffs by my house in the 1950s by Rocky Mountain College alumni, faithfully overlooks The Magic City. She gazes (I guess—she has no eyes) at the valley's human folly, her hands outstretched with fitting dolor and pity. "Please stop," she says. But the place just gets bigger.

Here in the angel's arms was the newborn town—purple, gasping, just arrived from eternity. It quivered, its lungs opened, it took a terrestrial breath, and it began the mortal journey. In its platting was the latent image of the city it has now become. Its birth, no less than the birth of a child, contains in its trajectory of growth the eventual downward slope of the parabola, the death of spontaneity, the estrangement from nature, and the emptiness of wealth. The anxiety of its being a foreign imposition, and the probability that incomprehensible forces working inside it writhe and curl unseen, trouble it only occasionally, if it's lucky.

Despite the buffeting tides of development that erode its edges, SCA still responds to natural rhythms and sacred surfaces, its "as if" continuation. Here is the impulse against order and ownership. Here is the regrowth of grassy fields, ponds, and cattail marshes. Here is where spiritual expansion does not give way to progress or anxiety. Here Mother Sessions's four thousand midwifed babies could have rested from their drive toward godhood. Here I—collateral victim of her eschatological ambitions—can also rest.

TRAIL 14

Succession on Lake Fork

General location: Red Lodge, Montana, Beartooth Mountains; about 70 miles from Yellowstone
Distance: 14 miles round trip
Elevation gain: 1,100+ feet
Terrain: Cottonwood groves to lodgepole pine forest

The first time I did the Lake Fork trail was in 1995, a rare instance of my taking bold action. The fourteen-mile hike—by just Rita and me—was going to be my last hurrah in the Beartooths. It's in my nature to want simultaneously to fight and fly—never to be bravely stoic. These countercurrents of desperation and cowardice mean I'm often paralyzed and do nothing. Maybe that's okay, if hardly conducive to relieving tension. I mean, I'm still here, though nervous. So why didn't I just stay safely at home?

Bernie had accepted a job offer in Maine that included editing a literary journal, something he'd always wanted to do. It was time, then, to move back to the "wrong" side of the Mississippi to serve his career. We'd come to Powell, Wyoming, months after my dad died of cancer, for Bernie's first "real" job. Being in the West again after grad school in Indiana was comforting. But because I was hampered by anxiety in my aspirations, such as they were, to be a poet and author, I remained dependent on Bernie's work and now felt at the mercy of someone else's aspirations as I contemplated leaving the Rockies again. I guess I was fed up with myself and my life. Selfish and helpless and sometimes resentful. I had something to prove, after all, in the face of the inevitable. I needed a valedictory hike.

While Bernie and ten-year-old Tom were visiting his family in New York, I loaded Rita—not yet burdened by arthritis and always eager to be with me—into our rickety 1980 powder-blue Ford Escort and drove to Lake Fork trailhead, where'd I'd never been, for a last glorious Montana adventure. I was thirty-six years old that summer—young, whiny, foolish. I couldn't rely on my dog for protection. Rita was smart and would hide behind me in the presence of any larger animal or let me go first on the trail at dusk. In the absence of canine security, I had to trust humans to be peaceable, the weather to be bountiful, the grizzlies to remain hidden. Of course, there were fewer bears then.

A montage of that nostalgic walk includes a turgid river; mountain laurel and round-leaved kinnikinnick; Lost Lake a steel platter below pale cliffs; the bridge, big enough for horses, that marked six miles up; Rita beside me at Keyser-Brown Lake as rain fell and she shivered after a dip in chill water; smoke from the fire of a horse camp smudging the fog; light-headedness on the sunny way down when handfuls of nuts and dried apricots no longer helped (Rita and I would go fourteen miles on half a baggie of trail mix and an apple—and a few Milkbones). I can still see Wyoming's Badger Basin as sun gripped the mountains in the rearview mirror and rain churned the desert in front of us to impenetrable mist when we drove home.

In a few weeks, we were on our way east. Leaving the mountains and the high deserts of the Greater Yellowstone was an exile that seemed almost too hard to take. I cried all the way through North Dakota, Minnesota, Ontario, Quebec, and New Brunswick—not to mention for a month after our arrival in Fort Kent, Maine, where we discovered that the house we'd rented long distance stood in the middle of a bog. Lacking human friends in the hard-to-fathom Acadian communities hugging the St. John River with its view of Canada, Tom got to know salamanders, but I couldn't acclimate to the brown well water and the odor emanating from purported bat feces in the attic. I didn't explore to find out if there were bats or their feces. We found another place after a month, one that had a lovely view of Eagle Lake—in the winter when leaves were off the trees.

There were no grizzlies to worry about in Maine but plenty of moose, even one in our backyard. They seemed mostly peaceable sorts. I don't know why the Wyoming/Montana variety is so surly. We loved the beavers and the river, the spring peepers and the warblers. But not the blackflies and the social isolation of being "from away" in Aroostook County. One good thing about life in the "crown of Maine" was that my anxiety vanished. Like *that*. Though there were plenty of real things to worry about, including icy roads, the aforementioned black flies, and the local pediatrician's lengthy absences, I endured few sleepless nights or bouts of palpitations. Maybe it was exactly because I had plenty of real things to worry about that my brain stopped catastrophizing.

After four cold years and seven warm ones in Florida (where my mental illness not only revived but flourished, along with palmetto bugs and water moccasins), we moved back to Greater Yellowstone. Just, really, to be here.

Two thousand twenty is, in fact, our fourteenth year in The Magic City, and today is the last day of our son Tom's pandemic visit to Billings. It is also the nineteenth year after my OCD diagnosis. There was a time—Tom was in college—when our reunions didn't go well. Someone would end up sulking. There were hurt feelings, or ideas that someone was mad at someone else. I don't remember why there was such friction, but it was probably a function of Florida and of age—Tom's, yes, of course, but mine as well. Bernie was, as always, even keeled, but I was disgruntled. My life hadn't taken off; it had, in fact, become burdened by OCD and, between bouts, the fear of OCD.

This year in Montana our visit sails along, and soon we're down to our last fifteen hours together. What else to do but go hiking! Our other walks have been short stints around the Yellowstone valley—so this will be the best one, the long one, the mountain one. We choose Lake Fork—an easy trail with lots of scenery. We can turn around at any point, satisfied with the trip. No fourteen-mile jaunt for us today. Tom wants to get back to Billings at a reasonable time to pack. We don't think he's ever been to

Lake Fork. He hopes to see a moose. I sort of hope not to.

The morning is cloudy—either thunderstorms are gathering or night clouds burning off. Sometimes it's hard to tell. I'm the only one troubled by anxious presentiments of disastrous lightning storms. Bernie and Tom do not catastrophize—or admit that they do. As we drive toward the trailhead and parking area, the clouds burn off. Still, smoke from California and Idaho wildfires makes such a thick haze on a westerly flow that the sunlight is a golden-ale sheen through the lodgepole pines as white voile unravels from the higher peaks.

We work the trail at Tom's blistering pace—or so it seems to me. He mentions that the lodgepoles I've always thought quintessential residents of the Greater Yellowstone are the same species as the pines that grow in coastal California, where he lives. He also recognizes mountain chickadees, Clark's nutcrackers, and a Townsend's warbler. Long ago he thought his father's and my birding habits were, to put it politely, annoying. Now? Not so much.

Other transformations in a quarter of a century? Earnest Rita has lived out her lifespan, and now here's Luke, the silly dog whom I can't trust off leash. At fifteen pounds, Luke, when I first saw him, was a brindled bit of puppy fuzz with a talent for fun and mischief. His first night home was a nightmare of claws on door, claws on desk, baby yelling, and uncontrolled slingshotting around the canine paradise we thought we'd set up for him, replete with kennel, water, and food. After that night, he slept in our room. Then on our bed. His good humor makes him virtually untrainable. Everything's a joke. Still, he has learned to dance with me (treats help) and knows five steps. If something appeals to him, he's fifty-five pounds of ready.

The forest we walk through has also been transformed—after a blowdown in this drainage around 2007, the new trees come in thick. The canyons beyond us have burned and wildflowers have taken over. Bark beetles and blister rust lay waste whitebark pines. Snowfields retreat. A drought has come and gone and come again. This year's temperatures have been extreme, as has the lack of precipitation. Grizzlies move onto the prairie—their ancestral homeland. Pikas scramble to higher elevations. There are more and more people on the trails—and in the world. Over eight billion, by last count. In 1995, the year of my first Lake Fork hike, there were a mere 5.7.

And, of course, I pack a better lunch now. Or at least a bigger one.

Our son, taller and stronger and smarter than we are—and wonderfully unburdened by OCD—walks ahead of us, pausing as we catch up. He's compassionate and conscientious. Funny, I remember him as a toddler—so slow he'd fall down.

Forest succession: Fireweed comes in after a burn and eventually gives way to aspens, who shade firs and pines until the conifers are strong enough to bear the sun and crowd out their benefactors. Human succession isn't much different. Tom no longer fits in what he used to call his "slot" between Bernie and me. He's the one who's thirty-six—a young father. And that human succession, like the vigor of young pines and firs among their elders, is as right and regular as the face of Whitetail Peak or the mayfly-dented surface of the calm broadwater we mark as our turnaround point.

Change is inevitable, and I will not fear it. Inevitable? Necessary. No use in fighting or trying to fly from it. I'm hoping for another—and better—psychological stage in my internal succession narrative. One good thing is that somehow in keeping the worst of my anxieties and obsessions from Tom as he grew up, I have protected him, allowed Bernie's imperturbability to flourish in him. Maybe I was somehow a good mother, sometimes successfully hiding my angst and sometimes letting him know that I was distressed and that it's okay to express one's emotions. Or maybe he was a healthy kid. Perhaps the anxiety genes skipped him. It's possible that he just doesn't talk about his issues. Compassion is his leitmotif. He's the only person I know who, when we lived in Maine, would rescue black flies if they got stuck in the house or car. The world has been on the skids since he was born, Tom has confided, and so it doesn't pay him to fall into despair or be anxious.

There's no despair or anxiety today at the Broadwater below Whitetail Peak and Mount Rearguard. Succession and elevation, climate change and soil type influence tree growth according to so many variables that accurate origin theories and predictions are difficult to make. For the forests or anyone else. At the beginning of my search to understand where my anxiety and OCD came from—the bubbling up of unwanted, even loathed, thoughts that make me feel evil or dangerous—I found just such a plethora of variables: the LDS heritage of conquest, the ambiguous nature of womankind in our culture, genetics, growing up an unbeliever in a theocracy, the whole array of successive generations. The salient point is that my son is a good man. The new forest has come in healthy.

As for me, I've learned a few helpful exercises over the years. You have to breathe, of course. Then you take another breath and hold it for seven seconds before exhaling. You call up your senses: touch, listen, see. Tap your fingers on your thighs: right-left, right-left. Air your obsessions on the screen of an old black-and-white mental TV and let them play in another room, another county, another biome, so that you can get on with life.

My exercise today is to relax in the sedge with beings I love where the land levels out for a while, the current slows, and the river itself, though still young, has room to breathe. The firs make a comforting green loom on which spiders string their webs and warblers imprint darting yellow paisleys between the silver filaments.

THREE

Chamberlains in the Wilderness

TRAIL 15

Mystic and Island Lakes

General Location: West Rosebud Trail, Beartooth Mountains; about 100 miles from Yellowstone
National Park
Hiking distance: 11 miles round trip
Elevation gain: 1,200+ feet
Terrain: Cottonwood meadow to lodgepole pine and fir forest, some boulder hopping required

I sit in the car with Bernie and Luke under a tantric Montana sky some twenty miles short of the Beartooth foothills, surrounded by pastures and a mix of summer homes and old-time cabins. Stopped by a road construction delay, I pull out my scruffy binoculars to see what I hope might be a Cassin's finch. Whoever it is flies off before I can even focus.

Imagine having binoculars that could see backward in time. If I had such a pair, I'd identify every bird. Plus, I could zero in on ancient causal chains, which would acquire shape and color and wouldn't fly like the alleged finch. I'm playing with this fancy, maybe, because my dad was born in 1924, as was the lake we are going to today. But hiking or driving the West always immerses me in the temporal flow. Nostalgia. Saudade. Solastalgia. The loss of the wild that has occurred just in my lifetime. My time-traveling binoculars would be as magical as Joseph Smith's Urim and Thummim, and they would take me back to an era when industrialization created the idea of wilderness, when that idea shaped human behavior.

It's 1853, let's say. Nine-year-old John Marvin Chamberlain leaves the textile mills of Leicester, England, to sail with his parents and brothers on the *Falcon* from Liverpool to New Orleans, eventually to reach LDS Deseret in the Great Basin of North America, where John's dad can use his carpentry skills to help build an agricultural paradise. Their passage is arranged by Cornelius Bagnall, president of an LDS emigrating company. Prayers and songs—"Praise God from Whom All Blessings Flow" and "Glorious Things Are Sung of Zion"—infuse their two-month journey, but passengers still snipe at each other and complain about the "Scotch Brethren," who, they say, get the best provisions. Food is redistributed—how much can you do with endless rounds of potatoes, pork, oatmeal, vinegar, and tea? Imagine being stuck on a small ship for weeks on end with such bland provisions and people you don't know.

The journey is predictably hard. Just four days out on the water, fourteen-month-old Isabella Steward dies and is "put overboard near the mouth of the Irish Channel." Another child, one-year-old Lorenzo Hendry Kendall, is "put overboard" at "Latitude 45. – Longitude 25. –" On April 15—the approximate halfway point—John, like everyone else, crunches on new rations of "biscuit" and is ordered, with other children, to "be off the deck at 9 o'clock" so their parents can discuss important matters, petty jealousies among them. A four-year-old, John Mason, dies of "the croup" on April 20. His grave is also a longitude/latitude reading.

As the ocean claims little children, does John stand on deck feeling large on the small ship? Or does he shrink as he looks at the unknowable and unstable horizon? Or perhaps practical concerns—like what to eat—preoccupy him. By May 6, for instance, the Saints are still barraged by oats, pork, and tea. But little John Chamberlain, musically inclined, may be one of those "pleased and satisfied" with a "first rate meeting" and concert of "the songs of Zion." On May 15, the chosen hymn is "Lo the Gentile Chain Is Broken," and the next day, the *Falcon* is "pulled by 2 steamers" into the Mississippi River. Does John lean on the deck rail, humming his favorite tune, as egrets and herons erupt from the marshy wilderness? Does he see mangroves and live oaks strung with Spanish moss? What does he think when he learns that, at 9:00 on May 19, James

McGregor of Glasgow goes overboard and drowns. Whether it was morning or evening, and what exactly happened, the official account doesn't say.

I imagine John having to contain his excitement as he and his parents and brothers exit the *Falcon* and board a "packet" called *Die Vernon* to be steam-powered or towed by mules to Keokuk. North through the heart of his new continent, John watches the Mississippi River barges and wooded islands stream past. Finally, the Saints reach Iowa and are provisioned with bacon instead of that old salt pork of the Atlantic crossing. From Keokuk, John penetrates the wooded shoreline, reaches the prairie, and skips to Great Salt Lake City and the spiky Wasatch Mountains that will define life for him, his children and grandchildren, and even his great-grandchildren.

All those hymns must have hit their mark. Or maybe he caught blues or gospel wafting through the Delta. The 1860s, at any rate, find John as a musician and composer, not a carpenter like his father. He ships in the first organ to pioneer Salt Lake and writes "We Are Marching to Glory," still included in Mormon hymnals. He founds Chamberlain Music on Main Street downtown, marries Louisa Margharetta Euphemia Rawlings (whose claim to fame in family history seems to be her thigh-length hair and equally elaborate name), and raises a family of seven boys. He and Louisa sing in the Tabernacle Choir. When neighborhood children come into the store while he's up to his elbows in sheet music, John stops to compose songs for them. He's good with kids and crazy about gardening. One old local newspaper story shows him sitting in his front yard (now the site of a car dealership), surrounded by flowers, a cello resting on his shoulder. A kindly man, and one self-assured in his modest talents, this mustachioed ancestor of mine doesn't bear a whiff of neurosis. As an artist, perhaps he rides above arguments between LDS leaders and gentile miners. But I like to think he, like Brigham Young, favored clean water and agriculture, while the hard-rock crews valued profits over prophets. No matter. Mines and smelters crept toward the city from the south.

The third of John Marvin Chamberlain's seven sons will become my grandfather, Leroy Rawlings. Born in 1882, he's known as Roy. He and his look-alike brothers take lots of Brownie camera snapshots. A common theme is for them to perch a laughing sweetheart on one shoulder. You can also find them by Wasatch Mountain lakes with a rifle, a pistol, a dead snake, a Model T, and various Navajo blankets; goofing around in rented black bathing suits at Great Salt Lake's Saltair resort; and in town striking unlikely martial poses in doughboy uniforms. One of the seven brothers becomes an alcoholic. My dad will sometimes find him a bit disoriented on Main Street and drive him home. Though the yearning for open space persists, whatever religious fervor caught up John's parents seems to have cooled in the third generation. By the fourth, my dad and his older brother—John Marvin's grandsons—leave the church before they're twenty-one.

I think about young John's ocean crossing, how hard it must have been and how patient he must have had to be, when here I am antsy because the laying down of pavement has interrupted us on the way to the Mystic Lake trailhead. We passed the quaint town of Fishtail and its obligatory Cowboy Bar and set off innocently past farms and ranches. We've reached pavement's end and, with it, a thirty-minute delay. Thirty minutes. That's nothing. Still, there's not much to do but roll the windows down, enjoy the scenery, scan for birds, and chat with the flagman as we wait for the pilot car and its optimistic "Follow me" sign. Luke has settled in the backseat. We seem transported to an era without engine sounds (except for the distant hum of the road grader). An era John Chamberlain knew. And then, just like that, the flagman smiles like the good friend he's become and waves us on.

The wait will be worth it. The reason I chose (it was my turn) Mystic Lake for our hike was its unearthly blue. At mile three of the path, you top a thousand-foot rise and look down at a tureen of water as blue as an entire emotional cosmos, its beauty the result of natural erosive forces and human tinkering.

If my mother's family was driven by the twined obsessions of progress and faith, my father's line (and my father himself) often sank into regret and depression, a mood-disorder cousin of OCD. The descent, pun intended, didn't begin with my great-grandfather John Marvin. Or even with John's son Roy, who seemed remarkably free of psychological constraints, even in the face of personal disaster. He wrote diary entries during his LDS mission to Switzerland, all in pencil and a difficult cursive. He attended lots of parties during his service to the Church. He also bought studio photos and postcards of reclining seductresses with stemmed cherries between their lips, nude female Greek sculptures, and other wonders. Perhaps a mission in 1909–1911 was not the earnest experience it is now—or is supposed to be. There's also a family rumor that Roy was expelled. Whether that's true or not (and the dates don't support the claim), it seems as if he had a lot of fun. He was a young man used to the urban swirl of an industrializing city, which Utah was in the early 1900s. In fact, just eighty years later, the city had gotten so big that it was deemed necessary to protect parts of the Wasatch as official wilderness.

Mystic Lake wild is inseparable from Mystic Lake industrialized. NorthWestern Energy, a pipeline, a generating station, and the hum of Pelton wheels dominate the trailhead. Indeed, the lake is a power-generating reservoir. Once you escape the initial press of posted warnings—"This is Bear Country!"; "Take Trail Straight Ahead Over Tram Bridge"; "Attention Anglers: Daily Limit on Mystic Lake is 5 Trout"—you may stop to read interpretive signage and find that, "To the delight of onlookers, rock debris and water were hurled several hundred yards as dynamite blew a hole in the bottom of Mystic Lake on September 25th, 1924," five months after my dad's birth. A lake exploded, and everybody cheered. The wild was upended, and wilderness created. A child was born, and his mother cried. History permeates this hike.

The powers of harnessed electricity were young in American culture in those Mystic Lake-TNT days, but people quickly accepted the new technology, according to Jill Jonnes in *Empires of Light*. Large population centers were almost 100 percent electrified by 1930. The Beartooth engineers helped speed modernization along, but they also blew stuff up. As you cross the boulder field leg of the trail, old impact scars form starlike impressions where yet more dynamite helped obliterate stubborn granite.

The first mile or so leads you below the dam—and, because of this, warning signs tell you to run for high ground if you feel vibrations. When you see that wall of water signifying a failure, it will be too late to save yourself. If not dissuaded, you'll parallel the flowline as you cross the tram track to an elegant generating station with arched windows and Georgian cornices. Back in the early 1900s, even utilitarian architecture was made to be beautiful. I suspect "making" was a revered endeavor only slowly giving way to Henry Ford's assembly line. Creating something was a matter of pride and perhaps involved a bit of individual flair. These days, pre-fab siding and a flat roof are enough to please.

If you read the signage here, you learn that the massive surge tank on the mountainside is a machine to regularize water pressure and that valves in the powerhouse more precisely control the flow. In total, the project hasn't changed much in over a hundred years, except that NorthWestern Energy now owns and operates it, and its megawatt production—"enough to energize about 10,500 homes"—seems modest. Turning water into power for human needs may involve desecration of a sort, but, while those Pelton waterwheels in their green steel casings go on rotating at 300 rpms, humans do go on walking past them into the contrasting wilderness. I'd rather the Pelton wheels weren't there, I guess, but I can think of worse ways to generate power.

In those years before Mystic Lake's transformation and my dad's birth, Roy Chamberlain developed a good sense of humor and cultivated a gentle manner. Or perhaps he emulated his father. He too became a connoisseur of beautiful things. On his mission, he picked out a fancy pair of Zeiss binoculars to take home, along with some of those artistic, if slightly erotic, postcards. A souvenir lithograph of the Castle of Chillon and Lake Geneva caught his fancy and now hangs in my bedroom in its heavy gold-painted frame. The blue is still so vibrant and the foliage so exquisitely limned that Roy, examining it today, would notice only a few new nicks and dings on the frame.

He remained unmarried until he was almost forty—unusual for an LDS man. How did he begin courting and why did he choose to marry my grandmother, Frances Viola Glenn? She was striking, of course, in a cloche hat, velour coat, and high-button boots. She was also a bob-haired flapper and the daughter of an Irish miner. I'll never know what attracted these unlikely people: My dad didn't talk about his parents. It was too painful.

The marriage was relatively short-lived. Roy died of cancer at the age of sixty in 1943, sixteen years before I was born. It was quite a big deal when, more than two decades after his death, Frances had him exhumed and moved from the crowded historic City Cemetery to the newer and more spacious Wasatch Lawn, where she'd purchased two side-by-side plots. Otherwise, there was no room for her beside him.

She probably met with the LDS bishop, applied to the city for permits, to the two respective cemeteries for permission and the staff and equipment to move him, to the Chamberlain family for approval. And it would have been expensive—not just buying the new plots but also paying for excavation, transportation, and perhaps a new coffin if the original wasn't sound. Everyone seemed to think that the new cemetery would be a vast improvement over the old, crowded one. At Wasatch Lawn, the headstones were flat and laid out in well-planned rows. Frances didn't move her husband without a lot of planning and expense. I think she liked the two plots she had, surrounded by trimmed Kentucky bluegrass. Then, she remarried.

I remember standing by the freshly dug grave while Roy's body was still at the City Cemetery, Frances telling my sister and me that he "would have been" our grandfather. I wasn't sure what that meant. A dead man who wasn't dead enough not to need reburying? I remember juniper hedges and dirt and grass, the snow-covered Wasatch and a steady blue sky.

A similar sky presides, almost six decades later as I go up along Mystic Lake trail's third mile, some twelve hundred feet pretty much all at once, and quantum physics makes sense—particles, waves, odd conjunctions.

Thimbleberry red in the shady stretches and granite aglitter in the rocky parts. West Rosebud Creek washing, squirting, sprinting, and flooding over boulders fallen into its bed. Water spiraling through the canyon. Water measuring time and energy.

As we move up, we go into the river's brightening past, into the vision of all the people who've hiked here, including those 1920s-era engineers. And yet we meet water hurrying down toward another kind of past that we've left. Behind us is a dark canyon, the nostalgia of history, and a family story tainted by exhumation. And still ahead, a brightening, high-altitude eternal present rises from the explosion that's now our future.

Explosion or not, dam break or not, hiking a popular trail can sometimes take a sinister turn. Maybe, in going to this particular romanticized wilderness, we think we can escape causality. Or, conversely, because it's such an industrialized thoroughfare at first, hikers forget to watch for primal hazards. Mystic Lake trail has claimed a few unlucky visitors, including a forty-seven-year-old man in 2016 and a twelve-year-old boy in 1979. The man collapsed and couldn't be revived. The Boy Scout fell in the boulder field. A plaque near the trailhead honors the boy and warns that, despite its pretty setting and popularity, any mountain terrain ought to be respected.

One of my friends has a story to show how unprepared some visitors are. She was doing volunteer maintenance work in the boulder field. As the crew tackled the switchbacks, putting mattocks in untested hands soon proved to be a mistake. Someone dropped one, and it became a steel weapon as it plunged and spun toward other volunteers. "That was when," my friend says, "I learned to be toward the head of a large group."

I like that piece of wisdom. Watch things behind you shrink and become inconsequential. Be the one to set the metal or rock or genetic predisposition rolling, not the one receiving said metal or rock or genetic predisposition. But your past will always threaten and your family's theme song play whenever you arrive somewhere, which is, basically, all the time. The mattock will rotate and clang. And so, maybe, there *was* a germinal event in my OCD narrative. It just wasn't something that happened to me.

Today, we make it through the boulders without incident (Luke, sans hiking boots, has the toughest time) and now come over the top, and here it is again, as I remembered it—Mystic Lake. Other colors pounce—yellow columbine and the pearlite half-moon—but the lake reflects the sky, and the intensified blue swamps slower frequencies. Water sheeting over the spillway edges the expanse with silver, but from far above at the vista point, it's hard not to see it as static—a uniformly industrial sapphire ice, cosmic turquoise, bonsai beach gloss.

As we descend to the shore, the two-hundred-foot-deep lake breaks and lunges against its restraining rock, churns silt, and browns around the edges. At 7,669 feet above sea level, Mystic Lake is not the highest, wildest, or most alpine in the Beartooths, but, because of that 1924 explosion, it holds the largest volume of water, and up close its roiling blue is marbled and flawed.

We take the path above the shore and away from the dam, a flat stint, with a few exhilarating stream crossings, a patch of slushy snow, and some fallen timber to keep our pace honest. We pass two side trails and cross a bridge wide enough for horses. Climbers reach Granite Peak, Montana's highest, that way. People like us—but very few—would rather saunter along, their goal Island or Silver Lake.

After the climb to Mystic, we cruise this section, get into a rhythm, alternately watching our steps and enjoying the scenery, particularly Mount Hague, which looks like a pyramid, one crafted by Mayans or Egyptians on performance-enhancing drugs. It's the wrong season for elderberries and raspberries, but as Luke gulps fresh grass shoots, calypso orchids, also known as fairy slippers or Venus's slippers, appear beside the trail. He ignores them. Not tasty, I guess.

The orchids grow in acidic soil under pines and firs—usually there's one plant, occasionally as many as three, sometimes an entire patch. Each individual produces a single flower in June to July (depending on elevation). A giant *Calypso bulbosa* is about eight inches tall and leaves no trace after blossom and foliage dry and disintegrate.

This evanescence—the corm safely underground—makes me want to touch the pink and white labellum (the wide, toe-end of the slipper), the striped pink and white heel, and the yellow tease of the slipper's arch. But, despite the flower's fragility, the corm persists, and, moreover, the blossom is cruel: Unlike most plants that rely on pollination, it doesn't offer good things to eat after its alluring colors trick bumblebees inside.

Memories, like orchids, occasionally flair into cruel blooms. I knew somehow Grandma Chamberlain didn't like me, and years later my mother confirmed this suspicion. My sister was her favorite. At least my sister got the best gifts, including a red negligée and robe—which I wore as hand-me-downs after their magic dissipated. My mother said they were inappropriate for a child of seven or eight: all that flowing crimson silk and voile. But she couldn't keep my sister from wearing the elegant clothes.

It's hard to believe that such sharp mental images of a woman I barely knew date from so long ago, near the beginning of my life: Grandma Chamie, as we were supposed to call her, sitting at our kitchen table, saying she wanted to be euthanized "like they do dogs"; before her visits, Mother placing ashtrays strategically so Grandma's cigarettes wouldn't burn the furniture; Grandma dressing more elegantly than Mother, her hair impeccably styled, her clothes straight-from-the-store clean; Grandma posing for my dad's camera beside a tree or sipping iced tea on our patio, her crossed legs slim in black pedal pushers, her eyes behind sunglasses.

I didn't understand the dynamics, but I somehow learned that Arch Wilde, whom she lived with in the Sara Lee Apartments, was her new husband but not my grandfather. He was tall and didn't say much to me, which was okay because I didn't really know who he was. When we visited, I liked standing on their balcony overlooking willow trees, ponds, and mallards.

There was carelessness under Frances Chamberlain Wilde's tailored good looks. She chain-smoked and often drove a hundred miles an hour to Reno, Nevada, to gamble. Twenty-five was her lucky number—Jesus's birthday. The only time Frances babysat me, my mother came back to find cigarette burns on my hands (I don't remember this). My mother was furious, but nothing in particular was done about it. Grandma

Chamie was a powerful force, though feckless with her cigarette ashes.

When we were older, Grandma Chamie sometimes took my sister and me for cheap hamburgers at Dee's Drive-in, the local Salt Lake fast-food chain, complete with carhops and window trays. We plunged through town in her turquoise Falcon, and she swung her arm to the right when she braked at an intersection, supposedly to keep us from crashing through the windshield in those pre-seatbelt days.

There were also trips to Wasatch Lanes. We'd leave the summer heat of a melting asphalt parking lot and enter the 3.2-beer- and cigarette-scented bowling heaven of cool blue carpet, shiny wooden alleys, racks of pins, ball-return machines. I received my rental shoes reverently, picked out the lightest ball in the place—one of the speckled black ones, though I admired the shiny red-and-blue-swirled jobs I couldn't even lift—and chose a blue or white plastic chair to use when it was my sister's turn. Most of my tosses wobbled to the gutter, but I didn't care. The machinery that picked up the remaining pins (usually ten, in my case) and set them back again was magical. I loved the hollow crash as the metal rake came down to sweep them all away after my second try. These outings with Grandma Chamie meant we got to drink lots of soda pop, which was largely unavailable at home.

As a coda to this part of my childhood, I remember all the exotic plants and flowers in our living room after her funeral, including the banner that read "Beloved Aunt Frannie" as it decorated a lavish bouquet. A little girl had, then, to be on her best behavior in that mysterious suspension of normal time.

If I want to understand our family sensitivity, its underground heart, its origin—how it fell from my grandmother to my dad to me like a gear or mattock—I have to train my temporal binoculars at a more distant past. I search, to be clear, for the color behind gray-on-gray records of a single, brief life: Clarence Pead of 77 West Third South, born March 16, 1891, the second son of Parley Pead.

An immigrant laborer, Parley, like John Chamberlain, converted as a boy to the LDS Church. His parents presumably gave away all they owned to steam from Liverpool to New York and via train to Utah—the Promised Land. The 1860s offered a relatively cushy version of the Mormon Trail. But the promise, despite that mechanized journey to reach it, proved empty.

For three years, before Clarence's birth, father Parley and his wife lived in the small agricultural settlement of Huntington as he worked on Church irrigation projects. Two of his children died there. Even in the bigger employment market of Salt Lake, his family wasn't prosperous. They probably rented their place—perhaps a bare wooden structure—downtown, a few blocks from the Rio Grande depot. The houses in that area are long gone, so I can only guess how noisy and drafty this by-the-tracks spot was, the windows ill-fitting, maybe, with snow powder sifting in at the sills, blue evenings dissolving like sugar into the Great Salt Lake.

Parley's wife paced the creaking floor, like any anxious mother, cradling the newborn Clarence, who wouldn't be appeased. Ghosts of her lost children—an infant daughter and a four-year-old son, named after their parents—haunted this evening, like so many others. Or maybe they were shadows of ghosts, the children buried far away in Emery County. Yet their mother had the very real needs of three living girls and the fussy baby to tend to. Despite her efforts, five brief months later Clarence died of dysentery and was interred in Plat S, Block 17, Lot 2 of the City Cemetery. All very documented and regular and recorded in a beautifully readable script.

Clarence's mother was my great-grandmother—Mary Elizabeth Vissing—who emigrated from Denmark in 1873 when she was fifteen and married seven years later. She and Parley had six children, of whom two survived past adolescence: Aunt Ivy and Aunt Viny (Lavina Comfort)—as I knew them, two sweet old women in capacious dresses with netted pillbox hats. Uncle Clarence is, for me, a birth and a death certificate in online Salt Lake archives. But it was his passing that seems to have exploded the family's collective psyche.

Mary Elizabeth's youngest child, Grandma Chamie, emerged from that catastrophe. Her relief came from sitting on a plastic chair in Wasatch Lanes, chain smoking and sheltered from the heat outside; feeding nickels into a slot machine; choosing twenty-five at the Nugget in Reno, urging Jesus to come through for her.

You leave the Mystic Lake shore and the calypso orchids to discover the fairy-like terrain of lodgepole pine understory. The trees are so dense, you might hear a nutcracker skrawk above the canopy, but you won't see her, not even with binoculars. You could be in another world, not in Montana at all. Or you could be in another time, one before Mystic Lake was deepened into a reservoir, before assembly lines, before the European invasion of this continent. Hell, why not go back before humans of any kind? Mountain laurel would have done what it's still doing with its green *horror vacui.*

When the lodgepole pines open, Island Lake spreads its little curl of a golden sand beach and its far wooded shoreline in front of us, two tired people and one still-eager dog. If Mystic is beautiful, Island Lake is sublime. And unexploded.

When the day is fair and warm (say, in the 60s), you gravitate to sand and sunshine. You go wading or tuck your knees under your chin and sit in front of a light show. Pewter-bellied clouds delineate the infinite sky; the mountains are fanged; the lake vanishes around a bend; the island is forested. But, mostly, there's the blue-gold water, which a dog like our Luke can wade through and bite. Pools, dips, ridges, and valleys of water gather, refract, imprison, reflect, pulling light this way and that. Slipping waves reticulate golden lines on the smooth lake bottom. Backlit sparks of sun turn the darker, more distant part of the lake into a planetarium, stars scooting along in the currents' drift, water showing off its virtuosity. Undammed Island Lake is golden and silver, timeless green, white, and blue.

Did industrialization change human behavior? Undoubtedly. But some patterns are as eternal as Island Lake. Grief, for example. And the desire to leave it behind. Mary Elizabeth Vissing Pead fled her home, marrying John Francis Glenn in 1894, three years after the death of baby Clarence. LDS divorce wasn't common in those days, and I don't know why the one between Mary and Parley occurred. Parley's girls went with their mother and her new husband, the youngest—Anna Johanna Pead—becoming in the 1900 census Annie Glenn. Parley died in his forties, seven years later.

Who was John Francis Glenn and how did he win Mary over? All recorded history yields is that, at least in 1900, he was a quartz mineral miner. I like to think he was a charming young Irishman who promised an escape from the mourning that pervaded Parley's world. I see John and Mary laughing and waltzing at first on the dance floor of the bright Union Pacific ballroom, and Mary full of tense joy when their daughter Frances passes milestones of survival: infancy, early childhood, the teen years (Annie Glenn died at sixteen), a wedding, and a first pregnancy. When John Glenn, by then lost to alcoholism, came to visit her in the 1920s, though, Frances—in phrasing that impressed my uncle, her oldest boy—told her father never to "darken my door again." As far as I know, he didn't.

Mary never met Frances's second child. My dad was born four days after his grandmother's funeral. Despite the nearly simultaneous events of her mother's death and her son's birth, Frances kept the usual baby book, more tentatively perhaps than some. She noted a first tooth, a stylish "romper"—a gift from an uncle or aunt. Her grief emerges in the pale blue script she wrote with, not even denting the page.

Frances doted on her children, to the point of stifling them. She got up the toddler Leroy Glenn—known as Bud throughout his life because as a child he was his "mamma's little rosebud" and as an adult he despised being known as "the king"—in airy white gowns and shiny patent-leather shoes, with a hairdo that involved shaving his nape to mid-ear. Three years later, little Tommy, my dad, was less sophisticated, a tousled blond boy with wide-set eyes like his mother and an imploring impish gaze. Clearly, baby fashions changed, and Frances was up on the latest trends. Or maybe she knew Tommy was destined for somberness, not flamboyance. After all, her mother's death had "poisoned" Frances's milk.

For a while, the Chamberlains did well financially. They lived in Los Angeles, where Roy sold insurance. But then 1929 happened, and Roy's business partner committed suicide as their company failed. The family returned to Salt Lake to be taken in by one of the six Chamberlain brothers. Economic ruin colored Utah's unrelenting desert harshness. For the rest of his life, Tommy—who was five at the time of the Crash and eventually would refer to himself as TMC, a habit he picked up in the Navy when the ordinariness of a grown-up "Tom" failed to distinguish him from a sea of other midshipmen—would believe, unlike his mother, that his physical and mental discomforts stemmed from his being made to leave the benign climate of Southern California. He'd say his physiology was "formed" in the mists of Huntington Beach and along the eucalyptus parkways of Pasadena and that he was unsuited to the cruel sunshine of Salt Lake, where it wasn't pioneer times anymore, the city having already scarfed up its farmlands. The refugees from industrial Leicester had helped build a new industrial Leicester, this one with heat and salt flats.

Returned to Zion in disgrace, Frances sent Bud and Tommy out to eat Concord grapes until they were sick of the readily available free fruit, and Little Tommy's job was to paint and repaint his aunt and uncle's porch steps. Poor in a neighborhood full of social elites, Bud had to attend "soirées," where he squirmed and made faces. Once, Frances gave her two sons—at the ages of seven and ten—streetcar tokens, and they rode from one end of the line to another all day.

A childhood with the run of the town could have been a happy time for the Chamberlain boys, but their parents' troubles weren't kept from them. In fact, Bud and Tommy were pained by their financial and social fall. Bud took that as a lifelong challenge, left the LDS Church (which he would ever afterward mock), drove without his parents' permission to Mexico in a Model A when he was still a teenager (and, by his own account, almost died of dysentery there, like his half-uncle Clarence), admired the Catholic kids at Judge Memorial High School because they sure could drink, served in the Navy in World War II, became a manager at Skaggs's flagship Salt Lake store (Skaggs is now Osco), and then moved to Reno, where he claimed the first membership card given out by the Nugget Casino. The difference between gambling Nevada and LDS Utah, he told me, was that Nevadans were honest about their grift. He conquered smoking, cold turkey, after he visited a cigarette warehouse and mourned all the money he'd burned over the years. He wrestled long and hard with the skin cancer that killed him.

Tommy, on the other hand, seemed centripetally pulled into the misery of his mother's world. He followed Bud in apostasy but remained intrigued by the lore of the Church. Morbidly hypochondriacal, he sometimes checked the temperature of his earlobes to make sure he wasn't coming down with a fever. He often felt "woozy." Though he made a few efforts to move away—Naval officer's training in Michigan and Texas; the Pennsylvania Academy of the Fine Arts; engineering work in Pennsylvania; a demoralizing, flea-infested stay in San Francisco—he rarely left the dark orbit Frances established for him when she simultaneously nursed him and mourned her mother, whose own life had been shortened by loss.

My dad's early paintings, with their dense turquoise skies, express an occasional despairing helplessness. He never made enough money to be what he considered "successful." He never traveled his father's route to Basel, as he aspired to do. His future broke when the civil engineering firm he worked for designing bridges and high schools fell victim to a collapse in the global market for steel. He left co-workers he'd known for two decades and found another career. His new job—checking the figures for sewage treatment designs—was soul destroying. Only the challenging math problems he solved kept him going. Sometimes he came home from work and slumped on the couch in the dark. My mother thought his depression was her fault and apologized profusely for "whatever she'd done." She was secretly exasperated. Because my dad got a new job so quickly, I don't think any of us understood how the second large humiliation of his life—the loss of his profession—ate at his already fragile self-esteem. Perhaps nothing so much as his death from cancer after forty years of smoking defined TMC. In one of my last memories of him, he sits in a kitchen chair, his skin greenish as shunts keep his kidneys functioning a little longer—mortality incarnate in the room. It's what he's been working toward his whole life—the misery he's earned through all his grasping after it.

But, according to my mother, he rose up in bed one week before the end. And there was spine in his words, "If he can do it, so can I." By "he" my dad meant a friend who'd recently died. And now here he was, finally reaching for personal triumph, his own bravely met death.

We have Island Lake to ourselves. We are, I should clarify, the only humans and dog. Gliding mayflies, high-keeled water striders, and plucky little water boatmen with their two oar-like legs sparkle up the surface. A red squirrel trills from the firs behind us. We comb the beach and play with the green marble floats of algae we call "lake grapes." Everything's bright, illuminated, radiant. Even Luke's occasional shouty bark is suitably archetypal. And we have to go home. It doesn't pay to be out at dusk in the Beartooths. There's always the possibility of griz.

So back we go. Or forward. It's unclear. The rhythm of walking defies "progress," engaging the timeless and inevitable passing of the day. Mystic Lake's lesson might be that past and future, nature and industry rely on each other for definition. Or, more specifically, that nothing erases the past or stalls the future, and the arrows of geological force and biological truth pierce both. Like Buster Keaton in his 1922 classic *The Electric House*, I go up and down successively on the same set of stairs, beginning and ending at the power station, at the beginning and end of Montana's industrialization, at my family's reckoning with infant mortality and a promising but ever-receding future.

Despite all the new gadgetry of the eponymous electric house, Buster Keaton plays a man as confused as anyone ever was in the preindustrialized world. What good do all the fancy appurtenances of progress do him? Terrifying and hilarious, the climactic scene features his deadpan character scrambling to escape an electrified staircase of his own invention. It has the authenticity of a true story: Keaton almost killed himself doing the stunt.

One of Mystic Lake's gifts is power-generating blue, wild and industrialized, but also redolent of the 1920s when my dad was launched into the world from a history of sadness: the deaths of a small baby named Clarence and his three siblings, and a rare nineteenth-century divorce. I am, like Keaton, unpersuaded by "progress." Frances Glenn Chamberlain Wilde, in the first half of the twentieth century, navigated a boulder field of mourning, shock after shock as the steel tool struck, its reverberations persisting for four generations. Everyone born into a family has something to reckon with. OCD is my own particular challenge, but I see its origin in me as if through binoculars turned backward. Disasters radiate into the future, as they have to, because they happened so long ago.

TRAILS 16 TO 18

Three Numbers on the Yellowstone

Etude #1: Pictograph Cave

General location: Billings, Montana; 172 miles from Yellowstone
Hiking distance: Up to 4 miles round trip
Elevation: 3,500 feet
Terrain: Shortgrass prairie with sage and ranchland

It must have been right up along the intermittent flow of Bitter Creek, a sometime tributary of the Yellowstone River, where the first human visitors made their way, men and women following the bison. Their children played games of skill and boasted, as kids do, about souvenirs—snakeskins, antlers, a bleached badger's claw, a clutch of porcupine quills. They cooled off in the spring south of the sandstone rims, their shouts of joy dancing. Maybe a young woman, freed from babysitting, left a poem here, its eddies shimmering still when the wind shakes the aged boxelder I sit beneath, stretched with my notebook beside a giant hunk of pale-yellow rock that peeled off the cliff above me who knows how long ago. Vines crisscross it, stunted saplings dig at it with tickling roots, and chipmunks balance on it to look for danger. Far above and behind, a pigeon coos, sandstone recesses amplifying those purrs. A yellow warbler—incarnate dab of sunshine—fusses in last winter's dead leaves, emerging with a caterpillar almost larger than his beak can hold. His ruby-splotched plumage swells.

I could come here every day, looking for lost poems.

As I walk, music, not poetry, cycles in my head—echoes from my childhood, mass-produced, commercial songs dating from the years right after my parents bought a console stereo, those years when my mother and father were vigorous and young.

Buying the console was a big deal. It was cutting edge. Tasteful fabric screens disguised the speakers, and a faux-walnut frame housed the turntable. A hidden storage shelf would hold the few albums we might purchase—the few that over the years spilled from bookshelves and tables. A flaw in the veneer of the front panel made a small "J." I often studied that cryptic symbol as I listened to LPs, its presence a mystery, an icon of our post-low-fidelity years. We were middle-class savvy. When the stereo caught fire one night, my parents pushed it out the front door—an event my sister and I slept through. It never played again and was soon replaced but somehow made its way to the basement, where it stayed for decades.

Not much of our old home remains now. After my mother's death, fifty-five years of family history was carted out the door, tossed into dumpsters, given away to neighbors and friends. The new people have gutted the house, dug up the roses and boxwoods, and, well, that's the nature of human attachment to place these days. It wasn't always so, even if those attachments were seasonal.

Five miles southeast of Billings, Pictograph Cave State Park is a twenty-three-acre gift box containing at least ten thousand years of migratory human history tied up in sandstone cliffs, a dried spring, intermittent Bitter Creek, and deep skies. The pictographs, some dating as far back as two thousand years, have become fainter since I've been visiting. They evoke ghostly voices of beings who always returned: ancient, unknown human moieties out of deep time; elk and bison herds; modern Apsáalooke, Blackfeet, and Lakota travelers and families; fur trappers; white ranchers. Then the movers came: WPA crews who "improved" the site by sand-blasting cave walls in a misdirected attempt to clean the artwork, and archeologists armed with toothbrushes and mesh who have, like descendants cleaning their parents' house (or, rather, someone else's parents' house), spirited away tens of thousands of fragments of the past.

And now kids visit on school and family outings, and tourists read the interpretive signs.

Yet you can lounge, as I'm doing, in boxelder shade below the three rock alcoves from which the park derives its somewhat erroneous name and feel the power of those past lives echoing off the rock. Or you can follow the short trail around the recesses the park calls Pictograph Cave, Ghost Cave—with its eerie round concretions—and Middle Cave. From the trail, you'll find views of dry Bitter Creek and intimations of the larger Yellowstone River Valley. On a calm day, heat shimmers. Prairie dogs gossip. Magpies shriek, flashing long tails. Lightning might inoculate a far-off knoll.

For at least ten thousand years—and probably much longer—Pictograph Cave has been a refuge, pilgrimage site, place of cultural expropriation, and archeologists' playground. Built in the colors and textures of the place with native-plant landscaping, a visitors center now highlights, among other wonders, the turtle pictograph salvaged after it fell from a cave panel. In 2021, a rockslide barely missed the new center, mocking its claim to permanence.

Speaking of which, who would have thought that vinyl records would give way to cassette tapes to 8-tracks to CDs to MP3s to streaming services? All in the space of a few decades? Back in the 1960s, as with any partakers of new technology, my family and I were in awe of our stereo, and we purchased and listened only to "stereophonic" albums, representing the culmination of science and industry. Due to some misunderstanding, I thought the older records would destroy the stereo, or vice versa, but I safely played *Bitter Tears* by Johnny Cash. Over and over and over. Until I remembered all the lyrics (which I mostly still do).

This groundbreaking album ranks as insensitive today—a white person's mishmash of incorrect "knowledge" regarding tribal cultures, though Cash claimed Cherokee heritage. When it came out in 1964, it was controversial for its "*pro*-Native American" lyrics and was blacklisted by radio stations around the country. Even so, its "Ballad of Ira Hayes" reached number three on the charts. I don't know how we ended up with it—my mother did like Johnny Cash—or why it fascinated me so much.

Tapping into a growing outrage, the album preceded key events in the recent history of the push for Indigenous rights: the founding of the American Indian Movement, the occupation of Alcatraz, the two-month standoff at the Pine Ridge Reservation. On YouTube, you can see footage of a very young Buffy Sainte-Marie in white go-go boots singing along with Cash to one of the album's standout songs: "Let me tell you, buster / That I ain't a fan of Custer / And the general he don't ride well anymore." It's one of the few songs on the LP that has, in my mind, aged well. Maybe, come to think of it, I liked *Bitter Tears*, because it spoke of permanence, of people who had deep roots in North America and traveled much of it—a richness that tested my imagination. And still tests it.

As much as I like sitting near the giant fallen sandstone monolith, the best thing to do at Pictograph Cave is to park at the gate two miles up and walk with a dog or two down the hill, past grazing cattle, through cottonwoods, and along the sandstone wall where the caves are. In summer it can be dauntingly hot, and in winter the road, though hardly traveled, is plowed, with oval ice rinks in the shady spots. But it's a great walk in all seasons. On the park's off days, I used to climb the locked gate, and Luke had to squeeze under. We don't do this anymore, because park personnel have become more suspicious of unauthorized visitors—for good reasons involving attacks on the barrier and drug dealing. Plus, my walking companion who had permission to enter has migrated to the coast.

Beyond the gate, turkeys stand sentinel on the hills or vanish into the ponderosas. Cougars wander the area, but I've never seen any. Maybe coyotes are enough to get the blood going. Luke has doubts about his cousins, and if he hears or sees one, he nestles closer. His interest lies in the culinary possibilities of the road: cattle feed fallen from ranch trucks, deer and horse turds, and various dead things. Oh, and once an alleged bit of edible marijuana, which landed him in the veterinary hospital for a night.

Luke and I often traveled the four-mile round trip to Pictograph Cave with a friend and her three rescues, whom she referred to as "The Deplorables." We measured distance by conversation: anthropomorphic discussions about our dogs and intellectual disagreements concerning poetry, dietary choices, and the pending end of civilization. At any time, we'd stop for local dramas: porcupines backing down a cottonwood trunk after, I suppose, munching away at new buds, or a raven pair harassing a much-beleaguered red-tailed hawk.

Now that my friend and The Deplorables have moved, I'm often alone with Luke. Since he's not much for conversation, the usual tunes and lyrics start up in my head, rhythms in keeping with my footsteps. A common refrain for me is from Peter La Farge's *Bitter Tears* song titled "The Vanishing Race." Cash moans the words in true Cash style: "I-I see an eagle in space / My people will follow-oh-oh—a vanishing race." I can't shake this tune once it starts, even though its lyrics are erroneous. The "vanished" never vanished.

Which comes first, the lyrics or the awareness all over again that I'm walking through someone else's history? By "someone else," I mean the Indigenous stewards, not the older rancher whose registered holdings surround Pictograph Cave and who turned his operation over to the next generation a while back. They have now built a house a mile past the park gate and run more cattle than their father did on the golden grasses, trying to make a profit, I suspect. Once, the daughter gave my friend and me and the dogs a ride in her ATV so we wouldn't get caught up or trampled as the herd moved to late-spring pasture. She was joyous and kind, and, as much as I missed the old dispensation of benign neglect, I hope she and her husband make a go of things because, otherwise, subdivision and development pend. Progress has already come for the surrounding countryside.

When Luke and I walk to the park from the gate, a ponderosa signals our imminent arrival from the tip-top of a sandstone pinnacle, desert cottontails scratch out "forms" in the clayey soil and lie in them on a warm day as if they've discovered the most wonderful spa treatment, and native bees collect pollen from skunkbush sumac. For them, nothing has changed.

Obsessions infected by social prejudices are especially disturbing. Consider my first one, which was fueled by antisemitism. I've never had another like it, but it seared a cleft in my brain—good, open-minded thoughts on one side and evil intolerance on the other. How can I ever be whole again? Is wholeness possible for anyone? It seems likely that most people are at one time or another exposed to some component of themselves that shocks them with its vileness. That is, I hope they're shocked. I hope they defeat the thing, and keep defeating it.

You could say *Bitter Tears* fought uniquely white prejudices, even while it provided fuel for them. When I was a kid, one particular song from *Bitter Tears* seemed aimed at me. In La Farge's lyrics to "White Girl," a tourist visits the narrator's pueblo, steals his heart, makes him a "pet," and rejects him when he asks her to marry him. The song, cutting through certain cultural values of the time, made me wonder. Was I a bitter white girl, cruel and unfair? I didn't want to be. I wanted to dive into the lyrics and tell the broken-hearted lover, "I'll marry you! Don't be sad." But I didn't have "bright blond hair." He wouldn't have wanted me. Racism cutting against sexism. More plausibly, instead of rescuing him, I wanted to *be* him—a happier him. After all, my hometown—holy as it might have been—lacked the rightness of his pueblo. Its Temple, Tabernacle, and state capitol don't belong where they are. But maybe, as seems possible in the way of human things, pueblos also were once shiny and new, the latest technology; they've simply been around so long that they've become suited to their place.

Twenty thousand years from now, will steel-and-glass Salt Lake be more or less incorporated into the Wasatch foothills, its people Indigenous—their biochemical heritage intertwined with and marked by an odd invasive suite of DNA from Europe, Africa, and Asia that will by then have receded to belongingness? Will the Chamberlains finally fit in? Will OCD be a thing of the past? And here in Montana, will the visitors center lie at last under a pile of sandstone? All I know right now is that I can't live at Pictograph Cave. It's a state park, of course. It's also a millennia-old waystation. People do not stay. They travel through, leaving sorrows and joys behind to swirl on updrafts and vanish like the vultures tacking overhead.

After a while—and despite the boulder and the lovely weather, the yellow warbler and the pigeons—the thing for a human to do, the thing apparently most have done, is to close the notebook or the parfleche and move on.

Before leaving, I scan the fading pictographs again. That line of smoking rifles seems to indicate a fight or a hunt, but what to make of the much older, drum-bellied anthropomorphic figure with spiked hair, the red complex-antlered elk, the hefty bison, the Spirit Being composed of fringe and an X, the round striped bird and the naturalistic one, or the turtle/man/bird composite? Based on advice an Apsáalooke elder gave me about finding arrowheads, the thing to do is let the images be. If I see them, I'm meant to. If I find meaning in them, that is what they want. If I long for the past, I will feel it stirring through the present. I should, in other words, leave things as they are.

Etude #2: Black Otter Trail (Swords Park)

General location: Billings, Montana; 172 miles from Yellowstone
Hiking distance: 6+ miles round trip
Elevation: 3,124 feet
Terrain: Shortgrass prairie and sandstone cliff

The wind is coming up. The wind is always coming up. If you're going west, chances are that the wind is in your face. "It's hell going this way," a woman once told me as we passed, she bending into the full brunt of a coming storm, me loping along with the gale at my back. But if you're going east, the wind might also be in your face. In winter, gusts whip a meringue of clouds along the Pryor Mountains forty miles south, and snow drives from all directions, biting into exposed skin. In summer, prairie storms from any quadrant churn purple as liatris, filigreed with lightning.

Weather dramas on Black Otter Trail, on the cliff above Billings and its Montana State University campus, belie the peaceful substrate below my feet: sandy remnants of an ancient, drowsy, tropical sea deposited when the earth was warmer and more peaceful than today. In those epochs, ocean surface temperatures languished at 100° Fahrenheit year-round. Because there was little contrast in temperature worldwide, there was very little wind. We mammals were tiny things, carrying on, in our conniving way, under leaves and in the footprints of dinosaurs. The latter didn't look like the grim, bloody, bare-fleshed monsters of my childhood plastic toy set, but, like birds, they brooded their young, groomed their feathers, and sang (what that sounded like is unknown). Plesiosaurs bumped to the ocean's surface. Clams, ammonites, and other shelled creatures washed ashore. Tropical sharks cruised where the trail now curves.

After the inland sea dried, a river worked at the sandy bottom. Judging by the size of the valley it cut, it would have dwarfed today's Yellowstone. It sliced a course eighteen hundred feet below the cliffs, then sank into the shifting bed that cradles today's remnant. *Isaiah*'s geological vision hasn't come true ("Every valley shall be exalted, and every mountain and hill shall be made low"), but, over the millennia, the Yellowstone River has made low a significant amount of mineral and silt. If you're lucky, you might find a leopard rock on the shore—a three-billion-year-old chunk of Beartooth Plateau from seventy-five miles or more to the west. Dark with raised crystals, rather like fudge with walnuts, your volcanic souvenir may have bounced down a hundred years ago or as far back as the Cretaceous, in a time without wind when ancient birds sang.

Rarely do I think about sound as a source of obsession, even though certain songs and melodies can be torturously repetitive. In fact, sometimes I've found that interrupting a visual obsession with a mental shout or a "to hell with you" sort of comment is pretty effective. Oscar Charles Dawson, OCD personified, is easy to rail against. *What a bastard,* I think. A fraudulent tent-revival preacher, he sets my teeth to aching with his word pictures and zoetropes and flip books. He says it's all or nothing, not a continuum along which humans oscillate. But most people, I tell him, have vile thoughts. Someone with OCD just happens to trap them, examine them, form sermons around them, let them escape the mental flow to fill the sufferer with horror. *How have you come to think that?* Oscar Charles Dawson interrogates. *You want music instead? Let me send a repetitive tune to roll across the infinite cavern of your brain, a tune you don't even like.*

My dad's family knew chords, played piano, sold sheet music. There was even a secret Chamberlain whistle, which sounded something like a western meadowlark call. How comforting to hear it when, as a little kid, I'd get caught up in a school of shoppers and be swept into the wilds of a mall or store. Of course, the whistle mortified my mother. But her family had its music, too, which joined and flowed alongside the Chamberlains' more accomplished talents.

Driving Mother's loose-steering brown Valiant or bicycling, I'd stop at the folks' house on my way home from classes at the University of Utah. I'd bring my latest library finds: Dylan Thomas on cassette, or an anonymous recording of old Scottish ballads. Or I might dig out one of my youngest uncle's LPs. My grandparents' portable turntable with tiny low-fi speakers struggled with Johnny Cash's "Folsom Prison Blues" and Neil Diamond's "Brother Love's Traveling Salvation Show." A more amenable favorite was a paleontological sherd from the dark ages of the 1950s: Hank Williams. "It's sure inspiring," my grandfather would say of "Your Cheatin' Heart" as we sat together, three on the old couch with the gold nylon throw over it.

Aside from a yarn about using stilts because the snow was too deep for boots, my grandfather didn't say much more about his past than he did about religion. He communicated in snippets, occasionally surprising ones. I was playing my guitar once and warbling after the manner, I hoped, of Joan Baez. He'd have joined in, he told me, if he'd still had a voice.

I could—and can—hardly imagine it. My grandfather sang? Yes, he did, my mother later confirmed.

So, it's 1948, let's say. Piloting his Ford truck across the Salt Flats, dark hair thick and wavy, Alma Tripp belts out "Honky Tonkin" as white playas zip past his tanned face and his arm rests on the opened window.

You can pick up Black Otter trail from any number of spots. One common access point is a sometimes muddy, unpaved lot across from the oddly named Logan *International* Airport. However, on a nice day, Luke and I walk out of our house, head east on Rimrock Road, and take a sharp left uphill along Twenty-Seventh Street. We climb beside a concrete barrier edging the four-lane drive, step over riprap netting, reach the top, find the asphalt path, and take the pedestrian underpass tunnel to our right. If no one is around, I sing, as is my wont, "Amazing Grace" as loudly as I can, to test the acoustics.

Luke and I take a doggy waste bag from the dispenser at the official beginning of the trail, and then we're set for the next three or four miles. The problem here is that the route trends downhill, so it's easy to keep going until you realize that you're out of time and have to huff it back, ascending into that hellish wind. Once we get into a rhythm, though, Luke and I lean thoughtlessly ahead—until he discovers some delectable odor. Despite his olfactory gossiping, we soon get away from busy Airport Road, which parallels the trail (artistically paved around rock outcrops).

At this distance, human activity in the valley seems benign. Oil refineries, traffic on I-90, the BNSF railyard and coal trains, the hospital corridor, the Big R store, feedlots, Crazy Mary's fish restaurant, and the Metra fairgrounds subside, their flat hum drowned out by a red-tailed hawk's sharp *key-err*. If it's a clear spring day, the formidable front of the Beartooth Mountains might seem closer than it is. To the south lie the Pryors and the Crow Indian Reservation. On his *Bitter Tears* album, Cash sang about "Indian drums that you can't hear." And I believed him. I thought of those Indian drums as mystical. I might very well have imagined them emanating from a place like Billings's South Hills.

What lyricist La Farge meant and Cash brought to life, though, was a Hollywood caricature. Today's drumming groups, like those of the past, create an overwhelming percussive landscape and sing in virtuoso harmonies. Plus, contemporary Native American artists work in many genres. Take Apsáalooke Supaman's online hip-hop teamed with jingle dancer Acosia Red Elk's choreography—the beauty gives me chills. Great Plains music probably always was diverse, musicians being musicians and all. Their music uncoils obsessions, releases Oscar Charles Dawson's hands from around my neck.

Our first landmark on Black Otter Trail is a double-trunk cottonwood, half dead. I often wonder if it stands on an old homestead or attempt at a city park. It doesn't belong here—with scorching sun, the constant pruning wind, bitter cold, and scarce water. Any sizable precipitation, in fact, turns the soil into what Montanans call "gumbo"—a gluey mess of slippery clay. But, though its largesse evaporates after a day or two, rain-water or snowmelt usually fills depressions in the rimrock with clean, temporary pools for the birds to drink from: chickadees, pigeons (a resident band of seven or eight seems the norm), and magpies. In summer, white-throated swifts beat past.

Related to hummingbirds, swifts hunt on the wing all day, gobbling insects and airborne spiders. They roost in the sandstone seams that sometimes separate large chunks of rock from rock, with the result that boulders and even sections of wall crash down, occasionally on houses. With forked tails, white fronts, and dark wings, swifts tumble and dance like gymnasts over a vaulting horse. Twenty or thirty of them skip up the rims—and zip almost through my hair before plummeting over the cliff. If you traced their flight paths with neon, you'd see scallops, feathery tumbles, flat-out dives. Their stiff-winged flight is a series of stalls and thrusts, a dervish approach to enlightenment.

Even before the weather turns cold and insects die off for the year, the swifts vanish. Like magic. After they leave, the rocks turn silent and still—and then you know you're in for it. All the storms and cold fronts of what could be a seven-month-long Montana winter will drive down at you from the Arctic. It's no coincidence that "this land's history" was once told in spiraling designs on buffalo robes. These multigenerational records were called "winter counts" for good reason, since it was in the cold and dark that tribal historians had time to reflect. Prairie years began and ended with the first snowfall of autumn.

Nothing so magisterial as a winter count dominates Black Otter Trail these days. The traditional halfway point of our walk is the second parking lot and a broken cottonwood tree. The city is sprucing the place up now, but it still seems a bit forlorn—an old campsite, abandoned park, or failed homestead. I think of the people who lived here two hundred years ago, before the forlornness took hold. And then I think of Luke's origins, his mother lying dead in a yard at Crow Agency where he was found. Right after his arrival at a private shelter, he came down with parvovirus, which he somehow survived. According to one of the volunteers, the white streak bisecting his face is, in Cheyenne culture, a sign of spiritual power.

Luke's story emphasizes the human pain that prevented his first family from seeing or being able to do anything about the misery of their dogs. Animal abuse is everywhere in Montana—some of the worst of it on white ranchers' lands and in the bigger towns among white animal hoarders. It's hardly confined to the reservations. But walking into people's yards, scooping up puppies, and leaving behind human suffering is, apparently, easier there. "How does that make the people feel?" a Native American friend of mine asks. "Their dogs are worthy of rescue, but not them?"

If you stand at Black Otter's revamped and redesigned gravesite of local "hero" Yellowstone Kelly, whose motto was "briskly venture," you can untangle the beginnings of the cultural tragedy that Luke was a tiny part of. Riding a wave of racism-inspired destruction, the well-educated Luther Sage Kelly has become no more than an interesting minor character, his grave an attraction for Western history buffs and marijuana smokers. To reach it, you follow a graceful brown side path uphill from the main trail, pass various interpretive signs extolling the exploits of this literate and handsome Euro-American army scout, and arrive at his remains, moved from their previous resting spot several yards away. When he asked to be buried above his "beloved" Yellowstone River, Bernie often notes, Kelly didn't count on having a view of the Conoco Refinery. It's cliché to observe that pioneers destroyed what they most loved. But maybe they didn't love it at all. Their loyal descendants certainly don't seem eager to "let buffalo run through the streets of Billings," as one of them put it at a Fish, Wildlife, and Parks scoping meeting I attended on the possible return of bison to certain isolated state lands.

Kelly not only briskly ventured into the genocide of Indigenous Americans but also served in the Philippines, where William McKinley's imperialist aims led to the deaths of more than a million residents. As we go on, I think about friends who can't walk in Montana for fear of being harassed because they're Native American. I think about my uncle's gift Jerusalem cricket I left to die—such a small colonialist tragedy, that one, but one I'm solely responsible for.

"Walk with me, Luke," I say, and he does.

Like many urban trails, Black Otter knots human and nonhuman. Golden sticky cups and purple gayfeather liatris grow trailside. Sage and hovering winter rough-legged hawks recall the prairie that used to be cared for by Indigenous people. Steep cliffs and sidewalk-flat sandstone bring back the Mesozoic. But passenger flights as well as giant UPS and FedEx planes queue up to land at the airport—helping to define what industrialization has done to the Elk River valley.

My family's stereophonic music phase (morphing into 8-track, cassette, and CD) taught me about that bitter white girl lurking inside most of us "random white women," a term I picked up from a mother in a Billings city park. When her daughter thought she saw someone she knew, "That's just some random white woman," the mother assured her as I walked behind. "Random White Women," I noted to myself, riffing on humorist Dave Barry, would be a good name for a band.

White females—including my ancestors—were in on all the colonialism every bit as much as white men. When historian Patricia Limerick gave a talk at the Buffalo Bill Museum in Cody, Wyoming, where I worked in the 1990s as a curatorial assistant, she seemed determined to absolve pioneer women of complicity, as if they were on a lark, trading recipes and sewing tips. But Euro-American midwives, schoolteachers, missionaries, and entrepreneurs had their hands all over the nasty business of Manifest Destiny. Random, bitter white girls. My Puritan ancestor Patience Throckmorton. My great-grandmother Mary Elizabeth Vissing. My grandmother Frances Viola Glenn, who married into the Chamberlain family with its seemingly kindly LDS faith and music store.

The sandstone rims on Black Otter stimulate creativity for good or ill and everything in between, like most things humans do. Pictographs, now faded to oblivion, used to decorate them. Artists still balance near the edge to photograph sunsets. Deranged people (even a recent gunman) choreograph police encounters. City paramedics practice acrobatic rescues. One evening, near dark, I watched a young man film a female dancer near the drop, highlighted against afterglow. Lately, I find pottery, white with cryptic black script, broken in widely spaced piles. The writing seems important and poetic, but it's hard to read. The smashing resembles an installation. Tonight, nothing but a humble poem unscrolls from evening primrose throats opening at sundown. Oh, and a man sits on a bench overlooking downtown and plays his saxophone.

The trail takes us to Alkali Creek or, as we choose now, Boot Hill Cemetery, across from Applebee's, Country Inn and Suites, Office Depot, and Target. Above early settlers' bones, the cemetery grass grows long. Many of the interred are unnamed. Roads surround the plots. I've driven by many times without thinking. Now I read the scant interpretive signs and walk between the graves. There's a makeshift quality, an impermanence that suits these unknown lives caught between "frontier" and contemporary urban sprawl.

In the shadow of the cliffs, Luke and I are sheltered from the wind's brunt. The endless repetition of lyrics quiets, too. Maybe it's the walk. Maybe it's the lateness of the evening. Maybe it's the sandstone. Or even a certain clarity of mind, however fleeting and hypoglycemic. I scan for incipient obsessions and find none. When I bend down to pet Luke and tell him we've got to go home now, I realize I could be any human and he could be any dog. We're archetypal, and we belong.

Etude #3: Along the Yellowstone: As Long as the Rivers Flow

General location: Billings and Laurel, Montana; about 172 miles from Yellowstone
Hiking distance: 2 miles round trip for Two Moon Park; 4 miles round trip for Sundance Lodge
Elevation gain: Negligible (depending on which trailhead you choose)
Terrain: Cottonwood river bottomland

I'm thigh-deep in almost seven hundred miles' worth of river. I hold my shoes and socks over my head to keep them dry. I rolled up my pantlegs, but they're getting soaked. My feet inch through the silt, toes searching for rocks and, worst of all, sharp limbs and roots drowned by the spring flood. I'm on the verge of losing my balance.

A friend and I teeter along like spotted sandpipers. At one deep section, I look back at her and at Bernie, and I'm reminded of a 1940s black-and-white film of gringo Amazon explorers. Burt Lancaster, maybe, and someone like Deborah Kerr. It's warm enough to evoke fantasies of anacondas slipping into the muddy current. The most I can brag about, though, is to have gone knee-to-tail with a few pollywogs.

Every year, the river's flooding of Two Moon Park and its subsequent receding surprise us. It's hard to understand how quickly the lazy Yellowstone obliterates its trails. Cottonwoods file further down the banks where the water turns away, until suddenly we're amazed by the small forest grown up in all of our favorite agate-hunting/dog-running spots. Undammed, the Yellowstone is in flux.

And maybe for that reason Billings isn't a town to embrace its river. In fact, you can live here for years and, unless you make a concerted effort to approach it, the prairie Yellowstone, entering old age, will remain an abstraction, a tiny curl of it visible here and there as you look down from the Heights, or a broad gushing stretch of it vanishing below the bridges along I-90. It took me a few years after moving to Billings to realize that, when I was feeling blue, anxious, or hemmed in, the river would be there to greet me with its broad and slatternly embrace, an absent-minded mother ready to say hello but also able to forget once I walked away.

The valley's most obvious features are the rimrocks—the old seashore. Visible all over town, the cliffs orient me to the north, their frosting of pale yellow giving the river some of its names: *Mi tse a dazay* (Minnetaree), *Roche Jaune* (French), and Yellowstone (English). In the Apsáalooke language it's the *E-chee-dick-karsh-ah-shay* (Elk River). It demurely skims the base of the South Hills, a dark, eroded series of ridges looking like slag piles. So, for the people of Billings, the river does not come to us. Rather we go to it.

Along the twisting, twirling course, cottonwood bottomlands shelter white-tailed deer, beavers and muskrats, great blue herons and bald eagles. In winter, pretty little common goldeneyes shoot the rapids, dive in any pools that remain open between ice shelves, and swim upstream to do it again. In spring, tree and violet-green swallows (Bernie and I inevitably call them "violent-greens") sparkle like tossed turquoise over the waters, which begin to swell with runoff from the high peaks. Summer's turgidity matches the swollen abdomens of the mosquitos who suck our blood, and it's possible to find a catfish hanging peacefully in a flooded inlet. Western toads pulse along the shore, hoping, probably, to avoid the invading bullfrogs local scientists want to control. I've seen wildlife people with jars full of the newcomers who've been "controlled"—meaning, killed. I doubt the bullfrog's trombone will be silenced by these methods, judging by the many tadpoles rippling through summer ponds.

Reptiles are common in the warm months, too. Once, at Norm's Island, a racer swooshed up the riverbank, dazzling me with its lemon-bright belly and lime-green back. And here at Two Moon Park, bullsnakes head through the shallows to the safety of deeper water. Rattlers are said to live along the rocks and in the deep grass. I've no reason to doubt that, but I've seen only one—a tan coil right on the trail, peaceable enough.

In fall, ring-billed gulls congregate by the hundreds just upriver at Norm's—surely happy with the best of all possible worlds: the landfill close by and the long flat islands and archipelagos of sand and stone exposed as snowmelt from higher elevations becomes a memory and water draws down into its contemplative ebbtide.

Not so well-provisioned are the suckers caught in autumn irrigation ditches, draining dry by mid-October. While the Yellowstone is famously undammed, it does have diversions, and one of these canals goes through Billings, a quarter mile from my house. A friend and I spent an afternoon scooping out the gray-pink fish with our bare hands and hauling tubs of them back to the river. Along with the handsome, glistening suckers—they have pink-veined, Betty Boop lips and velvety skin—we caught perch and tiny stinging catfishes that had thrived in the summer's muddy heat under the mallards' orange paddling but were now gasping in inches-deep pools.

Think of creativity as a canal—rising at first, then flowing and productive, and finally drawing down to reveal treasures or detritus. For me, music has been like that, starting with *Bitter Tears*, of course, but also with my dad's classical guitar career.

He decided to take lessons as an adult. This was when Andrès Segovia and Carlos Montoya first caused a sensation in America. My dad bought a $100 Goya guitar, a metal footstool, and a method book, and found a teacher. He practiced in the evenings and on weekends. As his unaccustomed fingers stretched along the fretboard, my sister and I made fun of his grimaces. Instead of admiring him—picking up an instrument in adulthood has got to be one of the hardest and bravest things to do—we thought he was funny.

Yet the guitar hooked me. My dad's fumbling couldn't disguise those percussive strings' potential. His ponderous Malagueña whispered the Spanish romance of an arpeggio. I hung around sometimes for the magic under his labored coaxing—he said he often felt like flinging his guitar out the window. But I loved the instrument's richness and its limitations. It wasn't like violin music that could bend and stretch. It wasn't like the bump-bump-bump of a drum. It was both, and neither. It ran through my bones like a blue cord of nostalgia for times and places I didn't know.

When I was nine, I started lessons on my own orange Hernandez. I could barely reach the first fret, let alone master a barre, but I kept at it. My early success must have led to my dad's discouragement. He mostly quit playing and ferried me every Saturday to my lessons. I don't think either of us realized that for me to become a professional musician would have taken more work than that: six or seven hours of practice every day and world-class instruction.

Two Moon Park's two-mile loop trail starts in Russian olives—an invasive species controversial because, though it sucks up water and nutrients native plants need, many birds like its cover and fruits. A project to clear away the gray-leaved trees has resulted in piles of brush but so far not much visible difference in the number of olives. They and the cottonwoods are rife, in late spring, with yellow warblers calling out their "sweet-sweet-sweet-I'm-so-sweets" and exotic peach-pulp-breasted chats whistling and, of course, chatting. The bottomland forest opens to a meadow, where you might see a red fox leap through the tall grass like a little spurt of fire.

Then you reach the Weeping Wall, a tablet of rock moistened by an exposed water table that splashes and drips all year. In spring and summer, it shelters black-headed grosbeaks, a brown thrasher or two, and a jungle-green growth of moss and forbs. In winter, slabs of ice still the tune to a subtle dripping.

Bitter Tears lyrics also slip through my mind as I walk, rising sometimes to consciousness, sometimes overwhelming external sounds. One of the album's songs was about a treaty that would last "as long as the rivers flow." The treaty was broken, like so many others, with the building of Kinzua Dam in New York State on Seneca land.

So far, the Yellowstone flows free. At this point in its career, it represents the watersheds of multiple mountain ranges and a plethora of smaller flows. When I look at it on a map, it reminds me of a feather—the solid shaft with a thousand filaments along its length. Of course, it's not exactly a thousand, but, like any river, the Yellowstone picks up more water as it goes, the accumulation of various strains and cultures.

If my particular river is the Chamberlain, it's just a chance name. Really, I'm the gathering together of many individuals and families, and they all sing and clamor in my DNA. One of the more dominant drives is the desire to create something tangible. But, after I took up the guitar, I ran into difficult rapids. The late sixties and early seventies were not guitar-girl friendly. Oh, at first, I cruised through Julio S. Sagreras's *Primeras* and *Segundas Lecciones,* ignoring the "women's pose" suggested by another method book and spreading my legs with the best of them as I cradled my guitar. This was long before Sharon Isben would pull a pick out of her bra to play a splashy Albéniz "Leyenda" in front of a cheering audience or Antigone Goni would stretch her left hand from the first to the seventh fret, intimidating male master-class students. By the time I made it to *Las Cuartos Lecciones,* I felt confident enough to enter the youth classical guitar competition at the Utah State Fair—ages nine through eighteen. I was ten and in fourth grade.

There were six contestants—two females and four males—and three judges, all men. I've no idea how well I played. I remember the sparse audience (my mother and grandfather among them), the white walls, the large windows. I remember opening my guitar case (which smelled of dusty velvet and rosewood). I remember taking out my guitar and trekking up to the podium in that sun-flooded practice room of Kingsbury Hall on the University of Utah campus. I remember sitting down, settling my left foot on the metal stool, cradling my guitar, and playing a measure or two of Fernando Sor's "Study No. 5"—and then I remember finishing a Bach minuet. There's nothing in between, though I think I played both pieces in their entirety. The winning contestant was an eighteen-year-old who went on to become a professional musician. The panel of judges complimented and encouraged the other male performers but not the females. My mother pointed this out to me, with suppressed rage.

I suppose I lacked the precisely driven current, had too many other interests, or hadn't been blessed with talent. Or happened to be a girl. That was my last guitar competition. I like to think I became a fair amateur player, anyway, and interested some people as background music at a wine bar in Florida, where I performed when I was in my forties. (Even as late as that, when I took lessons again, the other students were all male.)

After the Weeping Wall, the trail winds back to the river and the best spot to sit along the lower Yellowstone shoreline: a giant cottonwood log faded to white. Cormorants cruise with common mergansers and Canada geese.

Sometimes, the best days in Two Moon Park are in winter, with the glowing lapis sky, fallen stars dancing on snow, and bare tree limbs delineated against the blue. Bald eagles eye us dispassionately as they cruise past or perch in the tall cottonwoods. Someone once built what we called "icehenge" using huge crystalline slabs they chipped out and dragged from the river. One winter after an Exxon oil spill, rainbow hexagons of sheet ice were embedded in the larger frozen shelf that had run against the shore. Farther upstream, farm fields were contaminated.

Along this stretch, you can never forget you're in town, whether there's been a chemical spill or not. Refineries burn off methane and traffic streams, but a tough little sharp-shinned hawk might stalk the interstices, an otter might swim into the fastest under-ice currents after the very suckers my friend and I tried to save, and a family of deer might bed in the tangled buffaloberry. Most humans will never know those dramas are happening.

Cuddled under the arm of a river bluff, Two Moon Park is a crescent of meadow, bottomland, and shoreline, the whole thing waiting to be swallowed between the Yellowstone River's seasonal whims and the expanding city suburbs on the bluff above. It's a place visited by dog walkers, human traffickers, bird watchers, drug addicts, and swimming kids. Its magic is a curve in the water, the "witchety-witchety" of a yellowthroat in cattails, the quick and easy ultramarine of tree swallows copulating on a dead cottonwood branch. It's the tang and taffeta swish of cottonwood leaves, the chant of the flood-stage river, the swoosh of slush as ice melts in March and whisks by in the quickening current. It's the chirp of an osprey and the bass rumbling of an invasive frog. It's a forgotten tangle between city and industrial wasteland. Luke knows it, navigating its world of shape, scent, and texture, finding joy on this groaning planet, in this Valium-popping, THC-vaping vale of tears.

Two Moon's trail runs deeper than the depth of a three-mile-long park, its Weeping Wall bright with a silvery laugh.

In November, you can walk along the sand of a drained canal. Scalloped patterns suggest the energetic currents that once drew mallards, barn swallows, beavers. Plastic bags catch on the grasses of the shore. A tossed-out school notebook shreds itself on the old bed. Compositions erode, their promise drained by harsh weather.

I rarely pick up my guitar anymore. Albéniz's "Leyenda" and Granados's "Danza Espanola #5" echo somewhere along the back neural pathways of my mind. And my fingers sometimes itch to play. But my calluses are gone. And my guitar is old and creaky. And so are my metacarpals.

What really did me in was my adulthood teacher, who suggested that unless I was willing to perform—to be a genius-level player—what was the point? I was crushed. I couldn't enjoy working out a rhythm or highlighting a tune, the creation of imagery with chords and melody, the heartbeat bass percussion underneath a treble extravaganza. Maybe I overreacted, but the joy was gone. The concept of competition destroyed it. Achieving mediocrity, after all, is a pointless ambition.

Musicians compete. I know that. Sculptors and painters compete. A poet or a writer, I'm told, competes not only with other writers but also with X and Facebook and overproduced, commercial trade-paperback novels, and gut-wrenching essays that must start with a "hook" and end with a devastating clutch at the heart. Writers have to make money and appeal to audiences, or they devolve into hobbyists engaged in literary masturbation or useless compulsions. Such an "untalented" individual will soon be swept into the general flow and forgotten—something anxiety's crippling inertia seems to want for me—or stranded with other detritus on a drained canal bed.

. . . But what's so wrong with being swept into the flow? Why all the focus on plot and drama? My first guitar teacher introduced me once to a visiting friend of his, an old man (anyone over fifty was ancient to ten-year-old me) who played real Mexican flamenco. The guest didn't speak much English, just smiled mischievously between pieces, raised his eyebrows and rocked to get the rhythm going until he unleashed a swirling, pulsing duende. He was never famous, but he was part of an old-style song—a tributary running parallel to the mother current until finally it would be subsumed, the great river streaming service enriched and whispering on.

The lower Yellowstone could be jazz. Ellington's "jungle sound." An improvised rhapsody of power, not-so-subtle transitions between lyricism and raw beat, piano stylings and saxophone wails on an underlying percussion, an upswing of sound that catches in the trees and is carried off by a red-tailed hawk.

But folk and country music are in my head, and the old Johnny Cash tunes will escape their synaptic moorings in my brain. Especially on the four flat miles of the Sundance Lodge trail, a small plot of BLM land about twelve miles upriver from Two Moon Park. To be clear, Sundance Lodge isn't on the Yellowstone. It fronts the Clark's Fork, right before its confluence.

Though its birth in the mountains is as wild as it gets in the lower forty-eight, the Clark's Fork right here is a cozy run of tame water, the haunt of mergansers and Pomeranians, pheasant hunters and muskrats. Ancient cottonwoods tower and bow, forming a Salisbury Cathedral ceiling. In winter, the sky is a wispy blue or cloudy peach through lead-dark trunks. Where the trail veers west, a federal sign says that the Nez Perce band of Chief Joseph came by here in 1877.

And the cathedral image falls away. The grandeur. The fancy. The memory of those tired, hunted families whose footsteps I follow reminds me that I'm invasive, the pirate, the thief, the obsession. I'm injury walking, trapped by my portion of Manifest Destiny, by the treaties the Five Hundred Nations made with the United States over the years that proved worse than worthless. The motive force of this country has been coercion: Give us your _____ (fill in the blank) or we will take it and kill you, which we might do anyway. As I learn from the old country songs, my OCD orders me around with that settler imperative: Bow to me, or I'll strip you of the best of your humanity. It's meant to keep me within a prison of its own devising. But just as the condemned murderer or bank robber sings of his confinement, so can the sufferer from OCD. Sometimes it's music that sasses back at power. Sometimes it's music that exposes the unjust voices in our heads.

How dare we make white people feel bad about history, some say.

I demur. Guilt is a luxury, but it's not a perk to *know* that my life and leisure have come at the cost of other humans' pain and displacement. The knowledge obligates me and explains in part my damaged nervous system. How can one be an occupier and not be askew?

My family's invader legacy traps me, and I want to escape the pathologies I attribute to it. I wish I could hear my dad's first halting Malagueña, my grandfather's singing, or my great-grandfather's organ playing. Maybe there was joy and promise in those early efforts. A possibility of merging. A whiff of transcendence. Sometimes I want to be a ten-year-old guitar-girl phenom again. I'd like to be able to approach an Apsáalooke drumming group and say, musician to musician, "I appreciate what you're doing with that harmony." But never do guitar tunes get stuck in my head as I walk. Only the catchy, kitschy, old country-pop melodies. I still see that flaw in the form of a "J" in the veneer of my family's console stereo, and I remember that, finally, the machinery burst into flame while I slept.

January at Sundance Lodge. Bernie, Luke, and I come from the shore of the denim river spilling over two flat ice shelves that tried to contain it. A storm curls in the west. To the north, on private land, is a harvested field, small tussocks and remnant stalks rippling and puncturing the snow. We turn to follow the snow-packed trail to a ruined outbuilding of the old farm that was donated to make this public space. As we admire the old barn, a community materializes in the field in front of us like Kadmos's stones. I stop and stare, squinting against the shine, the cold breeze, my watery eyes. It's uncanny. Rocks are springing from the snow.

My vision clears. The rocks become sharp-tailed grouse, a flock breaking from the powder, slipping toward a windbreak of cottonwoods. As they reach the field's end, they fling themselves one by one into the highest branches. There are fifteen, twenty, thirty-three. They peck at the buds. They work silently, a companionable group. The trees shake as they pull at next years' leaves. But there must be some signal. After fifteen or twenty minutes, the grouse take off together, no longer a column of marchers but an avian storm beating across the field, over the ever-changing river, into the middle distance until they're lost against the hillside, off to another part of their home. They apparently have rounds to make. One valedictory bird, like the choreographer of a brilliant grouse ballet, admires their progress before following, the last of all. With any luck, they'll be back in a day or a week.

TRAIL 19

Killing Coyote at Shepherd Ah-Nei, with SARS-CoV-2

General location: Shepherd, Montana; 199 miles from Yellowstone
Hiking distance: 5+ miles
Elevation: 3,300–3,500 feet
Terrain: Shortgrass prairie and ponderosa pine breaks

There's something about a feedlot. The black substrate—a mixture of mud, feces, and feed resembling a high-pile carpet kept ten years in the dark under a running swamp cooler. The unsavory office-cubicle arrangement where animals are set to fatten. The smell—a particulate-dense, aromatic miasma redolent of shit, clay, and leather. Above all, it's the fate of the cattle themselves. Their purpose is to be sold and eaten. Part of the imperative of progress, cattle in a feedlot are de-animated, their family sensibility eliminated, their destinies denied. They might as well be born in Styrofoam and cellophane.

The feedlot I have in mind is small, nestled beneath sandstone and marked by a stacked promontory of bare, sculpted rock layers, tilting at the top like any good Western landmark. We drive by after passing the ranchettes of Shepherd, Montana, ten miles or so to the north and east of Billings, a mile beyond the Feedlot Steakhouse and Razor Creek Saloon.

The road goes straight for a mile or so after that. I tick off sights that over the years have become familiar: a small sapphire-and-diamond water impoundment marked by a single cottonwood, now leafless; a group of colorful metal sculptures—Woody from *Toy Story*, minions from the eponymous movie, a dragon—at the front gate of an otherwise hidden manor; and finally the turn at the top of the hill into the ponderosas.

Bernie, Luke, and I leave the feedlot far behind as we pass through a more natural gate: a gap in the sandstone-rim playground once visited by shellfish and copepods—all long gone, eighty-five million years ago. Sandstone shelves rise on either side of us, and then it's a downhill glide to the BLM reserve called Shepherd Ah-Nei (pronounced "aw-KNEE"). The first section is open to off-road vehicles, motorcycles, and other motorized toys. It's eroded, noisy, crowded. Escaping COVID-19 pandemic rules in Billings, folks come here to tear up the land and get a thrill. They congregate in the dusty parking lot, disregarding "social distancing." Like some liberal fuddy-duddy, I'm annoyed by that.

I was taught to obey and be thoughtful. That's my Chamberlain inheritance. Care about order and decorum, not, as my mother would, because you don't want to stick out, but because it's the right thing to do. Beat yourself up if you fail, and rage against those who take advantage, like the "me-firsters" my dad used to curse when he drove—the people who'd go too fast or cut in front of him on the freeway.

The rest of Shepherd Ah-Nei, a few miles further up the road, is open to hiking and horseback riding. It's a glorious stretch of high prairie, sprinkled at the seams with ponderosas. No one is here. Progress and feedlots are forgotten. There are few rules to constrain the old animal instinct, the reptile brain, and no strangers to offend. We park and go through the rusty, barred gate, replacing the chain that holds it in place once we're inside (or outside).

It's March, but, like the parking lot, the trail is dusty. We've had piddling bits of snow and rain—nothing to speak of for two months now. Unlike optimist Bernie, I think end times: pestilence and drought. A major earthquake hit Salt Lake a few days ago, about six hundred miles south. It knocked the gold-leaf Angel Moroni off the LDS Temple. Three horsemen so far.

Today is beautiful with the usual purple overcast, blue at its edges. The Beartooth Mountains foam with clouds and snow on one horizon, and the Bull Mountains rise closer and barren on the other. The long grass is golden, flicking against my pantlegs.

We don't say much. It's a relief to get away from the pandemic. Luke clowns, trying to gulp coyote scat. He leaps and prances when he finds a promising turd but spits it out if we feign outrage. And so we go. Down to an old water trough, which is as close to the ORV range as we'll get. The motorized whine bounces in and out of a coulee, rattles an old windmill, and fades as we climb the hill.

We go through yet another gate and down an overgrown ranch lane, repurposed into a hiking and horse trail. Through use, it resolved into several ruts, each new one made perhaps when the ground was wet and the older ruts impassable. Like cattle, humans tend to follow each other, tearing up the land. Even when we think we're wildly original, we're usually walking in the same old tracks—physical, mental, spiritual.

I wonder if birds follow ruts, places where the currents are easy. Here, for instance, are chipping sparrows, come back to us from points south. Meadowlarks. A kestrel. A red-tailed hawk. The coronavirus dread loosens its fist. Spring asserts itself. The natural rhythm of the biosphere is a power humans haven't figured out how to erase. Not even my GAD can minimize the beauty of a mountain bluebird in his new navy jacket, which turns gemlike when the light is perfect. He perches by the trail, ready to find love and make the next generation.

I've been feeling like Cassandra. Or, at least, like my father's daughter, taking on the style of the Vissing-Chamberlains. Pessimism and caution. I know things are going to get bad for all of us, not just for the sardine-packed city dwellers I see on the news. But it doesn't seem like anyone's listening. There's the virus, yes, and the political situation as the United States and other countries crave antidemocratic regimes. Topsoils are thinning, and mass extinction is ripping life's weavings. Already, such common birds as western meadowlarks and even starlings are declining. And there's the ever-present, if often denied, doom of climate change. But who wants to hear this goody-two-shoes, preachy stuff? So, we're out where the birds and grasses know the score and keep working against it.

We designate a particular juniper as the farthest extent of our escape. Too soon we're standing at the turnaround point, tracing the hills, the ponderosas, the sandstone, and the purple gap of the river valley where Billings (with its still-early seven coronavirus cases) lies. Beyond that is the billions-of-years-old rock of the Beartooths.

It starts as a single guffaw. We stop our uphill climb toward the car and try to parse the sound. Another guffaw. A trill. We smile. Coyote. Luke, though, doesn't look scared or worried, as he does when he hears his unfathomable cousins. We resume walking, but the single notes gather force and urgency. Then there's a whine, a scream. It's odd, but the tone's familiar and canid.

We pass two horses, saddled and serene, tied to a tree. They rest, as horses do, with a bent back leg and a sleepy eye. They look well cared for; their blankets are bright and striped. They're free of panniers. Incongruously, down the gentle slope and out of sight, the coyote cries turn to wails and shrieks. Bernie thinks the coyote might be caught, and, city slickers that we are, we wonder if trappers have to club animals they find in order to save the pelts. (Later I read that most animals are finished off with a shot to the head.) Have the two horseback riders discovered a coyote den? Are they killing an entire family? Besides those of the suffering animal(s), there are no sounds, no human voices, no firearms.

My pandemic chill, my native cautiousness, my habitual anxious scanning for danger return. Raw sadism, like the casual constricted violence of the feedlot, raises my hackles. Trapping or shooting coyotes isn't against the rules, state or federal. Their lives count for little. After a while, the screams either stop or we're out of earshot. Shaken, we finish our hike, the final ascent taking us past a small flock of Bohemian waxwings and a familiar art installation that's been in place for about two years. Someone tacked the skull of a domestic bull to a ponderosa and painted two concentric circles on it—one red, one blue.

Thinking back on them now as I write, I still can't make the parts of that day fit. The two calm horses, dressed for recreation, not work. The mid-day coyote screams. Luke's lack of reaction. … Eureka! What if it was spring for more creatures than the bluebirds? What if all weren't lost? Maybe Chamberlain pessimism is not always healthy (well, of course, it isn't!).

I wonder if those screams weren't shrieks of murder and fear but cries of the wildest equestrians-turned-lovers we've ever run across. Yes, now I think that's what they were up to, their horses patiently waiting and Luke not hunkering beside me. The Newbys who lived downstairs from an apartment Bernie and I rented when we were newly married have always been my world champions of loving. They were marathoners, and they've held their title for thirty-six years. But they weren't loud during their two-hour sessions. These Shepherd Ah-Nei folks, if that's what they'd been doing, were something else.

Having tossed their riding clothes, wool socks, and boots across the grasses like so much trash, they went naked to the wind. Protected from sight only by a single hill, they pirouetted while prone, danced supine, pounced on each other. Out on the prairie, they wailed to a world bound to renew itself. Their horses were talismans of love.

I ask Bernie about this latest interpretation. He says he'll keep an open mind.

In the car again and on our way back to Billings, we don't turn the radio on. People are dying in Italy, France, Spain, and New York City. Our son and his family live in California, and the coronavirus ripples out from Los Angeles, San Francisco, Sacramento. In the silence after we glide past the feedlot again and its shadow of death, my grim Chamberlain mood has turned everything grim.

We pass the feedlot in the shadows now and turn onto the last straightaway beside the cutbank complexity of Razor Creek. How might I explain the smugness of the Harlan's hawk sitting at her usual post overlooking fallow spring fields?

TRAIL 20

Sensory Extenders at Norm's Island

General location: Norm's Island, Billings, Montana; 172 miles from Yellowstone
Hiking distance: Up to 3.4 miles round trip
Elevation: 3,150 feet
Terrain: River bottomland

Afterglow yellows and spreads like a silkscreened scarf. The Yellowstone River pulls from shore, and the trail crunches as if we're walking on snakeskin. Cicadas stridulate from wild licorice. City lights vanish behind the reclaimed and forested berm of an old gravel pit. Most humans have gone home. Luke will feel hurt when we come back smelling of Norm's Island, but dogs aren't allowed on this educational walk hosted by the Montana Audubon Center.

Megan O'Reilly, a wildlife biologist with Montana's Department of Fish, Wildlife, and Parks, has given us a few basic facts, and now we're testing things for ourselves on this island that hugs the shore. When we started, it was still light enough to see a beaver from the footbridge. The privately owned park has a checkered past with beavers, who like to chew cottonwoods, but for now the large rodent is free to work.

There are about thirty of us, some with small glowing boxes. We might have stepped out of an adventure film where night vision in the form of red LEDs turns up spies or assassins. We happen, though, to be looking for bats. Our devices make their ultrasonic hunting clicks audible.

Ordinarily we can't hear them at all, but with their calls stepped below 20 kHz, we might pick up an incisive four-part series that trails off into shorter bursts. Unfortunately, our instruments won't be sensitive enough to tell us what *kind* of bats we'll "hear."

I dutifully search for clicks, but, ever my father's daughter, I'm not hopeful. White-nose disease—caused by an invasive fungus that killed millions of bats in eastern North America—has made it to Montana. When flying mammals come out of hibernation to the incessant itch *Pseudogymnoascus destructans* causes, they burn energy reserves that should have seen them through winter. And they die. Moreover, the fungus can remain on surfaces for up to four years, continuing to infect any erstwhile survivors. Solitary tree dwellers are safer than cave and mineshaft communities. I like to think that the bats we might hear tonight will be those tree lovers, safer and healthier.

My detector finally lights up with the four tones I've been told to pay attention to. And then four more. And more. The bats are here, doing what they are supposed to do: filling their stomachs. According to O'Reilly, they can eat upwards of twelve hundred invertebrates per hour. Each. The little rascals.

Adding to my enthusiasm, I realize I've been walking without pain.

The problem started subtly, as many things do. I got out of bed one morning and my left foot wouldn't bend without a twinge. After I'd walked on it a bit, everything was fine. But the next morning was the same. And many mornings after that.

Over a month, the foot pain intensified and lasted till noon. And then all day. Each step was a carnival of heel aches. Treading on loose rock while hiking, I was hit by troglodytic target practice. I kept walking, though. What else could I do? I couldn't let anxiety get the upper hand—plus, Luke would jump up every afternoon during the Covid closures whenever I left my desk and put on my hat. His electricity compelled me to get outside. "It's a walk!" his tail announced, sweeping the stale indoor air. Surely, the whole painful foot thing would quit at some indeterminate point in the future.

But it didn't. That internal poniard stabbed every step. It drew my consciousness to my left heel. Everything contracted and stuck there in a two-inch-square patch. I was acutely aware of terrain, sticks, exposed roots, changes in grade. My foot was a detector of minute surface features.

I remember my dad reading up on medical conditions in the *Encyclopedia Americana* and a home medical guide my mother had bought in some ill-considered moment. The reading fed his hypochondria, offering multiple diagnoses from dire to benign. He usually chose the dire ones. I have often followed in his footsteps, ratcheting up anxiety. Until the foot thing happened. I realized I couldn't find and didn't really care about the provenance of my problem. As I scanned the internet to self-diagnose, podiatric anatomy left me baffled. Tarsus, metatarsal, calcaneus, phalanx (proximal, middle, distal), cuboid, malleolus, abductor digiti minimi muscle, peroneus longus. It was so confusing I couldn't even scare myself. And what about intelligent design? Hammer toes, bunions, corns, blisters, plantar fasciitis, pronation, heel spurs, neuropathy, ingrown toenails? I questioned the omnipotence of a being who engineered such a system. And I just wanted relief.

Not being able to walk without pain, even around flat and easy Norm's Island, was a nuisance, a sharpening of my plantigrade sensors. But for hominins of the past, it might have been a death sentence, changing to disaster the easy stroll documented by three australopithecines—seventy footprints fossilized at what is now Laetoli, Tanzania, some three-ish million years ago. Eons later, a human mother alternately carried her toddler and let the tyke walk across a then-lush landscape in what is now New Mexico. She and the child navigated with sloths, camels, wolves, mammoths, lions—all left sturdy footprints that would persist for twenty-three thousand years. It might be that, in those days, one didn't live in fear. One couldn't.

So, anxiety is perhaps not a residual condition from a hunter-gatherer past. Maybe it and foot pain are products of this civilized era and I the flawed descendant of hearty explorers who crisscrossed African savannah, western Asian desert, European forests, Western Hemisphere steppe as they gathered roots, berries, bird eggs, and mammoths. Less-distant forebears may have had a hand in making Stonehenge. I'd have been with you, my mothers and fathers, as you rolled, prodded, floated, or pushed sarsen stones to Salisbury Plain. As you barbecued hogs (archeologists have found a *lot* of pig bones onsite) and measured the solstice. And you, my LDS foremothers and forefathers, I'd have crossed the Great American Desert with you to reach Zion, or heaven on earth, in Great Salt Lake City. But if the adventure were happening today, you'd have left me with a week's rations by some cholera-tainted stream.

Technology came to my aid now. So, there was that. Intelligent design anticipated bad feet and created the mental acuity that fashioned wheels. Luke, though, wondered why I was riding a bicycle while he and Bernie walked a neighborhood street. As I circled back and let them catch up, I got to see Luke from the front, for a change. He'd almost mastered the leash, and he pranced, half-erect ears flopping comically, eyes eagerly focused on me, feeding my ego, of course. He pulled when I pedaled ahead and twisted to see when I circled behind. I was happy to bike, which didn't hurt my heel, but I didn't touch the ground. From the saddle, I saw farther but much less clearly.

Finally, I went to a podiatrist.

I think Chamberlains are supposed to walk. When I visited our native England, I found octogenarians who set a brisk pace—uphill, too. My Chamberlain great-grandfather would probably have fit right in. He left Leicester, England, ready, as he put it in his memoir, "for our six months' journey to Utah." After that perilous sail across the Atlantic and the packet boat crawl to Keokuk, Iowa, his family set out overland to Utah, but their wagon was full of his father's carpentry tools. So, as young John Marvin Chamberlain remembered it, he "chose to walk" and sometimes run. Summer prairies "were covered with grass and flowers" as he sprinted through them, the ponderous Appleton M. Harmon Company rolling behind. He loved straddling a "big white ox" to cross creeks and rivers. After one of the other animals "stepped on" his foot, he had to ride for a day in the leader's wagon. He proudly explains, "With that only exception, I walked all the way to Salt Lake City" at a pace of fifteen to twenty-five miles a day.

His father "was an expert hunter" who helped feed the company. John witnessed the downing of "ducks, rabbits and prairie chickens" and even watched his dad singlehandedly kill and butcher a bison. Unselfconsciously, he remembered how "buffalo [were] so plentiful that they almost covered the prairie like a black cloud as far as the naked eye could reach." He doesn't mention how those herds smelled or sounded. How much, in fact, did he miss? Spiraling curlews' whistles? Prairie wolves' howls? He was a young English boy, his ears not primed for those sounds. He couldn't understand the greetings of polite Indigenous people and didn't see their stewardship at work in the health of the bison herds. The highlight of his long walk was meeting a supply wagon out of Fort Bridger, full of fresh vegetables from Great Salt Lake City: "The man [on the wagon] handed me a carrot and it was more delicious than any candy I had tasted before, or since." His first view of Deseret encompassed "the waters of its big inland sea shining in the rays of the setting sun." Walking for so long, it seems, enhanced his senses of taste and sight.

Once, unlike my great-grandfather and other pioneer ancestors, I cultivated and cherished a sedentary existence. An indolent college student, an impractical English major, no less, I read books all one summer and lolled in my parents' backyard in a cheap chaise longue, which I moved from shady patch to shady patch as the day advanced. I wonder what my great-grandfather would have thought about that lazy use of a sacred town, and I wonder equally what my work-ethic-serious mother thought when, preparing the pot roast or scouring pans, she looked out the kitchen window and saw me adrift on the lawn, mostly reading but occasionally studying a yellow warbler or light in the birch leaves.

No doubt the books I gobbled that summer of lollygagging helped me see and think farther than I could have alone. I was ambitious in that way. Mann's *Magic Mountain*. Globs of Dostoevsky and Tolstoy. George Eliot's *Romola*. Dreiser's hefty *An American Tragedy*. Probably a pastry course of *Les Fleurs du Mal*. I had a taste for the past, and those books took me there. The most important, though, was *The Tibetan Book of the Dead,* which obliterated time. I read it as a manifesto of liberation, the idea of the Bardo showing me how, when I was between lives, I'd be able to resist the various traps and demons seeking to tie me to what I'd known as "reality." I was gratified to find a religion in which fear was considered limited and unreal, a screen keeping "truth" prisoner.

The other prolonged time when I didn't walk was no idyll. I was pregnant and worked at a lumberyard in far northern California. At first, I went on foot to my job as a bookkeeper and home again when my shift was done. Sometimes I drove. Once during the weeks in which I had a bout of morning sickness, I threw up in the middle of the street. A neighbor's dog gave me a cunning smile. "Ah," I almost heard him saying, "I know just what that feels like."

Then I came down with early labor. My job was to keep the baby in utero for at least six more weeks. To effect this, I took a medicine that sped up my pulse, obliging me to lie on my right side to ease my heart. All day. All night. I could only get up to eat, go to the bathroom, brush my teeth. We had a few books, a boombox, and a thirteen-inch TV. The only static-free radio station was from Humboldt State University, which owned something like three albums, all folk music. For some reason, I later bought my own Silly Wizard LP. The town's sole TV channel aired Spookman Dan horror shows. I learned all the commercials by heart and still remember one catchphrase: "Max G. Arnold, a superior attorney." Strangely, I had little anxiety and no OCD during this time. Sure, I worried. Would the baby be healthy? But I had a mission, and that consumed all my thoughts.

As soon as the baby, born an acceptable four weeks early, was old enough, we wandered around town. I was, at best, a fearful mother. The walking was my postpartum salve and fit the level of fatigue I dragged through every day. That 6 a.m. feeding—when I'd finally reached REM sleep—was the toughest. But when I'm called on to do something, I seem to be able to do it. As when, at the other end of life's spectrum, I cared for my mother, let out of the hospital way too early following a craniotomy.

Somehow I learned to get her up, feed her, help her to the bathroom, cook for her, clean up her vomit. Fears of harming her only burst out when she was doing much, much better and less was required of me. The worries I'd had changed into images of her fireplace tools landing with force on her bald, stitched head, with my own hand directing the blow. I loathed myself all over again. More than loathed. I terrorized myself. Somehow I hung on, maybe because the mission was still clear: Keep Mother safe. I rarely went near the living room, and if I did, never looked at the wicked iron poker. I took walks when she was well enough to be left alone and read Jane Austen's *Emma* until I slept. Even as I write this, fifteen years later, the fear tightens my throat. Thankfully, my sister soon came to relieve me.

I was a would-be escapee from my own thoughts. I'd have left that mental country entirely if I could have, which gives me a hint—if only a slight one—of why people leave their homes when life there becomes unbearable. All over the world, refugees walk, not for aesthetics or personal health but to escape climate change, murderous regimes, economic oppression. By foot, by boat, across mountains, and through deserts, people leave their supplies, their hopes, and sometimes their bones along the tortured routes of their attempted escapes. They're hated and reviled, turned back at international borders: a desperate father carrying his little daughter hundreds of miles, worn flip-flops carving blisters on his skin; a woman longing for her cat, left behind, as she hides in a makeshift tent at night, the camp prowled by rapists and traffickers. Walking is the only relief they know. They have no time for reflection. They just have to move—and if they can't, it means they're either safe or never will be safe.

With my own walking difficulties, minor as they were, the pain was confined, and I was lucky to have a home and medical care. Still, I griped about it. The podiatrist I eventually visited gave me a steroid shot and sent me off, but the ache persisted. Another shot, and my heel remained hex screw-ridden. He proposed experimental shockwave therapy. The theory behind it was that causing more inflammation would rouse my immune system, which would remember to fight the original inflammation it had given up on. The machine for delivering this was a printer-looking box with a sort of gun attachment aimed at my heel. The treatment felt like ten-inch-long wasps stinging plantar nerves I didn't know I had. Would such a treatment work for OCD—stir up the harmful thoughts to obliterate them one by one? Don't think I'll try it. Fighting *them* is counterproductive—like trying to deck a grizzly with your fists. The best thing to do is to shrink them. "I'm on to you," I say. And they shrivel.

The ache persisted. The shockwave treatment course was about run. And then, one morning, my foot was almost okay. There were echoes of pain, shadows of achiness, twinges that whispered the onset of another bout. But I walked for several yards without being aware of my heel.

A month later I was almost back to normal, setting one foot in front of the other, seeing what was new, getting my hair wind scrambled, watching Luke trot ahead of me then find or make up some destination as he ran through the wild licorice at Norm's Island (the only place I let him go leashless), as he tore down the embankment to the river and returned for a treat. I was bound to see something rare—a hooded merganser, maybe, preening at nearby Lake Josephine. "Nearby," I could say now, despite still cataloging humans' faulty equipment. Upright posture. Scoliosis, lordosis, kyphosis of the spine. Vertebrae that compress and herniate. Nerves that sting. Torn ACLs. Troublesome feet. Limited vision. Seriously impaired high-frequency hearing (compared to what your average bat can discern). Misfiring brains. Self-destroying societies.

Walking beside the Yellowstone River again weeks after the bat excursion, with just my own unenhanced senses, I wondered about the little creatures sleeping under the bridge or in the cottonwoods. Without a detector, I'd probably see only one or two whirling through the dusk. In addition to that, how many tansy flowers and moths would I miss? What would owls notice that I couldn't? Would ants catalogue the chemistry of the world at my feet?

I think I know why cultures spin and sanction—even encourage—beliefs that obscure reality. They become subconscious images to live by, keeping humans from feeling or thinking too much, quashing natural empathy. We can't dwell on the deaths of millions of bats, can we? Or, for that matter, the sufferings of humans we have very little contact with—those in other cultures, for example. We'd go insane if we did. Thus, the curtailing of our perceptual abilities, the stricture against assigning emotional lives to many categories of beings. This prohibition is useful in enabling and justifying exploitation of the soulless inhabitants of the earth by those of us who do have souls—as defined by us, of course.

A few weeks ago, a crow sat on a fiber-optics box at a neighborhood intersection along the route of my again-usual morning walk, squawking without letup. I wondered why, until I saw the decimated body of another on the lawn near my feet; all that was left were outstretched wings, sprung and broken. The next day, I found a crow silently staring at the remains of the dead. I don't know how the bird felt, whether it was the same crow, or what the vigil involved. Meanwhile, cars drove by and no other humans paid attention. If all the deaths caused by traffic were tallied and recognized, no man or woman would get in a car again. So, culture carves out a space for us in which to act and dulls our senses, and the delusion that humans of certain groups are the only beings who count allows societies to function or, at least, careen from disaster to disaster. That same delusion enabled my Chamberlain great-grandfather—a kindly man—to watch his father slaughter a bison and later proudly tell about it. It allowed him to plant his own music on top of the songs of Shoshone residents of the Great Basin. It must be that, even for the Chamberlains of Leicester, immigration was a desperate gambit, not the pure nomadic joy of walking with giant ground sloths and mammoths and buffalo but the flight from political, economic, and environmental danger toward safety and promise.

The efficacy of mass fictions is clear. Defending home turf is a powerful incentive against tolerance. But why do personal obsessions still grip me and others like me, turning us into perpetual immigrants? I fear the world inside my head and miss the many hundreds of sensory borders outside it that I might cross. Yet I try to hear and see farther; walking is a kind of compulsion that offers real destinations.

As my mother lay dying at eighty-three in a care-center bed in Billings, and I sat beside her after a long day of witnessing her effort to stay in this world and an equally long evening while I talked to her and kept the lamp burning, something changed, some loss of desperation in her death struggle and my vigil. It occurred to me that she probably wanted to rest. It was one in the morning, after all. The nurse had assured me that the active dying process can take days. So, I kissed my mother, turned off the light, and resolved to stay awake beside her in the bedside chair. My sister, taking a well-deserved coffee break, would join me again soon.

Almost immediately, a whirl of voices came toward me from some far parsec of space. As it approached, the sonic upheaval grew round and heavy with an urgency that pressed me to the chair. I had no idea what it was. A globe of words, I could say. A joyous hum. It reached us with my mother's last exhalation, crescendoed, and vanished. In the resulting silence, I had the distinct impression that it took her with it. Because that was the moment she chose to leave, her dying energetic, a leap upward to join a spiritual engine of ancestral chants that my hyperawareness, unclouded right then by OCD or GAD, stepped down for me to hear. The sociable hubbub left me awestruck, and she joined it happily. I had no fear for her then. My mother died, I could say, ambitiously and well, shortly after I kissed her goodnight.

People have endured much more inherited and personal trauma than I have, so why does OCD grip *my* brain? The puzzle of this disease boils down to why me, why you, or why not this other person? So far, I can pin causality on a few epigenetic propensities and the liminal position of being neither Indigenous nor conscience-free occupier, neither LDS nor atheist nor believer. Being female in this culture doesn't help. Anxiety and obsessions feed on a desire for definition, certainty, and control. They make me observant, put me on the *qui vive*, as *Thirty Days to a More Powerful Vocabulary* would have it.

Sometimes as I walk, I look back to see what kind of footprints I'm making and to wonder what the next traveler might think of them. They seem part of a family chain. Tripp, Chamberlain, *Homo sapiens*, primate, mammal, vertebrate, animal. My extended family, all travelers of one sort or another.

Footprints rarely last. They're obliterated by other walkers' tracks, or, if fossilized and then uncovered, they erode. Those footprints at Laetoli and in White Sands, New Mexico? Precious because life moves, and they contradict that movement in the most ironic way. I fear change, but at our best we humans are time travelers. In the scheme of eons, we spin like dust, like bats, like cosmic immigrants.

TRAIL 21

West Fork, Where I Realize My Dad Was a Success

General Location: Red Lodge, Montana, Beartooth Mountains; about 70 miles from Yellowstone
Hiking distance: 12 miles round trip to Sundance Lake
Elevation gain: 350+ feet
Terrain: Lodgepole pine and fir forest to krummholz

Lightning nicked the ground a few miles behind us, and thunder scraped my nerves. The storm wasn't something to discuss—what could we do about it? Besides, talking would slow our pace. We put our heads down and hiked.

We'd been out three days. We'd driven the freeway and a maze of dirt roads through sagebrush flats to reach the trailhead. We'd walked ten miles in and were on our eighth out. We'd met the indescribable green of Dead Horse Lake in the Uinta Mountains. We'd slept to the sound of running spring water. We'd talked to squirrels and pikas. Now we were tired, trudging through wet pasture in wet boots. We were also hungry; in those days, freeze-dried dinners were barely edible. But we had a storm at our backs. We were on our way home. We carried gifts benign and terrifying: images of wildflowers, sunrises through Douglas-fir, snowfields, and atmospheric kilowatts.

One of just a few backpacking trips I'd make with my dad, our adventure had been troubled by a loud crew of Boy Scouts, by the cereal I'd packed for our lunches—not realizing how *dry* dry cereal is in the absence of milk—and by soggy, rainy nights. I thought the trip was about me and testing my anxious limits. The electrical storm fit right into my expectations.

Decades later, I'm on my way to another lightning round. I'm not sixteen. I'm with Bernie and Luke. I'll not be in the Uintas. But mountain elements are the same in Utah and Montana. Rock, wildflowers, streams, weather. The inevitable pilgrim's trail to the wild.

No one just drops you into the heights. For most Americans, the first leg usually involves a car. Unfortunately. To reach the Uintas' north slope from Salt Lake, my dad notched a corner of Wyoming. He was a good driver, and I didn't worry about anything in that long, suspended lull before our adventure. Getting to the West Fork of the Beartooths from Billings today, by contrast, takes only an hour and a half. I drive southwest along billboard-littered I-90 to the foothills. Bernie will drive home.

Long ago, the only urban tangle after Salt Lake and the exit from I-80 was Evanston, home of the Wyoming State Hospital. Past Evanston was sage flat and mountains and dirt road. Today, leaving the freeway at Laurel for Highway 212 promises a similar world without big-box stores or refineries. Transcendence pends, starting with the crossing of the Yellowstone River. Beyond that, ranchettes become farms, and people's lives gather in two nodes—the towns of Joliet and Roberts, which turn again into farms that turn into cottonwood groves, and then we're in Red Lodge, the last vortex of human "progress." I drive through town, turn past the ski resort, leave metastasizing trophy and vacation home subdivisions, and reach the end of "private" land. After the thick lodgepole stands of the West Fork canyon mouth, we enter a burn—everything from here to the trailhead and beyond transformed by the 2008 Cascade Fire. A disaster, we might think. An insult to the enduring sameness unanxious people expect from "nature" and, really, all the circumstances of our lives. But while it might perturb a human sensibility, fire nourishes insect-loving birds. Olive-sided flycatchers toast "Hic, three beers!" from burned hillsides; mountain bluebirds mate on bare limbs; and hairy woodpeckers, like binge-eaters, chase snag-dwelling prey so greedily that soot from the charred bark they've been rummaging through stains their white breast feathers gray.

For most of my teen years, my sanctum was Utah's Wasatch Mountains (our Uintas trip was anomalous and very ambitious), and my hiking partner was my dad. My mother stayed home. After leaving a ranch childhood at the age of seven, she never wanted to "rough it" again. She put scented soaps in her lingerie drawer and filed her nails every evening while watching *Mannix* or *Hawaii Five-O*. My sister preferred *not* crossing improvised log bridges or fending off mosquitoes that seemed interested only in her. So, it was usually my dad and me. I'd spent a year or so transitioning from calling him "Daddy" to the more mature "Dad," but as we walked, he was the adventurer, the wanderer, the Navy vet identified only by the initials of his name.

We didn't just hike, though. We collected transformative vistas. TMC conserved his energy by strolling as if he were walking a city sidewalk. He didn't like going through forests, but he would to get to the overlook, the summit, the ridge, the old juniper jutting above a thousand-foot chasm. Once, we went to Logan Canyon, Utah, to see the world's largest limber pine, and he was disappointed. The venerable being was one of a grove—not a lone giant with roots scrabbled down through a rocky promontory.

There's no rare limber pine or other superlative giant for Bernie and Luke and me today. But because every square inch is beautiful, the West Fork is the queen of Beartooth Mountain hikes. It starts at more than seventy-nine hundred feet. You can get a long way in without expending much effort—in six miles you gain only 350 feet in elevation. The trail can be "hiked through," over Sundance Pass and into the Lake Fork drainage to the south, but, like most people, I've never gone the full, eventually grueling nineteen miles, not even close.

In a recapitulation of my hiking partnership with TMC, a duo is coming down the West Fork trail as Bernie, Luke, and I start up. The father says he's been hiking here since he was twelve, and now he's brought his son. They'd spent four days backpacking, glissading ice fields, jumping into Sundance Lake, and scrambling over rocks. They're thinking of town and pizza, a final mountain-initiation rite. I nod, remembering a blessed hamburger in Evanston, Wyoming, after TMC's and my escape from the Uinta lightning storm. That back-to-civilization grease ball was the best I'd ever eaten.

Before he married, TMC joined the Wasatch Mountain Club (WAMOC)—a pioneering outdoor group. He may have signed up for the scenery and the adventure, but I think he wanted to meet adventure-loving girls. A black-and-white photo shows him in jeans jacket, cigarette in hand, looking dreamily at the camera. I never knew that man. Nor did I know the fellow on wooden skis at Germania Pass. Or that British heart-throb on the Ben Lomond trail, posing with a curly blond lass in shorts.

In stumbling across a few online, archival WAMOC publications, I'm surprised that TMC was not always at the forefront of climbing expeditions, as I'd have expected, given his fearless ability to scale knife ridges. In 1952, according to the *WAMOC Rambler*, he was one of three who "admired the mountains from their painting positions on the green roof" of the club's Brighton-area lodge. He was helping to weatherize the place—in my experience, he abhorred physical labor, doing it well but grudgingly. Another edition of the *Rambler* notes that one of his watercolors was raffled off, with high praise, at a party. His oil paintings from that era were slashes of rock and foliage—powerful but with errors of perspective. I never knew he used watercolors.

My dad inherited artistic passions. In addition to picking up classical guitar as an adult, he had sudden enthusiasms about Respighi and Andrew Wyeth and took perfectly exposed photos in the days when you worked with tables and light meters. Bursting with raw talent, he'd been accepted at the Pennsylvania Academy of the Fine Arts after the war. But he dropped out to become a civil engineer and avoid starvation. He told me he stood outside a closed gallery one night studying the paintings on display, which he thought were better than he could do. They were selling for a pittance. Figuring he lacked the stamina to face a lifetime of monetary and artistic disappointment, he saw the moment of his greatness flicker. I don't think TMC ever recovered. At least not fully. His tonic was hiking in the Wasatch Range. He even learned to be patient about my wildflower ecstasies, about the mint and black-eyed Susans twining below aspen trunks.

How vibrant life is almost fifty years after my Uinta trip, even in blackened woods. July butterflies—Western fritillaries, blues, painted ladies, angle wings—drift like painted ashes, tangle in ascending vortices, fan themselves on logs and horse manure, and are as flashy as the wildflowers—spikes of fireweed; rafts of mertensia, or mountain bluebells; pink-edged wintergreen; streamside Parry's primrose.

Luke, attached by a lead to my waist, pulls me forward, freezes, and lurches ahead, as always. His tail is up, ears cocked as we move through waves of floral perfume. After the Cascade Fire and the stripping away of forest shade, the smaller plants seem to have doubled down, pioneering new sites as if the world depends on them. And maybe it does.

Soon Luke resigns himself to my pace. In the heat of the open burn, his tail droops until he finds a runnel and goes in, paws and muzzle first, for a pick-me-up.

A WAMOC newsletter from 1953 reports that Tom Chamberlain was not an "ambitious climber" on a fall outing to Lake Blanche but that he and two companions (one female) "contented themselves with a lazy restful day beside one lake or another." There were other trips—to Mount Nebo and Mount Timpanogos. A *Rambler* from November 1955, a year after his marriage, identifies him as Lodge Director (having jumped to that position from Mountaineering Director) and includes his humorous report on "the annual wood gathering trip," featuring a chainsaw that "resisted efforts to make it run."

By the time TMC and I hiked, those WAMOC days were the stuff of legend. Utah's climbing elite still sent him Christmas cards, and I often went through his 3-D slides of a week he'd spent in the Wind River Mountains. Sitting on the cold basement floor in front of a cupboard where we stored such things, I'd open the door and pull out a precious box of two-paned positives in stainless steel rectangles, and the binocular viewer would insert me into those mountain meadows and onto his route up Fremont Peak.

Once, he'd almost summited the Grand Teton, turned back just short of his goal by icy weather. He'd suffered frostbite—an event that soured him on mountaineering. The closest I ever came to those days was when I got my courage up to climb Mount Superior in the Wasatch, overlooking Alta and Snowbird ski resorts—the scariest ascent TMC and I made together, along a deeply exposed ridge. Dad was steady and reassuring; he had a reputation for talking people through mountain nerves.

Thankfully, on the West Fork trail the plateaus rise gently and the valley is broad. Oh, a young TMC would have been crazy to get to the top of Mount Wood, Granite Peak, or Whitetail Peak, but I've never been eager to dangle by pitons or to strap on crampons. Bernie and I like walking through flowers and looking at birds. Luke likes finding strange snacks and smells.

Today starts out sunny and warm. I wonder if I'm going to make it with my hot-flash-prone metabolism. This isn't something Bernie would understand, obviously, and he swings easily along, stopping only to take a photo of a pine trunk sculpted by fire into a humanistic form with its base hollowed and its top broad. I figure if I keep walking, the rhythm itself will take over and the hot flashes will come and go without my noticing much. Luke keeps me on task. A current of excitement charges his spine even when he's walking sedately.

TMC quit the Wasatch Mountain Club in part because he didn't need to meet women anymore, in part because my mother didn't enjoy it. Naturally, she resented his hoarded photos of trailside girlfriends. But roughing it wasn't really for Dad. He was an urbanite at heart, descended from a line of British urbanites—an aesthete gathering views, not a mountaineer bagging peaks. A "flaneur," maybe (and that would make me a budding "flaneuse"). We prowled downtown alleys in Salt Lake, admiring historic brickwork. TMC pointed out keystones and decorative patterns.

Salt Lake has plenty of historic architecture: the Promised Valley Playhouse, the Devereaux Mansion, the Victorian Boston and Newhouse buildings, the Gothic McCune Mansion, the Eagle Gate and Lion House, and the Tabernacle (another touring aesthete, Oscar Wilde, called that domed concert hall a "soup-kettle" and compared it to Covent Garden in size). Above all was the Salt Lake LDS Temple, part Disney's Sleeping Beauty Castle and part Loire château. With less aplomb and less conversational glibness, TMC followed in Oscar Wilde's footsteps. And in Mark Twain's, who also made a visit to the curious home of the Saints and paused long enough to write a few pithy observations regarding Brigham Young. TMC fancied himself a quaint figure, an Edwardian gentleman, perhaps. We had philosophical conversations: Can beauty exist without being experienced? Is beauty always good? What is beauty, anyway? What made the Pfeifferhorn in the Wasatch such a pleasing form? And what made that pleasing form compel my dad to climb it?

After I left home for graduate school, TMC hiked with friends on occasion. But, at fifty-nine, he was diagnosed with lung cancer, which ended his mountain travels forever. After surgery, the oncologist told us that for someone with one remaining lung, my dad still had a large respiratory capacity—a fact my mother, sister, and I attributed to his WAMOC years. In the months between his retirement and his death, TMC sketched pages of lonely trees—cypresses, junipers, valley oaks, bristlecone pines, weeping willows. He'd often been able to ignore his hypochondria in his search for beauty, and now he used beauty against mortality.

My interaction with the West Fork trail is comforting, especially since we've almost made it to the cooler, unburned forest. My boots press the soil; my retinal cones register wood-lily orange; my dermal nerves calibrate the sun's heat and the trickle of sweat down my back; my tympanum sorts mountain chickadee, swooshing creek, human speech vibrations; the olfactory epithelium of my nose catalogs wild mint and Douglas-fir molecules. I'm alert for danger—moose, bear, thunder. The twist of a largish garter snake catches my breath. Almost as ecstatic as Luke is with all the odors and tastes he must be gathering, I radiate energy—and the world gives it back. Unlike Luke, I don't grab mouthfuls of grass.

When the burn ends, the creek hides behind a screen of needles. Hollow-sounding traverses echo my steps. Sentinel Falls shakes and vibrates. Farther along, a spring fans a single boulder with a Zen-like sheet. The first larkspurs purple a hillside that goes up to Red Lodge Creek Plateau. Three and a half miles in, a wide, slow place in the river attracts lush willows where Lincoln's sparrows or spotted sandpipers hunt. We let Luke splash at Quinnebaugh Meadows, and then we keep going until the medieval cathedral of Whitetail Peak comes out with its cross of snow, delicate clerestory, and golden, sun-gathering steeple. My dad would have appreciated those classic lines. Another widening of the creek before the switchback-climb to the pass is Sundance Lake, our pilgrimage's destination. One of TMC's sentinel pines, a whitebark, marks the krummholz, its trunk convoluted, its roots doubled into the rock.

The Wasatch Mountains were TMC's tonic after he lost his design career to international macroeconomics—that was the era when he and I hiked almost every weekend throughout the summer. But reading those old *WAMOC Ramblers* and especially TMC's account of wood-gathering, I realize that I didn't know him much. Not the young man full of hope, sociability, and adventure. The TMC I knew was like the cypresses or bristlecone pines he sketched: sculpted by weather, covered with a layer of sorrow and disappointment, leaning over an abyss, waiting for the fire. Hiking kept him pliable.

On the last camping trip I made with my dad, that one to Canyonlands National Park, I wore a halter top and shorts for fifteen miles of sandstone and dry washes, and I got so sunburned I couldn't lie in a sleeping bag or even eat that final night at the campground. I was nauseated and had chills. My dad didn't say anything critical. Didn't make me feel feckless. He packed up our tent, replaced our supplies in the car following precisely the reverse order in which they'd come out, and drove us to a motel in Moab. He paid for two rooms, and maybe he was glad he'd have a mattress and solitude that night as well.

I used to attribute all my anxiety to my dad's struggles and the lack of self-esteem I thought I'd inherited. Now I see in his sadness and hypochondria the traumas his mother passed down to him. But I realize too, many years later, that despite his patina of disappointment and failure, my dad was, in all the ways that matter, a success.

Camping that one time in the Uintas, I saw him irrepressible—someone, I understand now, to emulate and even admire. I wish I'd realized that then. When I write this, it shames me that I missed my chance to tell him so. But there's an inkling of something helpful in this realization. Maybe I'm no slouch myself, not with a dad like that. And, so, maybe I can be a success, too. It's a heady and liberating thought, but I'm not yet ready to accept it. I have too much of my mother in me for that. Do not love yourself until you have accomplished … X. An X that will never happen. Or, if it does, there'll be Y to achieve and then Z. And so on. Life is a battle against oneself, "fighting the good fight," as she used to say. But not, I understood, ever winning. (I doubt she'd approve of my occasional 3 a.m. dose of Xanax.) For her, OCD would have been a manifestation of weakness. If you try anything, Oscar Charles Dawson tsks, you'll screw up, in unimaginably horrendous ways. I have to admit it takes willpower for me to hike. Especially in a group where I might come up short. On the other hand, a hike with just my dad or with Bernie presupposed then, and requires now, no heroic feats of courage. Beyond the usual, that is.

It comes to pass that the clouds I've been watching tumble together over the Beartooth Plateau fill up the once-persistent blue spots that gave me confidence and conjured hot flashes. Still, we chat with a party of horseback riders until . . . a crack of thunder cleaves our words. At least I haven't seen lightning yet—the thought, of course, bringing it on just short of Sundance Lake. At my insistence, Bernie, Luke, and I race downhill chased by a volley of thunder and echoes and thunder, the wind kicking up, and the first tentative drops of rain. And more rain—serious now. And hail. And icy, Styrofoam-pellet graupel. And it seems that Bernie, in the lead, takes us into the storm, because it's brighter behind and darker before. But I can't talk over the thunder, and for a while I stumble along as Luke ploughs into growing puddles on the trail, puddles that become small tarns. He even gulps the luscious mix of horse dung and mud and water. His tail is up, ears alert.

He races, stops, prances. Having a grand time, and pulling me through muck that's now a stream. We're right below the thunder, but lightning remains high along Silver Run Peak.

Watching Luke's antics, I miss my dad's imperturbability. In the Uintas all those years ago, lightning spread out along the West Fork of Black's Fork like a wavery electric curtain. "What'll we do?" I'd asked at first. We seemed self-sufficient *and* helpless, with only our backpacks and hiking boots as tools. We were miles from the car.

"Keep walking," my dad shrugged.

Here was a man who felt beaten and crumpled at the end of almost every day at the dull job that replaced his creative one. Here was a man who felt he should have lived in his grandparents' England, who longed unreasonably for Los Angeles and the soft air of the Pacific Coast. Who'd been disappointed in just about everything he tried. Who often felt he was "coming down with something." But in the face of unrelenting mountain weather, here was a man I'd trust. "It's amazing how well the body works in the mountains," he'd said after our first night under the stars.

We kept walking.

When Bernie hears my question about going back up the trail, he asks if *I* want to. Hell, *I* don't know. So, we descend—at a rather breakneck pace. I'm swearing silently and thinking of storm-mortality statistics, and I'm fighting off the true enemy—my own swelling ego. The lightning is after *me*! My dad would have understood my fear, would have gutted it out. But Bernie seems oblivious to the danger. If lightning actually smote me, he'd shrug in wonderment and murmur, "I guess these things happen?" as he stood over my charred remains. I have no idea what Luke would do. Perhaps he'd eat me, charbroiled to perfection. I don't admit that lightning would take us all out.

We catch up to another group of hikers, and the six of us tag team down the trail. In a way, it's friendly that we're together. On the other hand, I wonder if six humans will attract lightning more than two. (Of course, humans don't *attract* lightning, my logical brain assures me.) Finally, it's brighter in front of us, and, possibly, the thunder is moving to another drainage. Possibly. I don't want to jinx things. We stop to put on raingear. I'm already soaked and so's Bernie. Luke's a muddy wet rag on four legs.

And then it's over. And I've survived. Lightning apparently didn't think I was *that* important. *We've* survived, I correct myself. Shrink, ego! Lightning has exfoliated my spirit, though, revealing my most inward fear: being seen. My dad used to warn against taking IQ tests. His score, he said, was so high that nothing he did in life ever seemed enough. He'd wasted his talents. And, in fact, his college transcript shows row after row of solid Cs and Bs.

I followed his advice and have deftly avoided IQ tests as well as many other official instruments of measurement. While I doubt my results would be high, I find this avoidance of challenge a good way to go. Mediocrity is better than trying and failing. Anxiety, OCD, and the constant mental movies of me being incompetent, cruel, or evil keep me out of the spotlight, out of the lightning path. I did not become a wildlife biologist as I wanted to, because I knew I would struggle with calculus. I might have even failed. I did not pursue a PhD because I would have had to take exams and be grilled by a panel of specialists. I might have failed. I don't drive alone on the freeway because I might not be able to do it. I don't fly alone because I might start panicking and make a spectacle of myself. When I first went to a psychologist for anxiety, she asked me why I was clinging to the chair I sat in. And I realized that I was. Would it hold me up? Another counselor insisted that OCD was there to protect me, which I never understood, until now when I see what she meant. Nothing is more important than keeping myself under wraps. If I don't, I might be shown to be a failure, just like TMC thought he was. Lightning will strike. And yet I've survived today by being cautious, I think, congratulating myself for my perspicacity. If it'd been up to him, I'll bet Bernie would have gone on higher, up to the very base of Whitetail Peak. When I ask him how he puts up with me, though, he counter-asks how I put up with him.

We devour the lunch we'd planned for Sundance Lake. Luke munches his kibble, spiked with a treat or two. I reassure myself that I made the right decision by looking toward the heights, where it's now socked in.

We dawdle to the trailhead, finding things we missed earlier. Chilled butterflies hide under leaves or logs—only a couple drift in the freshened air. But mushrooms have come out, especially giant orange boletes. Either they've jumped from the wet soil, or they show up only when you go down the trail, after you've earned them.

All the way back to our car, our jeans below orange ponchos are so wet they weigh about ten pounds per leg. Luke's stretched harness hangs around his waist. He looks like a bedraggled rodeo horse with a cinch strap, Bernie says. Or perhaps a clever dog Houdini wriggling out of his bonds. And I guess that's my task, too, now. Shaking loose for a minute, an hour, a day, a year.

Here's how I hope you'll picture my dad. On this short hike in our friendly old Wasatch, we've had good weather and good luck. Swinging a makeshift alpenstock, he reaches the summit of Sugarloaf Mountain. A green fishing hat covers his balding scalp; his plaid cotton shirt hangs from his broad shoulders damp with sweat; dark glasses screen his eyes. Cecret Lake sparkles a few hundred yards below, and in the clear sunny air Twin Peaks, Devil's Tower, Mount Superior, the Valley Twins, the Pfeifferhorn, and, past American Fork Canyon, Mount Timpanogos—all the peaks he's climbed—punch at the sky. Revealing the British gap between his front teeth, he smiles at his mountains.

"We should do Red Baldy next time," I say, thinking that it wouldn't be a technical climb, not even a hard one.

"We should," he says, eyeing the gentle, round, neighboring summit.

FOUR

The Gifts of Walking

TRAIL 22

Pygmy Panther and Insurrection 2021

General location: Warren, Montana; south slope of the Pryor Mountains; about 105 miles from Yellowstone
Hiking distance: 4.5+ miles
Elevation: up to 800 feet
Terrain: Juniper and sage with sandstone canyon

I see them almost every day from Billings, forty miles to the south. The Pryor Mountains. Getting closer to them hasn't gotten any easier than it was last year. Or the year before. Or in the 1990s, when we lived in Wyoming and they rose to our north. It's never been a straight shot from here to there. The main route to the cooler north slope and the Sage Creek Campground—the only "official" campground in that entire region of the Custer-Gallatin National Forest—is often soupy. Even four-wheel-drive trucks can slide and bog down. If it's not a morass, the road is corrugated by foot-deep ruts, dating from the soupy times, that have solidified and that a driver has to straddle to avoid high centering. It's much easier to curl around the mountains' west flank on Highway 310, as we're doing now, and head east to the spare, south-facing arid canyons.

We turn off the highway at the "town" of Warren, most easily identified by its location across from the Montana Limestone processing plant. The forlorn spot consists of the plant and a tarpaper house that used to shelter a couple of loose-jointed dogs and dreams of success before burning halfway down a few years ago. The house is still there, more or less stove-in and surrounded by a ragtag but somehow growing collection of cars and trucks. To the west of the ruin is the habitation of, occasionally, at least one snipe. That is, there's a slough of sorts with four or five cattails and lime-green grasses.

Past Warren, the road to the Pryors' south slope is, at first, a fine, paved thoroughfare, widening as the years go by to accommodate more and more trucks from the quarry that feeds the limestone plant, which produces "chemical grade" chunks in various sizes. From far off, the quarry looks like a gigantic arid version of Mammoth Hot Springs. Turbines of a new wind farm rotate along the sage flats farther west, causing no real disruption until dusk, when the light on top of each tower glows red.

The road leads straight to the mountains, specifically toward the Graham Trail—a rough dirt track we've hiked twice, the first time more than two decades ago when we discovered the Pryors, and the second time two years past when I kept thinking, "I lost my Kodak Instamatic somewhere around here." Instead of taking the Graham route, though, we steer east. Today—this warm and sunny January 6, 2021—our goal is the new Pygmy Panther Trail, so-named because a BLM scientist once found an exotic gecko there. How this creature arrived at and lived in these remote mountains hugging the Wyoming/Montana border is a mystery.

"Normal" people live in a "normal" world, and I envy them because neither my brain nor my world is normal. But how ordinary is it when a palm-sized reptile from Madagascar can rub noses with horned lizards in the desert of Montana? What if I'm a kind of pygmy panther myself, lost in an alien landscape, frightened, and just trying to get by? Maybe all of us OCDers are a bit out of place because we recognize the bizarre when we see it. Plus, we're lorded over by that internal voice saying, "You can't! You'll fail! The cosmos is watching you! You'll do something unspeakably wrong!" Oscar Charles Dawson again with his guilt-producing sermon.

Bernie and I only guess where to park on Bear Canyon Road, where the unmarked trail is, where to climb the first benchland below Big Pryor Mountain. Luckily, someone put up a series of cairns that seems to mark a faint track over, around, and through yucca, prickly pear, last year's prince's plume, and glittering rocks. From desert to fir forest to "prairie in the sky," as a friend calls the unique assemblage of plants high on the ridges and long, rounded summits, what hiker worth her salt would scoff at a place that offers sandstone and juniper, sooty-grouse-haunted coniferous forest, ice caves, green gentian meadows, and expansive views of the Bighorn Basin and the Beartooth Mountains—not to mention a Nabokovian wealth of butterflies, and black bears great and small? None of which, I remind myself, will be out today, mid-January.

Up and up, Bernie, Luke, and I follow a trace of a path and the zigzagging cairns. If these were meant as markers, then the builder may have been a bit touched by the spins. The air is crisp, the sky a Pacific Ocean without water or surf. Rocks shine as if sentient. And why not? Life isn't a "thing," I tell myself. It's an evolving interaction between "inorganic" and organic molecules, between migratory and sedentary, with, perhaps, no clear boundaries between the proverbial animal, vegetable, and mineral kingdoms. By this measure, no one is out of place.

And that is perhaps how we might see mental illness. It's not an internal glitch in a brain, not a characteristic of one person but a process involving many, both past and present. It waxes and wanes as substrates and stimuli revolve and evolve. It's one way of responding to time, to events, to history, to nucleotides, to DNA, to who knows what? Spirits? Electricity? Junipers? Minerals? Like the exotic gecko, though, I'm never quite at home with that interaction. Even when I'm walking.

Here the minerals lead us ... nowhere certain. We make the top of the first foothill, and then the trail and the cairns stop. Are we close to Pygmy Panther? We look right down into a lovely little draw and then across that draw at the higher elevation snow cornices. Should we go right or left? Straight ahead is impossibly steep. Do we even have a destination?

We choose left—for no better reason than what Robert Frost gives in "The Road Not Taken." And, like the poem's speaker, we discover that "way leads on to way." In our case, that means west, across the sage to a trace of a road, around the ridge we descended, and into the little draw we saw from above. It's lovely, yes, but what we couldn't see earlier are ten acres or more of cattle shit. Not just pies and flops but sculptural mounds, walls, and mazes of fecal matter.

I have nothing, in principle, against cattle grazing on public land, but the ammonia-rich ruin of the grassy draw is a surprise. I say "ruin," but that's not necessarily accurate. It's an aesthetic assault, but, not being a rangeland scientist, I will concede that the boxed-in, arid draw may not be ruinously fertilized by all that exotic waste. What it is, anyway, is an emergent relationship between elements. Fortunately, the dung has been in situ so long that this interaction doesn't reek. Not even Luke's dog nose is interested. At least, he doesn't try to gulp the flops or roll in them, the way he usually would.

As with a lot of things, no one has much understanding of how animals survive in strange habitats. That is to say, no one understands how a pygmy panther eked out a living here, any more than they understand how the pilgrim lost in Oscar Charles Dawson's land of OCD gets by. My mother said, when I told her about my diagnosis, that everybody is a little crazy. I guess she was right. Normalizing the oddities of human brains is a common tendency. People often say they're "OCD" about something, which seems to mean *diligent* or *concerned* or *meticulous*. Perhaps the people and animals who filled up this draw with solid waste would be said to be OCD. But that's obviously not what I'm talking about when I use the term. True OCD involves confusion, terror, and ultimately dissociation.

It's a relief when we escape the fecal draw and ascend a rocky slot in the far cliff. We're pretty well off the Pygmy Panther hunt, we imagine, but, as consolation, we find a bare-rock plaza for lunch and enjoy the sun and shelter from the breeze. Taking turns in this nondoggable terrain, Bernie and I scale to a miniature arch we crawl through, but we are both turned back by ice that persists in the shady spots. Smarter than we are, Luke lounges in the sun, head resting on his front paws in his relaxed-but-ready-for-adventure pose. It's fun to imagine we've rediscovered a place forgotten by modernity, one now known only to the Apsáalooke spirits referred to in English as "the Little People," whoever and whatever they are. This is not for me to know. I leave with a bow to their venerability and prescient good humor. I accept my incongruity.

My rational self says there is no normal. While the Little People belong here, the scores of European cattle that invaded the draw below do not. Do European humans belong? And if not here, then where? We've become nomads, attached to very little on this earth. The sanest, most rational humans do not seem sane and rational to me. To live in this death cult civilization has become, the well-adjusted person adjusts to insanity. Weapons sales, extractive industry, criminalization of freedom, private property as the core of our way of life, mass alienation. Billions of animals killed as economic collateral damage in the past thirty years. Wealth built on genocide and slavery. Piles of dung in the Pryor Mountains.

Like the pygmy panther gecko or any self-respecting sagebrush lizard, when I can, I avoid stress, hide in the metaphorical rocks. Wait out both those external disasters and those galloping thoughts of harm that've plagued me during OCD flare-ups for twenty years. *Here's how you could kill yourself*, my brain says. *I don't want to*, I reply, but the image and the words and the rebuttal play again and again—to torture me. Then, *Here's how you could kill someone else.* I have fought not to see myself stabbing my cats, bludgeoning my mother. Images repeat and words attach themselves to the loop. I hate them. Fight them. And they fight back. I feel like an evil freak. I feel inhabited by a demon. I feel foreign. Completely wrapped up in myself, I focus on maintaining control. And I do.

But we grapple for hours and days and weeks. Soon my thoughts in the grip of Oscar Charles Dawson circle so fast that everyone else moves in slow motion. No one looking at me would know this. If there were some physical symptom that flared up, too—a facial rash, for example—would there be more understanding? Or more jokes? Unlike many disorders, OCD gives rise to humor in TV shows and movies and on bumper stickers: Obsessive Chicken Disorder reads one designed for people who, I guess, like poultry. And then there's the word "obsession" itself. For most people, it means "preoccupation," as in "The Suspect Was Obsessed with Firearms." But, in psychology, an obsession is a very specific thing, an unwanted thought that occurs over and over, much to the thinker's disgust. While the criminal welcomes and enjoys whatever they're preoccupied with or fascinated by, the person who has OCD, to be clear, most definitely does not want that thought. My mental vortex is calm today, as it has been for a few years. But the possibility of its return keeps me as vigilant as an exotic gecko, and I reach out into the world for an anchor.

As we traipse back through the bovine droppings, another passageway off the main draw opens. We explore it on a whim. And, again, because it's got a four-foot step up, one of us humans explores as the other sits with Luke, who takes a second stretch in the sun. I go first through a slot and into a sort of theater-in-the-round. Its walls are bright sandstone, weathered smooth. But instead of Greek columns are two of the most ancient junipers I've ever seen. They're covered with berries—grandmother trees.

The wind speaks in their higher branches, the ones above the rock walls. Below, despite the good acoustics of the alcove, all is quiet shredding, the bark hanging and drifting like prayer flags made by the trees themselves—or by the mineral-tree complex they are part of. I like their persistence, their sandstone life, the way they belong here. How many centuries have these two been guarding this sacred site against all the human cultures and neuroses that have come and gone while they were moving deep, root hairs finding and being found by nitrogen, oxygen, and fungi, turning sand and rock into soil? Respirating and propagating?

Like the trees' root hairs, but less adroitly, my mind is always bumping into things below the surface, shoving them out of the way. The drama is invisible, as OCD burns into the fissures in my ego. I've been told that the disorder is idiosyncratic, and every sufferer has obsessions tailored for maximum personal discomfort. Some involve professional insecurity and some the dangers of plantlife. A scholar might come to believe her perfectly rational conclusions are too crazy to publish until she does just one more edit … and then another. A meticulous suburban woman thinks her new kitchen floor is sticky and perhaps covered with some kind of sap—and she imagines taking a hatchet to it. After reading a news story about a woman who drowned her baby, a loving stay-at-home father hates the recurring idea that he'll kill *his* three children.

I never saw myself harming my son, except by accident. Other vulnerable beings have haunted me. My pets, babies in carriers at the Post Office.

Although there was that long stretch of compulsion-driven OCD when I was a teen, it wasn't until my forties that the obsessive part of it gripped me hard, pulverizing my sense of self. Now I know that I will never act on those obsessions. They aren't impulses. They aren't the voices of psychosis. They are mental detritus. Or, better yet, they are bad films, obvious fictions, designed to torture me during my own private screenings. But I didn't know that at first.

My initial and worst bout of Pure O occurred when Bernie came back from a school trip to Italy, only to leave again for Rochester, New York, to visit family. Tom was through with the school year by then and went with him. How I loathed myself for feeling so lost without my males. I'd become an adult at a time when "A Woman Needs a Man Like a Fish Needs a Bicycle" T-shirts were popular. Maybe it was sheer anxiety. Maybe it was loneliness (we'd only recently moved and I had few friends). Maybe it was the urinary tract infection I had. Maybe it was the antibiotic I took to counter the infection. Maybe it was the summer humidity and the peninsular flatness of Polk County, Florida. Something kicked me into cantering madness and I responded and my brain kicked back. Okay, it wasn't madness. But erupting thoughts of harming myself or my dog Rita left me exhausted in the fight to eliminate those images. I somehow managed the ten days of Bernie's trip, but it took another three or four months to return my brain to something that resembled a steady pace and integration with what I would call normality.

I haven't since had another flare-up that severe. One was enough. I was exiled from everything that was in regular motion in the cosmos. It made me think that the depth of hell is not, as Dante suggested, complete frozen stasis but buzzing mental energy. It had no other mission except to swell my ego in the most harmful way—I was the worst of the worst. The record-holder for most horrific thoughts. I wish there were a foolproof practice to stop this from ever happening again. I've tried SSRIs for anxiety, and they exacerbate my fears. I've tried supplements. L-theanine. Chamomile. Ashwagandha. When my insomnia becomes crushing or my travel anxiety threatens, I take a Xanax. Or half a Xanax. Mostly I walk. For miles. I love to walk. It's the only medicine that works. That and having a therapist who won't give up on me.

As we leave Cow Dung Draw, my cellphone chimes. I'd forgotten to turn it off, and someone sent me a text when we were out of range. Against my better judgment, I glance at the sender's name: a friend in Binghamton, New York.

"I knew this would happen," she writes.

What? What would happen?

And then: "Trump will be forever linked to this."

The day's beautiful. The grandmother junipers' wisdom and cooperation with sandstone clutch my heart. But the political entity—the idea of it, anyway—that claims all of us has shifted. And, so, where are we now? In someone else's obsession?

"It's the same place you've always been," the junipers say. "Girl, we've seen it all change and change again. And nothing happens. You humans are like ants. Rearranging your busy hills. Put your roots in deeper, why don't you?"

"Easy for you to say," I answer the venerable ones. "You're trees, after all."

I check the news feed on my phone. A riotous mob of neo-Confederates and other white supremacists is sacking the US Capitol. There's a "shaman" in skins and horns. There are paramilitaries, Confederate wannabes, neo-Nazis, and guys with bear spray. We lose cell phone reception again. But somehow the Pryors don't seem so remote and intact. They seem, in fact, violated. Though not for the first time. There is that little matter of a quarry down the way. There are whining ORVs and a wind farm. There are white hikers, like me, who don't know who the Little People are or how to propitiate them. There was a pygmy panther. *Everything's madness,* I think. But that's an easy out. Human behavior does, though, walk a snaking boundary between healthy and unhealthy responses to vision, hearing, taste.

Much better to stay rooted like the grandparent junipers, sorting through minerals in the soil, gathering water and air. Not trying to control the world. Accepting change because what else is there? Humility and grandeur honestly come by. Community, I think it's called.

Shaken, we give up on the whole notion of the new trail and go back to the car. From there, we follow our usual route into Bear Canyon for a mile or two until the view opens: a widening of the defile into a broad, green, juniper-studded elevation that becomes fir forest and eventually snow scarves across the summit ridges. I can't enjoy it, the walk ruined by the antics of very little people in faraway Washington, DC.

But that's not right. Walks aren't perfect. Nor is the wild "wild." It never has been. There's no place to go today except this earth. There's no place that isn't inimitable. Diversity replaces obsession's simplicity. Like a family's or country's history, the Pryor Mountains are emergent, sometimes clashing, systems of thought and imagination, mineral life, vegetative wisdom, and pinyon jays' blue texts. Nothing about them is ever finished or complete. Getting too big (or too small) for the rock and soil you live in won't work. You just have to adapt. That's the trees' lesson. And Luke's as well—he's eaten dirt here, off and on, his whole life.

Right now, I'm seething with anxiety, and I certainly am not going to ingest the iron-red sand as enthusiastic Luke does. I'm too short-lived to accept the junipers' patience with a shining, crumbled, wind-drawn, rain-sluiced geological world that will persist in some form or other even as limestone once shipped by rail from Warren, Montana. What am I, though, but a mineral particle out of context? What is any modern human but that? So there, you perpetrators of political violence, you dancing bits of dust! We are all pygmy panthers.

TRAIL 23

A Petroglyph Canyon Snake (Plus Twelve or Thirteen Others)

General location: Warren, Montana, south of the Pryor Mountains; about 105 miles from Yellowstone
Hiking distance: 2+ miles
Elevation: 80 feet down and 80 feet up again
Terrain: Juniper scrub with sandstone canyon

In October 2020 we decide to escape the depressing news cycle and hike Petroglyph Canyon at the southern base of the Pryor Mountains, several miles from Pygmy Panther. We exit the highway at our old landmark, Warren, and look for the next turnoff—this time from the gravel onto a perilous, high-centering route optimistically called Helt Road. An even rougher way to the right and then a cattle guard and finally a massive, pyramidal hill. We can't go farther in our Rav4, so we park and load up our daypacks, setting off along the two-track flanking the hill where, Bernie helpfully suggests, there could be cougars we'll never see.

What we do see are fossils: bullet-shaped belemnite shells—the remains of ancient squid—and Triassic–Jurassic oysters, whose form has leant them the common name "devil's toenails." Actually, we find one-half of each oyster, the shells having disarticulated millennia ago.

We continue on an unremarkable sandy stretch—wind and sunshine battling. Soon it's hot. With his dark, raggedy fur (he's been "blowing his coat" for two months now, thank you), Luke pants, and his flag of a tail sags. I tie my jacket around my waist. Bernie, impervious to weather, continues in his heavy sweatshirt.

After a mile or so, we reach the Bureau of Land Management parking lot at the top of the canyon, discovering, to our disappointment, that occupants of a high-clearance SUV that passed us earlier have the look of humans who are going to stay a while. The foursome has beaten us to the trailhead. We stop to let them get decently in front of us (which we would do for their privacy and ours even without the COVID-19 pandemic), and while we wait, we read the interpretive sign mapping the sandstone canyon below us and describing the petroglyphs, which were pecked into the rocks some 850 to 1,275 years ago, between the reign of Alfred the Great in a newly Christianized Britain and the murder of Thomas à Beckett, between the invention of gunpowder in China and the birth of Genghis Khan, and between the artistic innovation of Igbo bronzes and the reign of Saladin.

Our own nation's recent past—and one reason we've decided to get the hell out of Billings—is sad and salacious, and menacing. Before the spring winds died in 2018, the leaves were out, and the first rattler hissed, I was primed for danger. Bernie and I were driving from Billings to Dillon, Montana, tuning the radio from one translator station to the next as Christine Blasey Ford and Brett Kavanaugh testified in the US Senate.

Blasey Ford started the day—and our climb to the snow-laden pass between Livingston and Bozeman. She talked about something none of her peers remembered because, presumably, it was so common: a boy sexually assaulting her at a party. Alcohol and young people—one of whom was now a nominee for the Supreme Court. Was it serious? A crime? Had it happened at all? As Blasey Ford's voice quavered above FM static, lodgepole pines shot by in vertical ranks, and two memories I'd almost put away met me as we crested the pass:

I'm twenty-two years old, a graduate student in Louisiana. I use my cheap big-box store bicycle to explore open spaces around Lake Charles. I've gotten off near Prien Lake for the subtropical birds, among them yellow-crowned night herons (awake and active though it's not night). As I admire their striped heads and red eyes, a blond boy—younger than I am—walks up from the shore, comes face-to-face with me, and abruptly presses the flat of his hand into my breast, saying, "I've never met anyone like you here."

And . . .

I'm married—three years past my Louisiana stint—and in two-months-too-early labor. It's nighttime, Bernie has been kicked out of the hospital at the end of visiting hours, and I'm lying in the twilight medical world of Northern California. The OB/GYN appears at my bedside, pulls down the sheet, and pushes his fingers into my vagina to see, he tells me, how much I've dilated. No permission asked or given. It's over in less than a minute. I cry when he's gone. Was he wearing gloves? Why was he staying so late? Why did he examine me in the half-light? Where was the nurse?

Decades later—as we made it to the Gallatin Valley bounded on all sides by cloud-strewn mountains—I wondered why I didn't do anything more than tell the Louisiana boy to stop, and why I accepted, as part of the indignities of medicine, the doctor's violation? More than that, I said nothing to anyone until years later. And the telling was met with a shrug—probably why I kept quiet.

Into the flat and barren steppes near Three Forks and the Wheat Montana truck stop, it was Kavanaugh's turn—his histrionics filled the car. I couldn't turn off the radio or try to find music on the dial with its sparse station selection. For me, what would stand out most from the hearing were Kavanaugh's self-righteous indignation and Blasey Ford's memory of boys laughing at her.

In fact, her testimony jarred loose memories that many women my age have carried privately for years. Random verbal abuse or inappropriate behavior at parties. "Normal," expected, and tolerated violations of women's physical agency. Decades ago, we lacked definitions—or even a sense that such things were aberrant. Clearly, we had no means of redress. Have no means. I'd have respected Kavanaugh if he'd simply admitted that he didn't remember the incident but that it was plausible and such things were relatively common occurrences, and if he'd been contrite.

The relationship between danger and anxiety disorders in general isn't clearcut. Sure, certain situations cause anxiety. But the deep, unshakable neurotic form that leads to OCD doesn't necessarily arise in response to actual physical stimuli—male aggression or anything else. Or I don't think it does. There's always anxiety pulsing around my joints, and I may worry about the likelihood that something will bring on obsessions, but the obsessions and their torments are what terrify me the most. Actually, I don't think I'm a particularly cowardly person. I've hiked alone in bear country (not that that's a good idea), I've walked through city streets at night (not the best idea either), and I've found humor in medical procedures, as when a nurse had to puncture a patch of cellulitis to "dig" for splinters embedded in my finger. I suggested she call it "probing." Once, I had to drive Tom by myself to Bangor to have a piece of metal removed from his eye, and I watched the ophthalmologist *probe* my son's cornea. The euphemism wasn't helpful.

Today is a case in point. Unlike our past wanderings into Petroglyph Canyon, we decide to follow the trail, but, as usual, we're soon going insouciantly sans cairns. We've never had luck with the established route, but all you have to do is go downhill, surfing the sand dunes. The terrain is a fantasy of red-orange pinnacles, knobs, sheer walls, and junipers.

As for the real snakes that summer of 2018, I found at least eleven—a fair haul. Not that I did anything but tally up sightings. I like snakes. I was ready for all but one of them. Something about the country's mood? Something about defense? Something about not quite understanding power? Snakes are daring action in fragile bodies. They're often shot, chopped into bits, "milked" in the case of rattlers, or run over deliberately when they get onto human byways. People are scared of them, though I think the feeling's mutual.

My 2018 list:

1–3) Three North American racers on the Molt-Rapelje Road (one a victim of county "traffic," one slaloming away to a culvert, one needing a nudge to reach safety)

4) A very active rattler at the mouth of Bear Canyon in the Pryor Mountains (coiled and hissing explosively at my ever-oblivious dog, as I did everything wrong simultaneously—pulled Luke by the leash toward me, leapt out of the trail, screamed; not my finest hour, but one clear reason I'm usually hypervigilant)
5) One bullsnake at Four Dances Natural Area near Billings (performing a bravura rattler imitation)
6–8) Three bullsnakes at Pictograph Cave State Park (including an eight-footer oozing along the back wall of the largest rock recess)
9–11) Three western prairie rattlesnakes at Hailstone National Wildlife Refuge (hidden in grass fringing the old road—hidden until they rattled after a languid fashion)

And what *about* those rattlers? Forget the fierce caricatures you see on bumper stickers around Billings. Pit vipers are generally relaxed. Because their venom is reserved for the small animals they hunt, their aggression toward us is for show. It's a misfortune for them if they have to use their valuable resource on creatures not even their expandable jaws can open wide enough to swallow. Some herpetologists speculate that adults can "dry bite" without using any toxins, the supply of which takes a long time to replenish. Younger snakes supposedly lack this control. I don't think I'll test the hypothesis.

With snakes, we're talking about prejudice and hatred. I remember my dad earnestly throwing rocks at a congress of rattlers near Hidden Falls in the Wasatch. It was important to scatter them before another party of hikers arrived. I can't recall him actually killing one. If the rock throwing was uncharacteristic, though, it was not borne of fear. It was simply the duty of a good hiker to clear the trail. For my part, I think I've always felt danger in witnessing "justified" displays of duty.

I say that, but as a child growing up in Salt Lake in the 1960s and 1970s, I was indoctrinated into a tacit racism and sexism that went largely unchallenged. Embracing them was our duty as citizens-to-be. I remember singing "Ten Little Indians" in school and showing with cupped hands, representing canoes, how their boats overturn when the second verse's

Indian girls, unlike the sailing boys, capsize. Naturally, the boys in our class mocked us girls, and we tried to fix the verse so that the females would "go sailing" too. But our version wasn't authentic. We were making it up, and erasing the sexism (if not the racism) was cheating. We all knew it. Deep down, we believed in our inferiority as surely as we believed in the vileness of snakes.

I can only imagine how awful that scene of first-grade music-making must have looked from the front of the classroom: twenty-five earnest little children—white boys in cotton shirts and slacks and white girls in dresses and knee socks—belting out "One little, two little, three little Indians . . ." while the number line and the American flag hung above them, and the teacher's cheery geraniums decorated the window sills.

It's hard to say whether Petroglyph Canyon trends uphill or not—the floor between high cliffs is that flat. Yet we climb boulders and then jump from them and over tangled debris that clogs the canyon with an overeager, leaping dog on a leash. We take turns belaying Luke down the more challenging jumbles. At one point, the air turns cooler—and I idly wonder about past flashfloods. Raindrops freckle the rock and then give up any pretense of falling.

At a tricky spot, I wait for Bernie and Luke, a bullsnake emerging beside me from background sand, stretched long and relaxed under sage, her pattern of interlocking ovals tidy camouflage. I know she'd be soft and smooth. But I won't touch her. Even if she's a bit sluggish, I'd never succeed before she conveyor-belted herself away. Still, she doesn't mind when I squat down to see her more closely. Must be a youngster, I think—not like the behemoths of two summers ago. This little one doesn't bother to look at me, world-weary already. She tastes the air once or twice. Her head lifts a few inches, but she remains quiescent. The genius of the place has met me, taken a languid one-lunged breath, and essentially shrugged. I point her out to Bernie when he and ever-oblivious Luke catch up. Then we leave her to her lidless ruminations.

Like bears, snakes are creatures to ponder and are prone to getting caught in thought loops; one doesn't simply dismiss them. Is it their lack of legs or eyelids, their unnerving length, or their sensitive tongues? Despite all the human turmoil in our world, what events make the front-page news? "198-pound Burmese Python Caught in Florida: 'It Was More Than a Snake, It Was a Monster'" or "Video Shows Hissing Snake Found in Arizona Woman's Toilet" or "Albino Python That Terrorized Trailer Park for Six Months Captured." Why is it that here in Montana we're not so worried about the Covid pandemic, but we shiver if a snake crawls out of a woman's toilet in faraway Florida? Is it a matter of scale? Though the virus has officially killed almost seven million people worldwide (most counts ended in 2023) and more than a million in the United States, the often-cited figure for the combined weight of all Sars-CoV2 viruses active during their 2021 heyday is only a bit more than that of a large Montana rattlesnake. Most of us wouldn't hesitate to squelch any rattlers we run across, but what to do about a microscopic virus? Somehow, getting a vaccination is not as easy as axing a snake to prove our *Homo sapiens* sapience.

Soon we pass the spot where one December we saw a weasel, all decked out in white and awaiting the first snow—discombobulated perhaps by the delayed winters of global climate change. We also meet up with the other hikers. They haven't found the art, but when we tell them it's a bit farther, they seem unenthusiastic.

Discombobulation was a major theme of my teen years. Perhaps that's true for everyone. While in junior high school I complained about male chauvinists, most LDS women in our neighborhood responded to the women's rights movement by continuing their Relief Society service and redoubling their housewifery, concocting mountains of Jell-O salads and fudge. When they began experimenting with a fermented fruitcake starter dough that took the Seventh Ward by storm, my mother suspected they were getting at least a little buzzed.

The general trajectory for LDS girls was to finish high school and marry, while that for the boys was to finish high school, go on a mission, go to college, establish themselves in a career, and marry. At Wasatch Junior High, it was clear that the eventual "MRS degree" was still much coveted, along with its required cooking and sewing skills. While the boys learned mysterious and important things in Shop and Technology, our all-female Home Economics classes taught us to concoct lollipops and make German pancakes: "6 eggs, 1 cup flour, 5 T butter, 1 cup milk, ½ t salt. Whip eggs till thick. Add milk, flour, and salt. Heat butter in a dripper pan in oven while preheating. Pour batter into pan. Bake at 450°F." The pancakes are very good, but I've never used a dripper pan, whatever that is. We sewed aprons and sometimes accidentally rammed a machine needle into our index fingernails. Unlike Janis Ian, I learned the truth far earlier than "At Seventeen." "Beautiful girls" were not only desirable; they were the ones who counted. A young LDS woman in Utah had two options: be a good housekeeper or be pretty.

In high school, boys lined the hallways and judged girls, LDS and gentile, by our looks on a one-to-ten scale as we walked past. My plain face full of acne didn't get me many points. Despite our fear and disgust, none of us females complained to the administration. Being subjected to such humiliation was just life, every bit as expected as the casual terror we'd known in grammar school when the boys hung around the sidewalks and pelted us with snowball-covered rocks or tried to stuff worms down our shirts or throats after a spring rain. In fact, the one-to-ten rankings were important to us. We had to know how we stacked up on the road to acceptability. The eventual goal for the LDS girls was to, in the words of *Genesis*, "be fruitful and multiply." I've since read *The Book of Mormon*, finding nary a named female character in the hundreds of pages of scripture. Given the all-male LDS priesthood and bureaucracy, gendered paths and male taunting fit Utah's culture. Yet people aren't ideologies. I know plenty of Church members who defy the typecasting.

In my gentile case, the 1970s were confusing. I never chose female authors or singers because they were female. I cheered on Barbara Jordan, my hero at the Watergate hearings, and in the shower I did a fair rendition of Helen Reddy: "I am woman, hear me roar." But I also liked Paul Simon's "Homeward Bound," where the singer's "love lies waiting silently" for him. And I longed to be beautiful.

Gentiles were perhaps "less than girls"—or more. We had dreams and options beyond immediate post-high school marriage. We could excel at academics or rebellion (chiefly by smoking behind the school building). We put Billy Joel lyrics on our lockers ("Only the good die young"!), drank Utah's 3.2 beer or even a parent's whiskey (to the point of vomiting in first-period biology class, in at least one instance), and went to the Blue Mouse "underground cinema" to watch *outré* movies such as *Harold and Maude*.

Occasionally, someone enhanced our female self-defensive venom. A police officer came to school to teach us how to avoid physical assault (one thing you're supposed to do is put your keys between your fingers so they stick out like pointy brass knuckles—advice I still follow when I'm in a parking lot at night). Our coed sex-education class, the first of its kind in the state, discussed contraception. But any female's job (LDS or gentile) was to *attract* males, not stave them off. As far as I know, I never questioned the state of things until I got a little older.

All the while, I hated those metaphorical pheromones: heavy blue or green eye shadow, itchy mascara that seemed to run at the slightest provocation, painful high heels, nausea-inducing perfume. I'm surprised by an old photo sent by a cousin, in which I appear very fashionable—nice blouse, flared pants, wide belt. My hair looks relatively combed. I doubt that the picture is of me, but she swears it is. I'm a perfect little snake, camouflaged and thereby secure.

Far into Petroglyph Canyon, the first rock art panel is maybe twenty feet up on the north-facing cliff. Though damaged by tourists who carved their names in the sandstone, it still clearly depicts beings with oblong, floating heads; occasional large penises; and elongate bodies. I leave a devil's toenail in tribute because I've forgotten to bring an offering of tobacco.

Another panel is at eye level on the path and seems more jolly than spiritual. It features the same horizontal row of enigmatic figures—tall and thin—this time holding, or almost holding, hands. Above their heads hovers a stylized bighorn sheep in profile. This mural, though also defaced, is beautiful and lively, and, unlike the first, invites us to participate.

I don't know how the artists of Petroglyph Canyon responded to serpents, who are not depicted. I don't know how they responded to bighorn sheep, who are. I suspect that the ancients had as many fears as anyone, but they probably weren't embodied by those Christian symbols of evil who crawl on their bellies as punishment. Did they pair women and snakes, beings of fertility and cyclical self-renewal?

In the eastern hemisphere, a god similar to Lucifer and associated with the planet Venus brought daylight and was also called Phosphorus. By the time Christian-influenced cultures began to come into their own, Lucifer had clearly developed "feminine" traits—a beguiling and persuasive manner, an intimate and empathic complicity. Milton in *Paradise Lost,* terrified of his own attraction (that voice! that shimmering!), reduces his hero to "a monstrous Serpent on his Belly prone," mellifluous whisper replaced by a hiss, beauty by slime (not even British adders are slimy, as he should have realized).

The Eurasian defeat of scary, feminine "pagan" gods—of whom perhaps Lucifer once was an ally—started eons past and is ongoing. Long before the Judaic "adversary" appeared on the scene, the Phrygian mother goddess Matar (otherwise known as Kybele or Cybele) traveled in veils and robes with an escort of lions, hawks, male musicians, eunuchs, and snakes. Perhaps Eve was one of her avatars. At any rate, Matar and Eve were humbled, and must still be kept down. By Zoroaster, Moses, Jesus, Mohammad, Brett Kavanaugh. Might makes right. All that women are left with for defense are disguises, wiles, and venom, which can, I admit, be potent. And scary, even for those who possess it. A 2019 study published in *Current Psychiatry Reports* concludes that boys have OCD early and worry about religion, while women tend to be diagnosed later with fears of pollution or committing violent acts.

There is no hint here that women of the rock art world cultivated wiles or anxiety. Or suffered from OCD, though some probably did. Perhaps the culture was matrilineal, its imagery, like old *Playgirl* magazines, fetishizing male potency. As the artists pecked and designed, far to the south Mayan cities were collapsing, and to the southeast the city of Cahokia in what is now Missouri was beginning its ascent. But the people in Petroglyph Canyon were men and women of the broad and bright sage flats, women and men and children who climbed mountains, knew where to find scarce water, danced, laughed, cried, got mad, and sang, and left, as mementos, not landscape-destroying monuments or world-classifying religious texts but alternately joyous and mystical intaglios carved into the heart of a snake-guarded canyon.

When I was sixteen, I went on a date with a guy who had gigantic biceps and nothing much to say. In the Youth Conservation Corps I lived in dormitory conditions in the Wasatch National Forest, and a boy always waited outside in the hallway while I showered. In college, I dated a paranoic communist who went around the city after the manner of a 1920s Bolshevik operative looking for capitalist outrages and flashed to anger when anyone cut in front of him while he was driving. I remember accepting this undercurrent of violence as an attribute of young males, and I tended to avoid them when possible.

I was never ready for their verbal aggressiveness. I often froze. Or, rather, like a snake, I laid low. It's taken me a long time to realize that when a man reverts to discussions of casual violence it probably means only that I've gotten too uppity or seemed unimpressed, and I have little to fear. A museum curator in Wyoming where I worked in the 1990s tossed out my rough draft of a brochure regarding female influence on firearms use and manufacture, replacing it with his own text filled with stories of women's gruesome deaths as underpaid munitions laborers. I had nothing to say about that, as I had no formal answer for the boy in Louisiana or the OB/GYN in California.

Would I stick up for myself at the museum now? Would I dial 911 regarding the boy? Would I, fragilely pregnant but infused with decades' worth of gusto, demand my doctor wear gloves, or, better yet, get the hell away from me? What *have* I learned from snakes? Recently someone regaled me with stories of brutally hunting down raccoons and blasting them with a shotgun. That was supposed to get a rise out of me. I didn't take the bait. In remaining silent, though, I may have been acquiescing to the psychological abuse, falling back on my desire to blend into the rocks because resistance is provocative and pointless. Though my obsessions are never about gender, they highlight helplessness and anger over that helplessness. And sometimes I do seem snakily manipulative.

One morning as he eats his customary bowl of cereal flakes, Bernie tells me that his quest for an academic career was a sacrifice for him. Pursuing a PhD in American Literature took him away from writing poetry, among other things. In response, I lament that I've failed to stick up for myself throughout my life—even in our marriage. I've been second fiddle to his career, which, I say, trying not to sound testy, I never asked him to follow. And would he have been happy staying at home with an infant? "*I* gave up a lot when we had Tom," I remind Bernie.

"Like what?" he asks.

"I wanted to be a wildlife biologist," I for-instance. That was the reason we'd moved to Arcata, to be near Humboldt State University, where I could establish California residency and then go to a school famous for its ecology programs. Instead, I became pregnant and was eager to return home to benefit from my mother's expertise with infants—a serpentine maneuver, as if the unexpected pregnancy provided an excuse to avoid confronting my background anxiety. I could have become a supermom, simultaneously tackling school, career, anxiety, and childrearing. I didn't.

"Oh," he says. For an instant, we're out of sync: I the snake trying with venomous threats to avoid danger, he the hapless victim of my defensive subterfuge.

After a brief lunch at the opposite end of the canyon, where a cutaway bank has eroded to reveal the long, snake-like roots of sage and where yellow-blooming rabbit brush fans its tease of staid bentonite, we go off-trail again, up the hill, skirting the sandstone slot. Neither Bernie nor I want to ruin our communion with the art by seeing it again so soon. But the terrain is more complex than we'd expected, and it takes a long time to cross hardened Mesozoic mudflats and wend our way around junipers and prickly pear. The Pryor Mountains eventually pop up to our north, and we find an old road at the top of the canyon that, after some discussion, we follow. There, a short-horned lizard emerges, like the snake, from camouflage—a tiny resident whose distant ancestors must have hidden from the rock artists' kids those many centuries ago.

As a final flourish, we leave the main road just as we return to it and climb the hill that heralded the beginning of our hike. Luke seems concerned at our unstructured approach, keeps looking back and staring in the direction of the canyon. The view from the top, which he doesn't seem to appreciate either, is fifty miles of arid spectacular. Four mountain ranges rumple the horizon: Pryors, Bighorns, Absarokas, and Beartooths. Mormon agricultural villages dot the sweeping and arid Bighorn Basin of Wyoming that lies below and between the peaks. Obsessions and anxiety slink away. This view is as clear and round as a drop of glycerin.

When I was eighteen, I had my first run-in with the medical patriarchy. I was sick with what turned out to be the flu, and a GP I admired told me to "take your beautiful body home and get some rest." What to do about that?

A year or two later, pain and cramps led me to several doctors who more or less patted me on the head. "You've been seeing too much of the medical profession," one told me, discounting my troubles. My mother sent me to her OB/GYN, who talked about what "we often see in young girls." Eventually someone took me somewhat seriously, and I had a laparoscopy. A frightening experience. The muscle relaxant went to work before the anesthetic, and I remember the panic as I tried to ask for help but couldn't move my lips, tongue, or throat. It was like being buried alive. I couldn't sleep again peacefully—ever. One of my anxiety symptoms remains a momentary inability to swallow.

The laparoscopy revealed endometriosis ("a real problem," the internist conceded), uterine tissue growing outside the uterus but in all other ways behaving like it's still inside, bleeding, shrinking, swelling. The disease is pretty well known now, but not so much in 1980. At the post-surgery follow-up, with my legs in the stirrups, I got a lecture about how to enhance my fertility, as if that was all I should care about. I assumed the doctor was LDS and sincerely wanted me to be fruitful. And I was. Though I was not supposed to get pregnant, I did several years and states later when the contraceptive foam I relied on as extra insurance failed.

I loved the ball of cells in my uterus immediately and didn't even consider having an abortion. It took Bernie a night of wandering Eureka (Arcata's sister city) to see things my way. I chose nurse practitioners for prenatal care and delivery, but because of my tendency to early labor they had to bring in the doctor to consult. He'd recently returned from Africa, they apologized, and had become very cynical. He referred to multiple births as "litters" and complained about "spoiled" American women. Fair enough. When you're a spoiled American woman, you can stave off a dangerously premature birth by devoting six weeks to bedrest. This was the doctor who invaded my privacy.

During those weeks when I lay all gravid and immobile, I wasn't scared. I just did what I had to do to protect the fetus as he grew nails and hair, as his lungs matured and fat grew beneath his skin. Still, being pregnant—in this culture, anyway—erodes women's power and individuality. Somehow when you're pregnant, strangers of all genders want to touch your abdomen, ask you about the due date, give you advice. You're community property. Your health isn't paramount; the baby's is—something most mothers agree with, of course. When I was losing weight because I couldn't get out of bed to prepare meals, my mother came to visit for ten days and fixed high-fat foods to "help the baby."

If before birth you're a vessel and a curiosity, afterward you're a milk factory and a curiosity—and will see a decline in your economic well-being and your freedom. It's hard work to breastfeed and hold another job—well, it was for me. My mother said my grandmother made her drink beer to "bring in the milk." In my case, it was the baby who took charge. He liked to nurse for hours on end, and I soon tired of daytime TV—*The Price Is Right* and *General Hospital*. Desperate, I consulted a baby book and found that only the first fifteen minutes of suckling per breast provided nutrition. (My mother hadn't been much help in this regard as, apparently, the beer didn't work and subsequently she followed the "modern" practice of bottle feeding with both her babies.) My own little con artist was, I learned, happy enough with a pacifier chaser, and

I tasted a bit of post-partum freedom at last. Until I had to become gainfully employed. But, as a mother, I found that my identity and name were still sometimes lost. I became "Tom's mom," "Mrs. Quetchenbach," or, as my dad took to labeling me, "the mama." That was, oddly, fine by me. I was hidden in purpose, disguised as a mom. OCD never attacked that role. Maybe Bernie was right, and I'd become confident in it. The mother goddess Matar maintained a formidable entourage. Society grants mothers certain powers, after all.

Back in the car, we drive to the end of Gyp Springs Road. On this late August day, we're determined to wring as much experience as possible from the long-waning light. We get out to inspect a slope we remember from when Tom was a child and we lived in Wyoming, where we first collected belemnites and devil's toenails.

We travel back through our own geological layers—Tom is little here and thrilled and happy with the day's treasures. He wants to be a volcanologist or a paleontologist. We are all heartbreakingly young. Our previous dog Rita is a puppy luxuriating in her first open-range cow flops. Three of our parents are still alive. How vulnerable we are. We believe in things we will come to be cynical about or no longer take for granted: the environmental movement, educational and religious freedom, women's rights, Martin Luther King, Jr.'s "arc of justice." Some things don't change, though. The world was and is filled with men who put their hands on young women's bodies without permission. The world, in other words, was and is marked by resentment, humiliation, and regret—the milieu for, if not the cause of, anxious neuroses of all kinds.

Back in the car, I look over at Bernie. He gazes forward behind sunglasses he will soon take off in the spreading dusk. His hands guide the wheel as he dodges potholes, eager for our next shared venture. Almost everything in our lives has been shared since 1982. We're surely past blame or wishing things had been different. "You better outlive me," I say, voicing my newest fear—being without him.

"You better outlive me," he counters.

We've decided to keep moving, on to Bighorn Canyon National Recreation Area, twenty miles east. Shadows purple and elongate as our car climbs the base of the escarpment called Syke's Ridge. We find the wild horses we'd wanted to see, four mares with a buckskin colt come down to graze on the lush grass of the river bottom. Farther up, we take the turnoff to Devil Canyon and get out at the overlook. The moon rises—two days short of full—over a pink boa of sunset clouds and a steadfast Venus. Perched on a pale cliff, a bighorn ram poses a thousand feet above the twisting river like the silhouetted petroglyph we'd seen earlier.

The thrill of recognizing a true spiritual vision shoots to my core. Those long-ago rock artists of Petroglyph Canyon knew how to depict a wild sheep at sunset. Of course they did. In this light, you could superimpose the image on the model and barely know the difference. What had seemed static in the art was static in the original. Life and movement and enigmatic male beauty held fast in rock—and in flesh. Seeing the art and the model on the same day confirms the genius of both and the failure of my concepts of time and binary gender. It's possible to transmute fear into awe, to sublimate anxiety into beauty. To watch a still image go round and round through the centuries.

Like the wild ram, we stop on the brink. I remember the little bullsnake and the horned lizard, and their age-old lineages. I think of Matar, with her fearless hand on a cougar's broad head, a bighorn ram at her side, her ankles braceleted by pit vipers.

TRAIL 24

Hailstone National Wildlife Refuge, with Owl and Eagle

General location: Molt-Rapelje Road, Montana; about 152 miles from Yellowstone
Driving distance (from Billings, MT): 90 miles round trip
Average elevation: 4,009 feet
Terrain: Shortgrass prairie, alkaline playa

We haven't even brought snacks for our drive to the prairie northwest of Billings. We've been out a lot longer than we thought we'd be, and we're hungry, Bernie and Luke and I. Luke, of course, is always hungry. It's 8:30 p.m., and, after rain and clouds all day, the lowering sun has finally slipped below the valence of dark cumulus that bedeviled the afternoon. It primps up the wheatfields, alfalfa rows, last year's crop stubble, and the remaining tracts of shortgrass prairie with a light so wise and cleansing we might have passed into an El Greco canvas or an Ovidian myth. Long-billed curlews rise, glimmer, and shimmy like kites—white against purple clouds scuttling off to the east. They lure their beloveds and charm us.

It's hard to comprehend that somewhere there are pavement and crowds and world affairs—and sumptuous dinners. It's June 11, 2018. It's also June 12 in Singapore, where President Donald J. Trump is dining on beef confit with Supreme Leader Kim Jong-un of North Korea. Fittingly, confit involves the slow cooking of muscle in its own fat, leaving the flesh tender and moist. The process usually happens to some sort of tough creature, like duck. But Mr. Kim and Mr. Trump are above the consumption of birds. Castrated cattle for those two. A dish for the powerful.

Not that we don't have our own sort of rulers here. This owl, for example. A short-eared owl, to be specific, on a ragged fencepost. We pull over and stop. He stares back at us with an innocent ferocity that's hard to endure. In the golden light, he shines like a natural zircon. He's glorious. Despite how close we are, he doesn't move, shake his head, raise his feathers. Pale and compact, he must be a male. I take in the whole of him: round, feathers blowing, head swiveled at a sharp angle to consider his world, ourselves included.

I linger over every bit of his beauty. He has two short "ears"—tiny, dark, pointed tufts of feather right on the top of his head. His facial disk is round as a crater and more clearly marked than a great horned owl's. His beak is a black line bisecting that disk. His eyes seem highlighted by Egyptian kohl. The owl's feathers are white and tawny, a spangle of gold-nugget freckles across his breast and flanks. His legs are covered in what look like golden fur tights. Splayed, his talons squeeze the fencepost he perches on as if he might pulverize it.

But I keep coming back to his eyes. Two round black pupils cut through circular yellow fields. Yellow? As in sulfur, egg yolk, sunflower, lemon, neon sign, emergency vehicle? Nothing I can think of compares to owl yellow—its own color, simile, and metaphor. The yellow that death looks like. Or love. Or the will to exist. A yellow that says, "I know you. Not who you are, to be sure, but what you are." We've driven and walked, bird-scanning and alert, and finally we've found and entered his flat-out stare. Usually, large birds take off when approached too closely on foot or in a car. This one doesn't.

However impressive, though, our owl is a single dab of energy on the prairie. He's a random bit of birdlife in the continental scheme of things. The tiniest smear of earnestness on the face of the wide, round earth. No more than a particle in the solar system. So infinitesimally small in the galactic wilds that he might as well not even exist.

"Say the same for yourself," the owl's eyes retort. And "Fool," he might say, if he cared enough to call me anything.

Years ago, Bernie and I (Luke had not yet been born) went to the prairie on an Audubon field trip out of our new home in Billings. Ever since, we've made at least one annual spring trek along the route we learned. Getting a late start this time (which, I suppose, makes us pretty feckless birdwatchers), we went due west along Rimrock Road—past subdivisions that grew larger and newer as we sped from town, past the LDS Temple and clusters of raw development. Near Phipps Park, a haven for disc golfers, and the BNSF tracks, I looked up the hill toward a little sandstone- and ponderosa-tiered cove. Below the green, public water-storage tank was a twenty-thousand-square-foot mansion. Vacant and ever for sale.

Not soon enough, we left all the tacky upper-class sprawl behind and scaled the draw until we emerged on the prairie to a Connemara-green spring. Lark buntings and vesper sparrows teased the county road as it paralleled a ranch—one that had taken to raising bison. The animals looked wondrously peaceful and wooly, their fur the kind of deep brown you'd find in Caravaggio pigments, belying the reality that buffalo can run thirty miles an hour, jump over a ten-foot fence, and gore annoying humans with a single careless thrust of a horn. These creatures (they seemed to be cows with a few barley-gold calves) no doubt had domestic cattle genes entwined in their wild DNA to make them a wee bit more pliable than their ancestors. They were plenty happy where they were, anyway, and displayed no eagerness to rush the ordinary barbed wire fence that held them.

Past the Yellowstone-Stillwater County line, we cheered our first destination: Molt, Montana. Now all but a ghost town, Molt got its official start in 1909 with the incorporation of a post office. It was called Stickley then, Molt being the name of someone who would give the railroad plenty of land to pass through. The early 1900s were a time when people from the Eastern United States and Northern Europe bought the developers' line that fortunes were to be had in dryland farming on the Montana high plains. Some made it for a while, in fact, until drought squeezed most settlers out to Billings, Laurel, Livingston, and points beyond. The land is inhabited primarily by lost memories, anxieties, and desires embodied in old caragana-and-lilac shelterbelts, doddering cabins slipping and sometimes falling from their foundations, and generations of discarded farming equipment. Before the settlers came, Sitting Bull's Hunkpapa Lakota hunted and camped on these prairies. Not that long ago, really.

Molt had a brief run of fame in the early 2010s (even appearing in *Parade Magazine*) for its Prairie Winds Café. Housed in an old hardware store with beautiful blond brickwork, the café featured live bluegrass music on weekend mornings, and homemade pie. But the café closed, and Molt was left with an uninhabitable old cabin, a few inhabited houses with pleasant yards, an abandoned teacherage, a fairly new post office, and a row of shiny metal grain silos recently augmented by three or four even larger ones. Glowing on the hill against lowering clouds, Molt gave an impression of prosperousness, but, as we drove through, I could imagine towns in China, Kyrgyzstan, or North Korea as forgotten as our Molt.

The road curved north and west, a graded gravel route that wasn't much worse than pavement despite the rain and hail we'd recently had—and looked to have again. We headed toward Wheat Basin and Hailstone National Wildlife Refuge and the little town of Rapelje (pronounced RAP-pull-jay), another spot with a renowned café said to offer good pie. For some reason, we've never stopped there. The prairie basin we'd be driving through stretched before us like a codex, bounded on all sides by mythical lands: the Yellowstone River breaks on the east and south, the Crazy Mountains poofed up with ice and snow on the west, and a variety of dry cliffs and badlands to the north.

Sometimes we've come here when the heat is crushing and sometimes when the air is so fresh, still, and clean we can't feel it on our faces. Today it was fifty-one degrees and falling, rainy and windy. In June. But the clouds did not menace as they had on Father's Day eight years earlier. While a vindictive tornado battered the roof off the city's MetraPark arena, we'd walked out to Grass Lake and stared back at the eastern sky. "That looks kinda bad," I'd thought. Even when there's no tornado, the sky can seem downright apocalyptic as a half-dozen thunderstorms wrack their own little corners of prairie simultaneously, like a half-dozen prophetic seals of the end times.

Obsessions can spike my mind and limit my possibilities, but why do some people *want* to cede their freedoms? Why does "might makes right" come back and back and back? Everybody, of course, wants to own or control things, or perhaps identify with those who do. Everybody wants power of one sort or another. But when you're out on the prairie, especially, such claims are beside the point. Better to ask what the prairie wants.

Today it must have admired migrating rattlesnakes crossing the gravel. Sharp-tailed grouse, dancing out of season and in midday. A badger and a ferruginous hawk—canny murderers stalking the prairie-dog towns. Prairie dogs, of course. A broad-daylight skunk. Bald eagles. Pronghorn. An upland sandpiper or two. Mule deer. Harriers. Swainson's hawks. Burying beetles. Chestnut-collared longspurs, the colorful little males with jet-black breasts and reddish necks, soared and spun. Once it was their cousins, thick-billed longspurs, plainer but natty with black bibs and bay wing patches—six males parleying on the road. The prairie loved horned larks, especially the ones scooting from the road margins, challenging the car, or zipping like unmotorized Evel Knievels in front of us. Not to be outdone, western meadowlark arias cantilevered up from the sage or trickled down from a power pole.

The prairie wanted abundance.

When we turned at the "intersection" of Molt-Rapelje and Dannenberg Roads, we were happy to see lingering water in the ditches gathered into languid sloughs and one or two shallow pools. This flooding portended Wilson's phalaropes, ducks, and curlews. Sure enough, after we'd turned north away from Wheat Basin, they appeared. Not just phalaropes but coots, cinnamon and blue-winged teal, shoveler ducks, gadwalls, pintails, mallards, killdeer, willets, godwits, avocets, and the anticipated curlews. Red-winged blackbirds cheered on the churning swimmers and efficiently escorted a raven to drier land, away from mating and nesting neighbors. The race is not always to the swift and powerful. Often, the weak own the field.

Thinking about ownership gets ridiculous, though, like an obsession. On one of our previous spring prairie expeditions, there were so many mosquitoes we could hear them from inside the closed car with the windows rolled up tight as they went zinging and whining in a dance of a million hungry bellies. Their individual fragility belied the power of their swarms. Just how many mosquitoes was that, anyway, I wondered? But they would not own me. It would be the other way around. How wealthy and powerful I would be then! Not that I'd be Queen of the Mosquitoes or anything. But I do have something in common with Mr. Kim and Mr. Trump in this *Lord of the Flies* universe we're tumbling into. According to entomologist Erica McAlister, there are so many flies on earth that each human can claim seventeen million. Every human, no matter where we live, how lowly we are, or how exalted.

In addition to flies, every human on earth could have billions of grains of sand and salt crystals. Then consider the Milky Way. At over one hundred billion stars and only eight billion people, we can each call at least twelve billion our own. Cells in the body? Of course, we have exclusive rights to these (in theory and temporarily), tens of trillions of them in all their diversity and color (a goodly number are red blood cells, apparently). What's my allotment of squirrels? Some estimates say I get three and so does every other human. Ants? We could gloat over a million each—at least.

So I was thinking of power and ownership. All the things I could erroneously claim—land, water, wildlife—as the car glided through a small section of prairie worked by wheat farmers. Their places are both private in their isolation and public in their situation by the road. One man was building a straw-bale house. I wanted to stop and ask him when he'd be finished and why he'd chosen to use straw—questions that were, of course, none of my business—or offer him encouragement. The place seemed a long way from completion, and there were kids' trikes and a little play area with bright plastic colors. The elaborate makeshiftness of it suggested that it might be a while until the house would be livable. In the meantime, the kids could play and watch their parents work. (Years later, the place is a shambles of equipment, decomposing bales, and puddles; the children's toys are long gone.)

Wheat planted out in a checkerboard of green winter stuff and last year's brown stubble means prosperity, profit, and an endless food supply. They're feeding the world, Montana farmers like to say, with the land they own. Thanks to them and our modern supply chains, I grow only herbs and berries in my small Billings backyard without ever going hungry.

We all own a fraction of an acre here and there, way past the city limits, in the form of national wildlife refuges. We can't grow crops there, but we can visit them without permission. In that regard, they confer freedom on any American who'll appreciate it. As Bernie, Luke, and I turned off the road at Hailstone National Wildlife Refuge, I felt immensely wealthy and privileged. This was my place—and maybe I could even say a share of that shrike looking down sardonically from the telephone wire along the road was mine. Sadly, I also have to admit that my ancestors stole this land long ago. Or thought they did.

While our birdwatching drive had been enlightening for Bernie and me, Luke had suffered in the backseat, I can't say patiently waiting, as we stopped for birds. To Luke, gravel roads mean imminent fun in the form of a hiking adventure or at least a walk, but we'd been going slowly off pavement for about twenty-five miles without that exciting canine moment when a leap from the car would be a leap into the riches of coyote scat, grass, and deer smell. Now, as we stopped, Luke's demeanor changed. He knew Hailstone National Wildlife Refuge, and he liked it, from its rickety cattle guard that he would puzzle over until he decided to skirt it entirely to the salty water that would bloom in crusty mud across the undrivable road a mile or so ahead. He was standing up, at last, wagging, alert, ears primed, nose wriggling. Ready! Hailstone was his place, too. And, as an innocent dog, he'd come by it honestly.

Clouds still glowering, we hiked the overgrown two-track into Hailstone, bundled against the cold and bent into the wind. As unseasonably rainy and cool as it was, there were signs of summer. Orange mallow bloomed at our feet. Little pink gaura flowers spun in the wind. Yellow and red clovers scented the old road, and the grass grew knee-high. Up in the rocks above us, lark buntings called, vertical white wing bars streamlining the males' onyx bodies.

Ruts wound through grasses made tall by a late spring until they were briefly erased by the flow of what remains of Hailstone Lake. The product of a Works Projects Administration earthen dam built in the 1930s, the lake was originally meant to provide and enhance a migratory way station for the kinds of birds we'd been seeing all day: pintails, teal, gadwalls, mallards. Our birds. Over time, however, the water's natural cycles of evaporation led to the accumulation of salts and selenium metals, which were, ironically, toxic to the very creatures the dam had been designed to help. Not to worry. A friend of ours, microbiologist Amaya Garcia Costas, studied the community of microorganisms at Hailstone and found helpful bacteria species that can "eat" selenite when given the time.

On our first visit, Hailstone had been a Delft-blue flooded playa filled with salty white inroads, phalaropes, and other shorebirds. On our next visit, it was a dry, black-and-white barren made manic by the foraging of horned larks seeking gnats or grit in the vacuumed lakebed. For a long time after that, the refuge was closed as managers tinkered with the drainage. Today, Hailstone's little stream threaded past watchful avocets. It was flowing again, cleansing itself with the help of Amaya's bacteria, its dam having been dismantled. The basin it traversed was green, studded with locoweed and orange daisies. If my math is correct, .00000882 of an acre of the refuge's total three thousand was "mine" as an American citizen, but I could claim even less ownership of the two golden eagles we'd watched two months ago, climbing into the clouds, plummeting, grappling with talons outstretched. One of the birds was a subadult, so the whole affair seemed a bit illicit.

Part of the Charles M. Russell complex of national wildlife refuges originally envisioned as stopping points for the ducks that hunters want, Hailstone seemed about as obscure and humble as public land in the United States gets. I'd rarely seen another human party here. The two-track was overgrown and crumbling, its drying mud surface curling into clay scrolls you could pick up intact and, if you'd been so inclined and knew how, inscribe with cuneiform. As I looked across the basin, though, I noticed an occasional farm truck burdened with hay bales and groaning toward the town of Broadview, raising a wedding train of dust behind it on the far county road.

Last time we'd been out, the ridge above Hailstone Basin had been laced with a few remnant snowdrifts and pierced by a makeshift cross that had blown over. Put together with baling wire and two rough poles stuck onto a tractor wheel, the cross seemed the work of a person who hadn't taken much aesthetic thought but was handy with wire cutters and wrenches. I'd put it back up, wondering why and knowing it would probably get blown down again. I didn't see it on the ridgeline today.

How many Americans would ever lay eyes on their own .00000882 acre of Hailstone National Wildlife Refuge, or even care if they missed it, this little valley east of the Crazy Mountains and south of meandering sandstone rims where golden eagles pursued May–December romances, this heart of the cross, this center of the universe, this navel of the cosmos? Lives came and went under the passage of clouds, the rising and setting of sun, moon, and stars. Meteors threw down their spears in globes of turquoise combustion, to the delight of badgers and skunks. Deer slipped in and out of grassy folds. Kids from Molt and Broadview took target practice on the hills beyond the refuge and then scuttled off in rusty old Dodge Ram trucks. Missouri foxtail cacti rose less than an inch above the soil, took in the world, and hid.

As the sun began stretching below the day's overcast, five avocets wading the now-released stream strutted around like *they* owned the place. They could each, I'll bet, claim hundreds of thousands of humans. If they wanted to.

Who controls what? Who will prevail, the few or the many? Is life an either/or proposition—hope or suicide, as one friend puts it? Should every country develop nukes, and, if the whole world were bristling with doomsday machines and dictators, would everyone be equal? Is mass suicide our species' fate? Why do Montanans kill themselves in far greater numbers per capita than almost any other group of American citizens? Are all Americans unconsciously anxious because of our violent past? How can stolen property be returned, when Manifest Destiny involved so many thieves and the property is so scattered?

We were driving smoothly home through the sunlight that had burst through the gloom, the glow taking on power as if it were a thing of depth and dimension. I was alert to the textures and topography of the place, but I was thinking in a jumbled way of cultural preconceptions and personal obsessions stoked, as I saw it now, by insecurity.

And then, finally, the short-eared owl.

Consider two ways—the first rational, the second mystical—of looking at an owl glaring at you from a fencepost. We're dealing here with *Asio flammeus*, an efficient dawn-and-dusk hunter of mice, sparrows, and insects. A ground nester, the female lays as few as one or as many as eleven eggs. Despite these facts, the short-eared owl is, like the proverbial Other, unknowable.

His power scorches you with yellow flare. His eyes catch the last-chance solar storms rending our mere earthly ones into tatters. But what does he think? What does he yearn for? Does he see more clearly than we do, thereby avoiding obsession and ego? The owl's an observer, and he's got the optical equipment to prove it. He's not someone I'd want to tangle with. *Look*, I tell him, *I'd give everything back if I could.*

How arrogant that sounds. As if I get to adjudicate anything. I could never run a planet, as my LDS ancestors aspired to do. And anyway, the birds already have it all figured out. They know that control is a dead end, that the good hunting of today might become the fast of tomorrow. They know when to exert their power and when to abide.

"I know you," the owl's eyes tell me. I'm no longer Oscar Charles Dawson's plaything. I belong to the owl.

On our previous trip out here in March, we'd stopped at a large prairie pond. That day was sunny, warm, and calm, the water a brocade of blue tones with darker ripples for seams. We'd set up our scopes to spy out intimate moments of waterfowl life. Everybody had been pleased with the day, swimming, lazing, occasionally feeding or preening. Full of enough happy bird images for a week, I was carrying my scope and tripod back to the car when Bernie said, calmly enough as usual, "There's an avocet flying your way." (He knows I like avocets.)

I turned around and, yes, there was the characteristic apricot head and black-and-white-striped wings of an avocet, but, in fact, the whole peaceful community was coming apart. Avocets were zooming my way, but also ducks and yellowlegs, ducks and phalaropes, ducks and killdeer. They caromed from invisible corners of air, panicked and united only in their desire to escape. The ballerinas—off point and out of sync—were pitching forward. It was every bird for her- or himself as a bald eagle coursed behind the multitude. Unlike humans, these waterbirds knew enough to get out of the way.

The eagle wheeled and spurted ahead and flung her weight toward the mob until, satisfied that her flying skills were outmatched by the smaller, more maneuverable creatures, she circled back to the pond where four coots, too awkward on takeoff to escape, were forced to make a stand.

The eagle veered toward them and feigned a dive, separating one coot from his companions. That was all she needed to do, as it turned out. She came around again and dove, this time for real. The coot she'd chosen (or whose bad judgment had chosen for her) plunged under the water, and the eagle rose empty-taloned, took a lap over the pond, and stooped again as the coot came up for air. He skittered below the surface this time, right as the eagle landed. She rummaged a bit in the disturbed water and struggled up, the coot—still already, perhaps fainted away or dead—gripped in her toes. As powerful and lithe as she'd proven herself to be, the eagle had a time churning over the pond carrying such a fat, furry, chicken-sized bird. She landed on the far shore like an Olympian plunging onto a warm beach, the decathlon's athletic feats of strength mastered. She worked contemplatively at the coot's glossy black feathers and began dining on his muscle, heart, kidneys, and lungs. I wondered if she even ate the pale-green lobed feet. She knew, of course, that she was subject, like everyone else, to chance and scarcity.

The three surviving coots swam toward grassy lake margins, their world and confidence shattered. Or were they feeling foolishly smug to have survived the attack? No one else seemed to have stuck around. A shaft of power had burst from the heavens and broken the community as well as the life of one unlucky citizen. How terrifying it must have been: the eagle's talons raking at him underwater, pushing and finally holding. When did he give up? When did he know? Probably the moment he found himself alone on the pond, his companions having turned the other way as the eagle dove. I tend to think he might logically have surrendered right then. But even after that he tried two diving gambits, and if the pond had been deeper, he'd have made it, a testament to his sturdy heritage.

Think of the gauntlet he'd run just to grow up, and the courage and clarity future coots will need to survive the human era, no matter how widespread and numerous they have been. Perhaps not thinking any the less of themselves for their plain black plumage and small white beaks—and for being slow on takeoff—is the coot formula. That and sheer numbers. The eagle can't get them all.

Godspeed, dear coots.

TRAILS 25 TO 28

Bighorn Mountains—Water in a Dry State

General location: Bighorn Mountains
Shell Falls: 21 miles from Burgess Junction and 26 miles from Greybull, WY; 152 miles from Yellowstone
Melody Falls: 5 miles from Lovell, WY; 98 miles from Yellowstone
Porcupine Falls: 35 scary miles from Lovell
Bucking Mule Falls: 35+ scary miles from Lovell

Hiking distance
Shell Falls: less than ¼ mile
Melody Falls: 1.5 miles, one-way
Porcupine Falls: .8 mile one-way (though estimates vary)
Bucking Mule Falls: 4.9 miles round-trip (some hikers say 5.4)

Elevation Gain
Shell Falls: negligible (elevation 6,200 feet)
Melody Falls: ~1,000-foot gain (elevation 4,800 to 5,800 feet)
Porcupine Falls: 440-foot loss/gain (elevation ~8,400 to 8,000 feet)
Bucking Mule Falls: negligible (elevation ~8,500 feet)

Terrain
Shell Falls: coniferous forest; the falls is 75 feet high with a 3,600-gallons-per-second flow
Melody Falls: dry juniper foothills; the falls is 40 feet high with variable flow
Porcupine Falls: coniferous forest; the falls is more than 100 feet high
Bucking Mule Falls: lodgepole pine forest to sage meadow; the falls is ~200–600 feet high

It closes in. Everyone says we'll pay for these warm, sunny winter days with a cold spring or summer. But we don't. The expected cold spell lasts barely a week, its snow so thin and dry you can sweep it off the sidewalk with a kitchen broom. Come spring, rain holes up in the clouds like gray lace. Thunderstorms are sparse and often dry, starting fires rather than dousing them. People don't even need to replace their roofs—there is none of the shingle-chafing hail we usually get. Summer comes early, and the prairie grass no sooner greens up than it turns brittle and beige.

Bernie and I drive a dirt road northwest of Billings, looking for lark buntings. We find them. We also find a family of Hungarian partridges. The mother gathers together a confusion of downy cheepers and escorts them off the embankment as we go by. A mile or so later, we get out to walk beside masses of yellow sunflowers covered with what must be hundreds of suckling bee flies, furry little insects that act and look like plain versions of their namesakes. I think they're cute, but some species have the antisocial habit of laying their eggs in the nests of other insects. According to the *Pollinator Conservation Handbook*, when the larvae hatch, the little tykes drill the hemolymph right out of their neighbors' bodies, a fact that seems fitting today.

It's 90° Fahrenheit. There's no water and hardly any shade. Our stroll along the roadside blossoms doesn't last very long. Driving back, I wonder how those twelve partridge chicks will survive. June looks like August.

A waterfall is gravity's proof. Stand, for instance, at Shell Falls in the Bighorn Mountains. Physics produces seventy-five vertical feet of turbulence, trapped air pockets, eddies, temporary backflows, and slurries. Lean over the handrail that lines the paved walk and imagine the tragedies or triumphs of hydrogen and oxygen, the cumulative history of Shell Creek, the steady gathering—from cloudburst to rivulet, from freshet to creek, with quickening speed down stairstep grades until the final crash, the freefall over Precambrian rock.

For weeks, daytime temperatures in Billings rarely drop below their initial 90° and sometimes jump above 100°. Two days are among the hottest I've known here. You wouldn't think there'd be much difference between 100° and 105°, but there is. At 100°, you're pretty damn hot—"sweltering," as the National Weather Service puts it. At 105°, the sky presses like sheet metal; birds pant; squirrels stretch their bellies against bare dirt for any shred of coolness; milkweed flowers dangle like pink rags. There are no butterflies. In fact, the only insects seem to be grasshoppers and loud, grating cicadas. The humidity stands at 10 percent, low enough to make your nose bleed. Sometimes it's scorching at midnight. Sometimes the sky is umber with smoke. From 2018 through 2021, our local rainfall, measured January to September, shrank from an already-spare sixteen to a throat-burning eleven inches, the drop graphed like a mountain slope. Down. Each year drier than the one before.

We're not as hard hit as other parts of the world. In southern Madagascar it hasn't rained in four years. A million people may starve. In central Chile, it's too dry for prickly pear cactus. In Mexico's Sonora, the rain hasn't come in months. This couldn't happen here, I used to think. Now, I walk by the Bighorn or Yellowstone River, murmurs subdued, gravel shores broad, islands wider than the flow. Such a low diastolic pressure—the relaxed beat of summer contracture—indicates morbidity.

Weeks later, the steel sky in Billings relents. I run outside and rub a light drizzle on my arms.

A waterfall is causality. There's rock to be eroded. There's a jagged bed to land in. There're snow and rain to bring the water that'll foam and lace and bead continuously in a way no camera or human eye can satisfactorily record. Knowing these causes would exist, I used to take the result for granted.

As kids, my friends and I would go two blocks over from my house and a few blocks up to find our hidden refuge. We'd leave the asphalt of Mill Creek Road, squeeze behind yards, twist around scrub oak, and scramble down gravel, picking waterleaf, dogtooth violets, and chokecherries—whatever was blooming—until we got to the gully bottom and the whispery little stream that carved it. Hiking! We never told our parents where we went, exaggerating the risks we deemed they'd never allow of wading in a foot of flowing mountain runoff.

It was there I saw my first muskrat, there a friend and I wondered what two dogs were doing stuck together and yelping—were they in pain?—and there we played at female renditions of Lewis and Clark. In the summer, "green worms" (really caterpillars) dangled from silk threads, and, in the winter, ice made the paths treacherous. Weather permitting, we'd take off our shoes and wade, water's gadding cutting us off from our parents, the city, time itself. We'd rearrange river rocks to make waterfalls and reservoirs. We'd wonder about the pheasant striding around with his red lores and long tail. We'd fall under water's spell for hours. Linear causality exalted us. Mystics are said to come down from the mountaintops, but in our case, we'd climb up from the creek before dusk, entering the summer heat and happenstance of the homes we knew.

A waterfall is prophecy. Last autumn, I found only an empty trace of Melody Falls up Cottonwood Canyon in the Bighorn Mountain foothills southeast of Billings, five miles from the town of Lovell, Wyoming, and part of that state's long central mountain spine.

Dubbed "The Rose City" because planters of flowers line Main Street, Lovell is home to a Western Sugar refinery and, in fall, hills of sugar beets waiting to be processed. It's home to Hy-Art Cinema, the Brandin' Iron restaurant, the Bighorn Canyon National Recreation Area visitors center (closed as of 2025 due to federal budget cuts), and the long, wide streets that mark every pioneer LDS town. Its population has hovered just above and below twenty-two hundred souls since the 1990s. Its sidewalks are empty, its homes well-kept, its businesses hanging on. The mighty escarpment of the Bighorn Mountains flanks the east. A good road goes in that direction, from Lovell over the Bighorn River—widened to lake breadth by the Yellowtail dam some seventy-two miles north—probes to the mouth of Cottonwood Canyon, and ends at a well-maintained campground complete with gazebo.

After parking, we entered the canyon on foot. It's a giant gash in the headwall of the Bighorn Mountains, and it was all dancing and sparkly with cottonwood leaves and pale cliffs. It's also a steep climb, but I stopped and took photographs as an excuse to catch my breath. The canyon remains narrow, a straight shot, until four miles up.

Melody Falls, when we reached it, was nothing but a dark line over rock—the path of its former prosperity twisted and plowed from the plateau above to a dry gravel field below. Now, no one was there to see it—or, rather, its absence—except for me, my two hiking companions, and two chocolate-bodied, white-rumped bighorn sheep. I must say, it was a bit intimidating to be stared at (or looked through) by a pair of two- or three-hundred-pound rams. I felt in the middle of a fragile détente, with an impressive being on either side. Eventually, one bighorn trotted across the trail, wandered up the opposite cliffside, and paralleled our route as we continued, except that he browsed below the rock overhang to our north while we humans followed the footpath along the canyon bottom to the south. The other bighorn vanished downhill.

When had Melody Falls dried up, and how did the sheep manage in summer and fall without abundant water? Perhaps they'd get the hydration they needed from the vegetation they ate—the vegetation itself none too lush, though, what with the region's average annual precipitation of six inches. And there *was* water, a glissading bit of a creek that a ram might wet his whistle in. There just wasn't enough to power a falls. The rams made do, but what would happen to the twenty-two hundred humans in Lovell if drought really kicked in someday? Planters of dried roses on Main Street? Skeletal shops? The Mormon ward with a "For Sale" sign hanging crookedly in front?

I'm reminded of the musk ox vertebra fossil found nearby. "Nought may endure," wrote Percy Shelley, "but / Mutability."

A waterfall is time made palpable.

The Porcupine Falls trail in the Bighorn Mountains of Wyoming follows a short, steeply wicked way to the bottom of a narrow canyon. It's hard not to slide on the loose rock. Harder still to find a place to step aside and let others pass. We make the trip late in the day as the usual rain and thunderstorms threaten. The trail starts at 8,440 feet above sea level and ends at 8,000. All well and good (except for the knees and Luke pulling on his leash)—but, of course, you have to climb out again.

Despite its ragged lodgepoles and firs, Porcupine Falls has a subtropical flavor. Like a Maui cascade, it leaps over a pale multifaceted cliff, stretches long, and creates at its base a greenish pool where on a hot day families swim. Hidden and lovely, it may once have watered tree ferns and horsetails, and it might do so again as the climate heats. There ought to be a brontosaurus lapping at the broken rocks and pool below. Who knows what the world will look like and what rough beast will slouch or paddle or fly here in another 145 million years?

Solid chunks of time, as set out in the rocks of the Bighorn Mountains, are, paradoxically, slippery to think about. I try to get a handle on the past, when living clams and mussels filtered seawater through what is now solid rock. But the image pixilates. Water seems the one constant. An ever-transforming constant. As if Earth were a giant water clock measuring the flow from airy vapor to rain to stream to deer mouth to deer urine to luxuriant grama grass to packrat kidney to coyote belly to a leap across snow.

An ancient technology and aesthetic, clepsydras, or water clocks, tolled elapsed hours according to the path of water through often elaborate and elegant internal mechanisms. The elephant clock, for instance, was an invention of Ismail al-Jazari (1136–1236), author of *The Book of Knowledge of Ingenious Mechanical Devices*. It took the form of a graven Asian elephant with water-driven bowls, levers, and lead weights inside. It kept time by the half hour. The process continued as long as there was water in the reservoir. This instrument undoubtedly required a now-vanished occupation: clepsydra tender, a career that ought to be revived. Today's clocks wouldn't be ingenious devices, though. They'd be the timepieces of life: hydrology, ecosystems, geological upheavals.

A waterfall is metaphysics made visible.

Bernie, Luke, and I take the wrong route to another elegant gash in the side of the Bighorns. Somehow we miss the trailhead and set out on an old road through a fairytale lodgepole/fir forest deepened by sun shafts. We end up in the sagebrush heat of an open hillside, traipse along the sunbaked side of a steep gully, and stumble across the official Forest Service overlook, which thrusts like a prow into a dry ocean of air filling convoluted Devil Canyon. The vista point for Bucking Mull Falls is so exposed, Bernie and I don't walk silly Luke to the edge but take turns inching out alone. Someone told me that a rockslide swept a child away here, but no news account confirms the story, which gives the place an uncertain, somber aura.

Also somber, on our first visit, was the thick smoke blown in from massive wildfires in Idaho. We could see the falls, but not much else. So, we've come back during a clearer month. And the canyon is a gap in the world with its geological layers, vertigo, echo of death, and beauty.

I settle on the promontory with a few lonely pines and junipers, and a warm updraft. I crane to look below: hundreds of feet into nothing. I take it on faith that there is a bottom. Across the chasm (empty unless a swallow rolls by or a raven shoulders past), a sheen of water as thin as graphine papers the opposite rock wall, marked on either side by a pale teal border of what may be moss.

I don't know how high Bucking Mule Falls is. Estimates differ, from 200 to 600 feet. If the 600 is correct, it's three times as tall as Niagara Falls. Unlike Niagara, Bucking Mule makes a smooth, untroubled drop—or at least the part that I can see does. From the vista, you can't hear it, feel it, or watch it flow. It marks language's vanishing point.

And then there's the canyon: high walls with secret crevices and rock art, unviewable depths, Bighorn and Pryor Mountains' blue above. Magnified by the labyrinth, silence vibrates. The world dissolves like mineral crumbs winking on the promontory where I balance. Shelley called this the Sublime. In German, it's *unheimlich*. Uncanny. It's a better tonic for OCD than Xanax. I'm so small here that the obsessions inside me become insignificant. Their power huffs and then blows away into the canyon.

Waterfalls have become reminiscences, phantasms. We're more than nine months into the drought. What if the rain never comes back? With the exception of Melody, the Bighorn Mountain cascades, as I remember them, were luxurious, their lavishness in a semi-arid region now as distant as a conversion experience squeezed away by days of laundry and dishwashing, sweeping and vacuuming.

In the middle of September, I go down to the Yellowstone River, its shoreline rocks green and brown with algae. The smaller channels are not quite still but might be after another month without rain. The Earthly Paradise drains, putrefies, toxifies. Good luck being led beside the still waters. I'm thinking cyanobacteria, blue-green algae that can kill a dog almost instantly and sicken humans who breathe airborne particles.

The next week, we take a friend upstream to the park and it's 80° Fahrenheit, the land sere, the snow all but gone from the high Beartooths, the Lower Falls lankier than I've seen it, the canyon still, brown, and dreadful. An hour or two later, we find elk knee-deep in the Gardiner River's once-churning rapids. Unmoving, they're stunned in the autumn heat. Like the vista at Bucking Mule Falls, the magnitude of climate change again shrinks my personal anxieties to nothing. Faced with oblivion and biosphere collapse, of what use or interest are my cycling internal images of harm and dread?

In eight months, a flood will wash away the road and close Yellowstone, stranding tourists and residents of the gateway town below. And humans will mark another milestone as water and time cycle beyond our comprehension.

TRAIL 29

Lost Twin Lakes, with the Coward and the Valiant

General location: West Tensleep Lake Campground, Bighorn Mountains, WY; approximately 180 miles from Yellowstone
Hiking distance: 11–13 miles (written and online sources disagree)
Elevation gain: 1,524 feet
Terrain: Alpine forest to krummholz to tundra

I was angsty. My old sorrow for the world nestled in my heart: I couldn't envision the silky ideal without also fearing reality's grit. Yet that was background noise, and I was used to it. What was unusual was that I'd become overwrought about things that never bother me, like the elevation of the campground Bernie had picked for us. And then there was the catastrophizing: What if I couldn't breathe at that altitude? What if I had a heart attack? I've been higher for longer periods, and I've never labored to breathe. I have no known cardiac conditions—except for these palpitations. Yikes!

So, I'm not cut out for wilderness adventures. My brain-nestled hypothalamus senses danger from my anxious thoughts and tells my adrenal glands, which deliver adrenaline in spades to my cardiovascular system and muscles. My hippocampus resolves to remember the fear of my pounding heart, and my burdened amygdala projects distress as it tries to handle the entire emotional download. An endless loop develops, which my neocortex translates into words, e.g., "You're pushing sixty now. You never know when the heart attack is coming. Women are more prone than men. Women have unusual symptoms. You're pushing sixty now. Heart attack. Sixty. Women more than men." Or something like that. On and on it goes, the merry-go-round of self-absorbed, evolutionary, prey-animal programming. Another bout of OCD? No, just a return of the Generalized Anxiety Disorder (with its happy acronym GAD) that has plagued me, I think, since I entered my mother's birth canal elbow-first, trying to inch my way out, maybe, instead of barreling through head-on as a brave neonate should. When am I ever going to "get over" anxiety, OCD, and everything else I've been born or nudged into? All the pioneer baggage? To be honest, I'm not cut out for homebound quietude any more than I am for the challenge of the wild. Anxiety stalks me anywhere. I could be choosing pasta in Albertsons, and anxiety will bully me into sensing my own mortality.

The obvious source of my anxiety now was our pending camping trip. With my mind squeezed to the size of a rabbit's pituitary and working twice as fast, I thought about moose, for which the Bighorn Mountains are famous. I thought of the 6 percent grades on the road to the plateau and of brake failures. I thought of my old nemesis, lightning. Inevitably, I was thinking about thinking. Do rabbits catastrophize? I'll bet they do.

Where we were going was the Lost Twin Lakes trail in the Cloud Peak Wilderness Area—the longest round-trip eleven miles I've ever walked. It's a moderate day hike, according to most guides. It's not arduous. The route isn't terrifying. There's no serious exposure. No dangerous stream crossing—not, at least, in late summer. There aren't any grizzlies. There aren't even endless switchbacks. But it would take us two days to reach the top.

What Lost Twin Lakes trail has (and what my hypothalamus-hippocampus-amygdala trio was trying to make me afraid of) is elevation—all of it more than nine thousand feet. But that's not really what would stretch our travel there into an ordeal. The problem was that the trail would have me on it.

Last August we determined to camp in the Bighorns. We'd been talking about it for three years. Going camping is the summer goal Bernie and I find hardest to reach. Why we can't get away puzzles us. Once, we kept all our gear in the car for two months. That helped, a little. What holds us back? Housecats, work, gardening, laziness and inertia, my mental state.

Bernie chose the West Tensleep Lake campground. We'd sleep well and wake up early and rested. We'd have plenty of time to enjoy its beautiful, adjacent trail. We reserved a site online, arranged for Big Sky Animal Nanny, LLC, to watch our cats, and collected more junk food than we eat in a year at home (drinking Sunny D is like an intravenous shot of glucose). We jammed the trunk full of tent, cots, sleeping bags, camp chairs, coolers, and all sorts of superfluous stuff. Once Luke had jumped into the backseat with his own gear (bed, harness and leash, water bottle, kibble, treats), we were set. The only thing I forgot to pack was Xanax.

The Bighorns are a geological wonder, an uplifted hunk of sedimentary rock on top of older strata. Mostly locals haunt these realms—the two hundred-mile-long range gives Wyoming residents hunting, fishing, dispersed camping (a nice way of saying you can park your RV anywhere for a week or two), and hiking opportunities. Many visitors to the Bighorns have been taken there by grandpas and grandmas and often return years later as grandpas and grandmas themselves. On the trail, we would meet people from Sheridan, Casper, Laramie—we seemed exotics with our homeland in far-off Montana.

To get into the Bighorns, I rejected the route from Lovell, the radiator- and brake-destroying Oh-My-God Highway otherwise known as the Medicine Wheel Passage, a relentless, gravity-defying ascent that we did once when we were young and innocent, and will, I hope, never have to do again. Our best option was to drive south along the eastern escarpment of the Bighorns through Crazy Horse's country—where the Lakota leader made a heroic last-ditch effort to save his unique, grand-hearted way of life. We passed Sheridan and Buffalo—the TV series *Longmire* was filmed in the latter—and paused to walk Luke in Clear Creek Canyon on the way up. We met a pleasant guy from Texas—he'd recently moved to Wyoming, so, in that sense, he was a local. He loved the deciduous beauty of the canyon and wondered how, come hunting season, he could live-truss a moose as he was used to doing with wild hogs. We weren't any help in that regard.

The easiest way into the Bighorns, the road from Buffalo slid us into the high country without too much exposure or too many ridiculously steep pitches—by Bighorn standards, anyway. Soon we were cruising along the flat top of the plateau through lodgepole pines and past occasional views of the peaks. Rain came and went, and we stopped for elk burgers at Deer Haven Lodge. Now, an elk burger is the meat world's equivalent of a neutron star: heavy, dense, gravity-bending. We would be good to go for days.

All this while, I was filled with angst, terror, and a biting sense of my own inadequacy. My skin was sore to the touch because of it, as if that fragile dermal layer could barely contain such anxiety or keep out pulses of fear. I've noticed that phenomenon my whole life. I continued to blame this current distress on the altitude, but that wasn't right. Fear for fear's sake was about it. I like to think irrational fear serves some purpose beyond torturing me, but why does the old hypothalamus crank up fear when fear isn't necessary? If I were a human of the Pleistocene—that world of giant bears and badass deer like the North American stag-moose (weighing fifteen hundred pounds and standing eight feet tall at the shoulder)—I'd be the rare type who'd hide in a cave. And I'd survive, with a pounding heart, to spread my genes throughout whatever clan I belonged to. When everyone else was valiant, we'd form a tribe of the fearful. Maybe that's why we're still around, albeit cowering. But, I tell myself, we don't have stag-moose anymore, just the petite modern kind.

West Tensleep Lake Campground turned out to be a little circle of sites guarding its treasure: an outhouse. There were so many "hard-sided units," though, replete with their own facilities, that Bernie and I would have the pit toilet to ourselves. I later tested the acoustics with my standard rendition on such occasions of "Amazing Grace." They were very good. But this revelation came later, because the moment we arrived at the campground, the clouds let loose. We waited in the car while lightning shot around the hills and rain thunked the windshield. When it was over, we scrambled to set up the tent and shelter our beds inside before another storm hit (while we scrambled, Luke snapped up scones intended for the next day's breakfast).

A word about cots. When some people hear about going camping, they assume that they'd have to "rough it" in a tent. However, three years ago we discovered the advanced technology that lifts a tired body above both the ground and the roots that can press like bad memories into flanks and spines. Topped with a one-inch pad and a lofty sleeping bag, a cot means I can't ever say I'm uncomfortable—unless I get cold. But I've developed a method for keeping frigid air from settling against my back: Tucking a sweatshirt around my shoulders seals in the heat. I've also discovered that a sleeping bag listed as "good to -20°F" is quite adequate when it's +35°.

But, despite all my luxuries, I couldn't sleep that first night at West Tensleep Lake. Between Bernie's snoring and the antics of my heart and lungs, the peace of the wild didn't enter. Our fellow campers obeyed "quiet hours"—10:00 p.m. to 6:00 a.m.—sending kids and generators to bed. But their considerateness didn't help me. I had no Xanax. It was probably on the kitchen counter.

There was also the Problem of the Outhouse. Generally, I think nothing of getting up in the night. But that's because the bathroom is twenty steps from my bed. When a trip to the toilet involves a headlamp, the unzipping of numerous sleeping bag and tent coverings, the craziness of shadows, and the rare but possible moose or predatory black bear, I do think about it, dread it, and wait until waiting is no longer an option. The Problem is more acute now than it was when I was twenty—or forty. It doesn't help that, when Luke goes with me, he stares into the dark, hackles rising, and sniffs the air.

Before sunrise and before Bernie woke up, I walked Luke along the road, startling a snowshoe hare, who bounded away so fast all I saw were her legs and feet. After cold granola and boxed milk (and a single scone shared between Bernie and me, and nothing but kibble for Luke)—everything damp from the night's showers—we faced a clear morning and set out on the trail to Lost Twin Lakes, allegedly a mere five and a half miles to get to something like 10,330 feet. We'd seen photos of the lake with its dramatic, fortress-like cirque. It would be beautiful.

Clomping through the campground, we soon entered a lakeside forest, looked for moose (none), and reached the official Cloud Peak Wilderness sign. The trail was a pleasant way through pines and firs. Remarkably, everything on the low ridge we followed was dry. We'd come too late in the year for a wildflower extravaganza (and, thankfully, too late for a mosquito one), but when we emerged from the trees, meadows of lush grass spread like the green shag carpeting that was all over everyone's house in my 1970s childhood. Little puffy clouds and low ridges lofted above us. A few stones to teeter along over a shallow stream crossing. All bucolic and beautiful.

I was a nervous wreck, walking faster, breathing harder, and getting a drier mouth than I usually do on a hike. Trying to outwalk my own overreacting nerves and impending demise. Anxiety doesn't ever make sense—or, if it's justifiable, my response to it isn't. I knew that going higher and faster wouldn't stave off a heart attack, and neither would driving Bernie crazy with sardonic comments about my health. He thought I was blaming him for bringing us camping. Thing is, he didn't "bring us." If anything, it was the elk burger powering me along. I walked so fast, my mouth felt as if it was lined with wool batting.

Anxiety made me a diligent watcher of clouds. They started as innocent little wisps. When I looked again, they were curdling like fat in a pan. Next thing I knew, they began piling up on the peaks in front of us. After two hours or so, they coagulated right overhead, shoved forward by the mountains, metamorphosing from white to blue to a few ornery patches of battleship gray. Once, they'd been flat and skimming, happy and young. Now they were 3-D, stubborn, jostling each other like angry Christmas shoppers. Anxiety mixed my metaphors.

I started praying with every breath to the elemental forces of electricity. I didn't know how to pray to lightning and thunder, and I worried that it might be disrespectful to do so. But I kept on. I got it into my head that I needed to help clean the trail. That might make the storm gods happy. When I admitted to Bernie that I was invoking this force both immanent and ancient, he warned that I might be drawing it down. I intensified my prayers and my picking up of gum wrappers and twisty ties. I realized that my conception of weather was all wrong and shallow, but I thought that even if I understood a quintillionth of what it was, the lightning might be amused enough to be helpful. *Please keep us safe, dear clashing air masses. I don't know the etiquette at all, and I'm ill-equipped and boorish, and I'm doing my best. But you are more real than any other deities I can think of right now. So, keep us safe. Please. (But will you?)*

I walked faster. Prayed more fervently. Breathed harder. Felt my mouth tissues further desiccating. Suggested to Bernie that we should go back. I didn't like the looks of the sky. He didn't want to humor my pitiful whining (which, to be fair, had been going on since we'd headed into the mountains). We kept hiking, coming down off the ridge and out into the open, along a pretty little meadow. Pretty, though, to a point. It was dimmed now by gathering clouds.

In the 1990s we watched a TV show called *Tales from the Dark Side* (one episode starred Kareem Abdul-Jabbar as a genie). In the opening credits, a sunny scene is instantly changed to a menacing shadowland: "Man lives in the sunlit world of what he believes to be reality, but there is . . . a place that is just as real but not as brightly lit: a dark side." I was paralyzed by the show's either/or fallacy: light or dark. Fortunately, we were close to a destination of sorts, Mirror Lake—not our goal, but a worthy body of water in its own right. "How about," I suggested, "if we stay here a while and see what the weather's going to do?"

It was a good compromise and a good move on my part. We left the main path for a narrow cove, about three miles from the trailhead, and came out to quite an acceptable view of lapping waves and green hills. There wasn't a good place to sit, though, because of the pointy boulders clogging the shore. Plus, a dead fish—enticing to Luke—bobbed in the darkening water. Darkening as the storm came on. A shadow of an obsessive thought: Was the bouncing piscine corpse a bad omen? For that matter, had my pleas to the storm gods tipped into OCD territory?

I didn't want another repeat of our West Fork hike a year or two ago, where we were below simultaneous thunder and lightning. I didn't know if I could trust my bumbling prayers to the weather. I made us go back when the lightning began. I chose flight rather than my usual paralysis.

When we returned to the crest of the rocky ridge that split the bigger valley in two, we were met by a volley of atmospheric kettle drums. *See?* On the other hand, I felt cowardly to note that a party of six, including a baby and a young child, weren't fazed by the weather. I sure annoyed myself when a judgmental voice came up inside me, *What kind of mother . . . ?* We exchanged pleasant greetings, put on rain gear, and parted—they went up; we descended. At the stream crossing, we met a pair of hikers who said we were smarter than they were to have put the thunder at our backs rather than walk right into it. Still, they ascended. The brave, clearly. Shakespeare has Julius Caesar warn that, "Cowards die many times before their deaths. The valiant taste of death but once." All right. I was dying many times, but didn't Caesar end up stabbed and bleeding on the Roman Senate floor—et tu Brute, and all that?

By the time we got back to camp, the three of us—Bernie, Luke, and I—were wet and soggy. Determined to salvage some of the day for my disappointed fellow hikers, I suggested we drive down Tensleep Canyon. Which we did, leaving the electric weather behind. I breathed deeply as we descended and warmed my itchy-cold skin. In fact, it was Saharan at the Salt Lick trail near the mouth of the canyon. Climbing at what seemed a sixty-five-degree angle through junipers, we were soon heated up, and all our clothes were dry. Ironically, my mouth was now moisturized with thick saliva. Luke looked miserable, probably wondering what had happened to our cool mountain day and on the point of heat stroke. I turned us around. Too hot.

Disgusted with my cowardice as we drove back to the campground, Bernie didn't say anything, but I could tell. I'd kept curtailing our hikes. Crispy critters either way you looked at it, I'd thought. Optimist that he is, he didn't agree.

The sense of dread still hung around my heart. My brain was shrunken and petty, and wildness was preserving neither me nor the world. But when we got back to camp, the air was clear and the lake still. On the far shore, a bull moose browsed peacefully, never bothering to look up at his human visitors. We settled in our chairs that night, watched the stars, and heard the bats clicking. I wish I could say what sort of bats make audible calls, but I can't. The little creatures loop-de-looped through the firs as the night and the moon came up, and then they were silent. Not a stargazer, Luke was eager to get into the tent. He stared at it and clearly disliked our lingering in the damp shadows. So, we all went to bed. The night was silent. Luke settled on his pillow under my down coat, gave his usual big, day-ending sigh, and relaxed. Bernie didn't snore. I could breathe. My heart entered normal sinus rhythm. I slept, even without Xanax.

Next morning, Bernie had plans for a "safer," shorter, less high-altitude hike. Uh-uh. "Let's do Lost Twin Lakes again," my voice said. "Let's get to the lakes this time." I sent a quiet prayer to the lightning. Bernie seemed grateful.

We covered familiar terrain, at least for three miles. Again, I felt like I was almost running, trying to beat the clouds, which were more lackadaisical today but following the same basic mountain pattern: puffy, coagulating, graying. At least I was less obsessed by the elevation. I thought I might live (but compulsively knocked on wood[s] anyway).

Past Mirror Lake, where we'd stopped before, we made it into the krummholz, the trail following West Tensleep Creek into ever-higher fastnesses adorned by late-season wildflowers—a slope of Gunnison's mariposa lilies, one of the most beautiful things I've ever seen. For years, I've been trying to capture the "perfect" photo of their lower-altitude cousins, the sego lilies. I'm afraid I never will. How can a photograph comprehend the creamy wax petals; the furry, red-accented centers; the starry architecture of pistil and stamens? All swaying in the breeze on thin stems?

I'm partial to sego lilies because they're Utah's state flower and helped the pioneers avoid starvation. Maybe I exist because of them. Eating the bulbs reportedly wasn't even unpleasant. I saw the blossoms for the first time in the Oquirrh Mountains, behind Kennecott Copper pit's big smelter stack. I was on a school outing to a "sea cave," a remnant of the old, Pleistocene-era Lake Bonneville shoreline. As any Salt Lake schoolchild knew, the various lake levels of that ancient inland sea run horizontally like giant bathtub rings all along the Wasatch Front. Hundreds of sego lilies dotted the wasteland, sassing at the notion that they were in any way delicate.

And now here were their close cousins growing below the gathering clouds, singing in the breeze, turning open-faced to the weather, as they had to. I crawled among them, stretching for a good photo, not thinking at all about their edible roots or about the macabre fact that the man they are named after, Captain J. W. Gunnison, was murdered along with seven others in an attack by Pahvant Ute Indians, perhaps put to the task by Brigham Young and his Danite militia. No, I didn't think about Gunnison at all or about the ambitious theocracy of Utah Territory and my family's role in it. I even forgot my anxiety. If something as small and delicate as a mariposa lily could face the dangerous world, then maybe I could, too. As my mind expanded, my ego withered.

And then clouds passed across the sun, turning joy into a stern reality of short-growing-season desperation, and we were about to enter a narrow defile. I lost my little access of courage and humility.

Like many bodies of water in the mountains, the Lost Twin Lakes sit within a cirque or bowl. The setting is more dramatic than the usual, with a big blocky table rising to the south of the lower lake and a more conventional but no less imposing 12,281-foot pyramid flanking the upper of the two lakes to the southeast.

We could see this cirque for a mile, beckoning and welcoming as if it were close. But there were still small meadows to pass, wet pastures to cross, and rocky hills to ascend. At one point, when I thought we were at the last rise, I stopped my mad dash (a relative term) up the trail to let Bernie go in front. The hike had been his choice, after all, and I thought he should be first to see the lakes. But we hadn't come to the lakes. And then I realized that we were going to have to go right up the side of a willow-fringed, bare-rock slope to reach the cirque proper. I glanced at the clouds. We weren't socked in yet. Maybe my heart would hold out for this last ascent. I made these observations tentatively and kept them to myself. An odd feature of my anxiety disorders is that if I expect the worst, I feel that I magically stop it from happening.

Turned out the last ascent was easy, like walking three abreast on a sidewalk. Luke jumped past the willows, over the boulders and cliffs, happy as a mountain sheep, while I kept admonishing him to "wait" for me, a command he sometimes obeys and sometimes doesn't. I'd broken my ankle two summers before, after he decided to feign ignorance of the word and fell from a ledge near Pictograph Cave, landing in my arms and putting on my left ankle the whole torque of a 122-pound woman grabbing a fifty-pound dog rocketing downward.

The trail petered out, but, by that time, we knew where to go, and the lower lake smiled up at us with a harebell sheen and a gentle ripple. The sun was brisking in and out of the industrious clouds, but there was little wind on the ground. We sat by the shore, deciding that the lower of the lakes was sufficient beauty for one day. We dipped into our food supplies and daydreamed as we chewed on a carbohydrate feast of "Beartooth Bars" from our neighborhood bakery. Two young men lazed down the shore from us. Other than that, we were alone. In a world of almost eight billion people and untold millions of dogs, we were alone and very small.

How long can an epiphany take? Too long for an afternoon threatening storms. I did not become one with the scene, though it was beautiful. I did not overcome my anxiety while mingling with the particles of lake water, light, rock, willow. I didn't mingle much. I knew lightning and thunder were closing in. And so we left, feeling vindicated, maybe, but not, at least in my case—I can't speak to Luke's and Bernie's spiritual endeavors—uplifted. The whole puzzle of existence had dwindled to two options: Be nervous or be valiant. Though I was putting up a brave front today, I was stuck in nervous mode. Et tu, indeed.

Our progress downhill was fast. I suppose it was good exercise, our continuing race with the now earnest clouds. It's sad how soon all the work of climbing is undone as one descends a trail. But it's also comforting to know how soon one can escape the ramparts.

We were past Mirror Lake before we knew it and retracing our steps of the previous day. Then we were resting at a small cascade off to the side of the main route, a place we'd passed three times before without paying it much attention. The sky was a uniform gray, and, because of that, less terrifying. I thanked the storm, begging further mercy. Granted a reprieve, we stayed for a bit, and I started watching the falls in the two ways Bernie has taught me: Follow a single mote of water down (dizzying), or visually step back and see the cascade as a whole (not dizzying). The first is empathy; the second, aesthetics. Combining the two would involve mental antics I'm not ready for. Stuck in an either/or universe, I see the droplet *or* the sheet of falling water.

But there has to be something beyond rods and cones. Something beyond adrenal glands and pounding hearts and fear. An unbounded wilderness I've been searching for throughout my life. With little success. Until primal electricity imparted a gift. Or maybe it was the native genius of the little creek itself.

As I struggled with the two ways of viewing a waterfall, I noticed small fish leaping from the crushing tumble, aiming for a rocky ledge halfway to the top, flinging themselves onward as if their fins would become wings. It was a David Attenborough moment: "These salmonids have one chance to reach the calmer waters above if they are to spawn ..." What the fish were doing cut through the tension that had held my gut and heart in illogical terror for two days. To hell with it, the fish might have been saying. To hell with genes, ecological imperatives, and maximizing our reproductive capacities. To hell with mass extinctions and climate change. To hell, finally, with a jump onto rocks that could rip our swim bladders to shreds. To hell with desiccation, strangulation, lightning, and a current that might kill us. To hell with a binary world. Particle or cascade? We take both. By gum, said the fish (they suddenly cursed quaintly), we've got to fly and so we will. And so they did!

We made it to the car just as the lightning kindled. We'd already struck the tent and packed the trunk. All we needed to do as we took off our hiking boots and sweaty socks—and Luke, without those duties, muddied up the backseat—was enjoy how the first raindrops fell. The sheets of water came as we drove out toward the highway. Lightning put on a show as we skirted the high peaks, safe in our car. I was exhilarated, Bernie had forgiven me my griping and complaining (I think), and Luke had achieved the sweet rest of a trail-weary dog. He recovered enough by the time we stopped for gas in Sheridan to strain at the leash when I walked him past a fragrant sushi restaurant.

What I was feeling at last was the antidote to either/or equations: an unencumbered consciousness. Oh, I knew it wouldn't last. In a week or two, I'd be back to charging up the old obsession generator in my head, imprisoning myself in a dichotomous jail. Sanity/insanity. Coward/valiant. But I accepted the reprieve and the camaraderie Bernie, Luke, and I had deepened by camping together. And I'd remember it. Maybe next time anxiety or pettiness cranked up, I'd recapture this peaceful moment and squash the next round of obsessions or squabbling. I'd stop projecting my insecurities onto Bernie. Or maybe not. Chronic disease is chronic disease. And marriage is a hike, with new routes every day.

So, after all of this, I can't say that walking shores up the mind, though maybe the mass release of endorphins after a fast jaunt is Xanax's equal. At worst, it's a harmless compulsion. But I'd like to assert that mariposa lilies and living, jumping fishes teach a better ordering of thought than what I usually attempt. You don't have to be a super wilderness adventurer to gain the boon of extra-human knowledge, to understand and emulate courage, to forge peace deals with yourself and others. Mountains and prairie are not for the strong, the male, the healthy. Or not exclusively. Their hidden corners in or beyond wilderness are for those who suffer, those who worry, those who need them.

To beings the size of my handspan, the twenty-foot waterfall must have looked and sounded like the unlocking of the seventh seal. But those West Tensleep fish leapt into the crush, rose beyond it, and made it to the calm waters above. They demonstrated the better purposes of faith, those airborne water creatures in the birthplace of electricity.

Epilogue

TRAIL 22 (AGAIN)

Pygmy Panther and Luke

Now there's a trailhead sign, arrows, and a Pryors' Coalition map to follow. No more searching for the route. In one way, I know exactly where I am. In another, I'm in the true wilderness. Luke is dead. This is his commemorative hike.

I've always hated books that end with the nonhuman hero's death. But having read this far, you've been walking with Luke, too, and you might want to know what happened to him and what walking is like without him. Luke did not enjoy the full lifespan of an average dog. He was jumping and playing in the Yellowstone River on a Tuesday, became sick on Wednesday night, and within six days he'd been diagnosed with metastatic liver cancer. He was nine years and four months old.

I spent his last day telling him how much I loved him and reminding him of his adventures. As I petted and kissed him, I assured him again and again how good he was, and how beautiful. When it was time, Bernie and I lifted him into the car and drove the five minutes to his favorite vet. The doctor confirmed again that it was beyond her ability to help him. She administered a sedative. Soon Luke stopped pacing and lay between Bernie and me on the floor. We caressed him as his amber eyes, though open, ceased to focus. I've read that the dying can hear almost until the end, so I reminded him again that we'd had more than a lifetime of fun together and that I was proud of my curly boy. The vet scooped him onto the examination table as if he didn't weigh fifty-five pounds and administered the opioid overdose that would still his heart. His lids never closed. It's fitting that he went open-eyed into eternity. He didn't do things by half-measures. He wasn't ever shy about a new adventure.

I kissed him one last time, caressed his beautiful fur again, admired his spotted feet, and left him behind. But not really.

The official Pygmy Panther trail unravels through a red-sand draw. Twisted junipers weep along the outcrops, and wind calms in this sheltered place. How Luke would have loved it here: the rabbit droppings, the pure air, the sense of his pack on a mission.

When our son was little, he used to walk an Indiana forest trail with his arm around the caretaker's collie, who was about as tall as Tom was. Tom called it "going with a dog" and chanted the words in a rudimentary hip-hop. The phrase became part of our family language, and over the years I've often thought about what "going with a dog" means.

Of course, dogs recognize places and objects they've experienced before. But they don't appear to have a mythology that obscures their excitement and curiosity. What I want to say is that Luke didn't *walk*. He leapt, jumped, lunged, tasted. He waded rivers and streams, biting at the water and gulping sometimes, especially in his younger years, to the point of vomiting. He drooled when running with other dogs. He growled, tussled, fell, and hopped to his feet, tail up and smiling, when those other dogs chased him. He sometimes froze on a trail, sniffing in apprehension—always a tense moment. Was he smelling bear? Cougar? Deer? Squirrel?

Maybe the point of going with a dog is to imagine the world from a foot or two off the ground. To puzzle out the hint of another passing creature. To consider what you might eat, what you should eat, what you can get away with eating. It means not worrying much about consequences—unless you happen to go with a dog like our Rita. She'd shadow us on an evening path, or slip to my right if there was anything threatening on the left.

But Luke … Luke was spontaneous joy in action. Sometimes when we'd been walking for a long time in town—me proud as an honor-roll parent with my "perfect" dog (a bystander once actually called him that)—Luke would reach some Zen moment. He'd pounce at a random stick, toss it, twist to catch it, chew at it, carry it for a bit, and then lapse into his well-behaved prance.

Every step strikes me to the heart. The place is beautiful. We descend a reddish draw, wind around junipers lush or bonsai-twisted, the rocks they grow on jumbled. The place where Luke walked for nine years—at my left side or, when a trail narrowed, directly in front of me—registers his absence as if an historic era has been overturned. Despite the emptiness, some sort of body memory keeps him with me, except that he isn't.

Luke walked nearly every day of his life. He led me into and out of OCD episodes. He took me to city parks on winter days when I didn't want to go. He loved any river bank or dog beach, but—amazingly—he was too wise to jump into strong currents. That was about the only way he was wise. He loved snow and mud and tall grasses but was never fond of brome or burrs. Still, he ran heedlessly into thickets, emerging with a prickly tail or snarled foreleg feathers.

Luke was oblivious to the several moose we saw in our years together, scared of coyotes' voices, and puzzled by marmots. Once, he found a raccoon hanging by her front feet on the far side of our chain-link fence. He'd caught her in the act of coming into our yard. His bark for her was one I'd never heard before—a raccoon yell. He ignored birds and reptiles—except for that one time he and some non-bird-dog buddies flushed a dove. They stopped and stared, certain they ought to do something. But what? On another trail, a garter snake wriggled between his legs. He didn't notice.

Luke splashed in Lake Fork, scrambled over rocks at Mystic Lake, climbed to the heights and depths in the Pryors. He liked cross-country rambles, even if being off-trail insulted his sense of tradition. He'd keep looking back, not uncertain but maybe disappointed. He'd miss out on the scents and tastes he'd been hoping to find again. But he was more than a solitary dog of the wilderness. He pranced around the dog park, welcoming all the newcomers, checking back with those he'd already greeted, hoping someone might chase him. The quintessential emcee of the festivities—a canine Cary Grant, with whatever the canine equivalent of a martini in hand might be.

Despite its beauty, Pygmy Panther is a subdued place without Luke. I've lost my supersensory abilities. The hills are simply hills. An inert quality deadens the clouds and stills the breeze. No one is here to warn me of dangerous smells. No one digs and eats dirt or snatches at bear turds. No one jerks me forward when he spots a cottontail.

I don't know what became of the energy and joy and love that was Luke. I like to think he's now a "hound of heaven," as a friend of mine puts it. He's running through the cosmos, chasing rabbits who can never be caught (not that he could catch them in this life, either). But every so often I feel him come back to me. He's at my feet in bed. He's at my side on a walk.

I can't make him stay, of course. He's got things to do. Important galactic concerns. As we used to say after he'd put in some time walking sedately down a neighborhood street, "Luke! Sniff and play!" Then we'd let the leash run out as far as it would go so he could enjoy whatever the world had to offer. I admired him for his fearlessness and his lack of complaint.

As we reach the trail's apex, look down at the gulf Bear Canyon cuts in the Pryor Mountains, and begin our descent, a brindled collie mix dances in front of me. His tail is high, his ears bounce, and his shadow is comical and dear. No longer on the leash, he outpaces me. Getting farther and farther away. I close my eyes for a second, and when I open them Luke isn't there.

I'm no longer going with a dog.

Acknowledgments

My thanks go to Martha Cochrane, Lee Cooper, Tami Haaland, Danell Jones, Anna Paige, Julie Schultz, Virginia Tranel, and Ashley Warren for their critique of parts of this book. Those who reviewed it, among them Susan Marsh and Mary Emerick, spent time and effort to offer me valuable advice on improving the manuscript. Kim Hogeland, Micki Reaman, and Katherine White at Oregon State University Press shepherded the book (and me) along the trail to publication. Rick Cooper was a sensible and sensitive copyeditor.

I acknowledge the University of Utah's Marriott Library for records concerning Mormon polygamy, and Bryce Tripp and Ann Shedden for compiling family history and photographs. Any unfounded speculation or outright errors regarding ancestry are my own. I'm grateful to the person who posted seventy-year-old issues of the Wasatch Mountain Club's newsletter, the *WAMOC Rambler*, online, allowing me to learn more about the 1950s version of my dad than the few stories he told me allowed. All those who help preserve the Beartooth Wilderness, who write trail guides for the Custer-Gallatin National Forest, and who ardently advocate for the Pryor Mountains (www.pryormountains.org) deserve recognition—as do the American people, for holding public lands in common.

Special recognition goes to Kate Cohen-Posey and Tara Sorenson, my counselors in Florida and Montana, respectively, who taught me to find resources within my mind that I would never have found on my own.

And, as always, my hiking partner Bernie Quetchenbach offered sharp and useful suggestions as well as moral support throughout many anxious times.

"Yellowtail Wildlife Management Area" (then titled "One") appeared in *Palo Alto Review*; "Shepherd Ah-Nei Recreation Area: Killing Coyote" was featured in This House of Books' Simply Poetry series; and "Hailstone National Wildlife Refuge, with Owl and Eagle" appeared in *Great Plains Quarterly*. I am happy to acknowledge these publications. Quotes from *Everything as It Happens* (Bernard Quetchenbach, FootHills Publishing) are used by permission of the author.

These sources have enhanced my knowledge of natural history and the history of Mormonism and my family:

Alexander, Thomas G. *Brigham Young and the Expansion of the Mormon Faith.* Norman: University of Oklahoma Press, 2019.

Cheney, Brock. *Plain but Wholesome: Foodways of the Mormon Pioneers.* Salt Lake City: University of Utah Press, 2012.

Jack, James, Secretary of the Cornelius Bagnall Emigrating Company. *Saints by Sea.* https://saintsbysea.lib.byu.edu/mii/account/413

Jonnes, Jill. *Empires of Light: Edison, Tesla, Westinghouse and the Race to Electrify the World.* New York: Random House, 2004, pp. 367, 368.

All quotations of songs by Peter La Farge refer to this recording: Johnny Cash, vocalist. *Bitter Tears: Ballads of the American Indian,* Columbia Records, recorded 1964. Peter La Farge was the son of anthropologist/writer Oliver La Farge (who wrote *Laughing Boy*) and Wandan Matthews, a wealthy Rhode Islander. The documentary *We're Still Here: Johnny Cash's Bitter Tears Revisited* was a 2016 response to the album, as was 2014's *Look Again to the Wind: Johnny Cash's Bitter Tears Revisited.* Formerly of the Carolina Chocolate Drops, Rhiannon Giddens's version of "Vanishing Race" is powerful.

Mathes, Brittany M., Danielle M. Morabito, and Norman B. Schmidt. "Epidemiological and Clinical Gender Differences in OCD," *Current Psychiatry Reports* 21.5 (April 23, 2019).

McAlister, Erica. "Making the Case for Flies," *Natural History*, February 2018, 24–29.

Nichols, Jeffrey. *Prostitution, Polygamy, and Power: Salt Lake City, 1847–1918.* Urbana: University of Illinois Press, 2002.

For information on Japanese miners in Utah see Helen Papanikolas and Alice Kasai, "Japanese Life in Utah," *The Peoples of Utah*, edited by Helen Papanikolas, Utah State Historical Society, 1981, pp. 333–362.

"Rio Tinto Blasts 46,000-Year-Old Aboriginal Site to Expand Iron Ore Mine," *The Guardian*, accessed September 12, 2025. www.theguardian.com/australia-news/2020/may/26/rio-tinto-blasts-46000-year-old-aboriginal-site-to-expand-iron-ore-mine

Robert N. Reynolds Family History, accessed April 13, 2022, https://robertn-reynolds.weebly.com/warren-ford-reynolds.html

Shephard, Matthew, Stephen L. Buchmann, Mace Vaughan, and Scott Hoffman Black. *Pollinator Conservation Handbook*, Portland, OR: The Xerces Society, 2003.

Stone, Robert. *Day Hikes in the Beartooth Mountains*, 4th ed. Red Lodge, MT: Day Hike Books, Inc., 2006.

Supaman's hiphop teamed with jingle dancer Acosia Red Elk's choreography, www.youtube.com/watch?app=desktop&v=OiVU-W9VT7Q

Taylor, Suzi. "MSU Researcher Investigates Potential Role for Microbes in Central Montana Refuge," December 2014, accessed January 24, 2022. www.montana.edu/news/15268/msu-researcher-investigates-potential-role-for-microbes-in-central-montana-refuge

Van Wagoner, Richard S. *Mormon Polygamy: A History*, 2nd ed. New York: Signature, 1989.